THE TROPOHOLIC'S GUIDE TO HOOK ROMANCE TROPES

CINDY DEES

CYNTHIA DEES PUBLISHING INC

CONTENTS

Introduction	v
1. Arranged Marriage	1
2. Baby On The Doorstep	15
3. Boss-Employee	29
4. Bodyguard/Protector	43
5. Celibate/Unconsummated Marriage	57
6. Coming Home	69
7. Deathbed Confession	85
8. Disguised As Male/Female	97
9. Drunk/Vegas Wedding	109
10. Fake Fiance/Boyfriend/Girlfriend	121
11. False Identity	133
12. Fated Mates/Soul Mates	147
13. Fling/One Night Stand	161
14. Forced Proximity	173
15. Grumpy-Sunshine	187
16. Hate/Snark To Love	199
17. Innocent Cohabitation	215
18. Love At First Sight	227
19. Matchmaker Gone Wrong	241
20. May-December	255
21. Mistaken Identity	267
22. Nanny/Teacher-Single Parent	281
23. Online Love/Pen Pal	295
24. Opposites Attract	307
25. Raising Child Together	321
26. Right Under Your Nose	337
27. Road Trip/Adventure	351
28. Secret Crush/Secret Admirer	365
29. Stop The Wedding	379
30. Terms Of The Will	395
31. Tricked Into Marriage	413

32. Unrequited Love 427
33. Appendix A - Universal Romance Tropes Listed By Volume 443

Also by Cindy Dees 449
About the Author 451

INTRODUCTION

I'm assuming that, if you're opening this, the fourth volume of universal romance tropes, you've probably got or have read at least one of the other three volumes. Hence, I'm going to assume you know what tropes are, you know why they're important, and you have an excellent idea of how you use them most effectively in your writing process.

If you haven't read any of the other volumes, I'd encourage you to at least take a look at the rather lengthy introduction in the front of one of them where I:

- properly define what tropes are
- show how they're the vital building blocks of all storytelling
- demonstrate why they're the key to creating unforgettable stories that resonate
- powerfully with readers and viewers

Keep in mind that *universal* romance tropes apply to every genre and sub-genre of romance, and they apply equally well to **romantic**

relationships in any kind of fiction, be it thrillers, mystery, sci-fi, fantasy, adventure, westerns, melodrama...I could go on but you get the idea.

Because there are so many universal romance tropes, I have divided them into four categories and written an entire book of tropes for each category:

INTERNAL TROPES – These are the tropes of personal affliction: the wounds, fears, and personality traits that form obstacles to love inside the hearts and minds of your story's hero and heroine.

EXTERNAL TROPES – These are comprised of people, situations, and problems around your hero and heroine that prevent them from blissfully and naturally falling in love and finding their happily ever after.

BACKSTORY TROPES – As the name implies, these tropes are made up of the lingering problems, scars, and needs from your hero's and heroine's pasts that must be overcome before they can achieve happiness and true love.

HOOK TROPES – These tropes might more accurately be called Inciting Incident Tropes. They're the trope-based way your hero and heroine meet and come together as a couple and how that initial meeting establishes a set of problems that must be overcome before the hero and heroine can achieve their happily ever after.

In this book, the two main love interests in each trope are referred to by the terms "hero" and "heroine" purely as a device for telling apart the main protagonists. Gender identity is interchangeable and exchangeable in every example, and not limited to just two people.

The table of contents lists in alphabetical order every trope included in this volume. An appendix at the back of this book includes a list of all the universal romance tropes I've analyzed and which volume they appear in.

I've developed this book as a handy guide for working writers. It's meant to streamline your plotting and planning, speed up your drafting, keep you from getting stuck or unstick you when you do stall mid-story, ensure your revisions catch all the big plot holes and pitfalls, and help you aim your story squarely at your audience in a way that will be deeply satisfying to your readers or viewers.

Here's a sample of how each trope entry is constructed with a few notes (in bold type) about each section of the analysis that you might find helpful:

FORBIDDEN LOVE

I've tried to choose the most common names in use today that are also the most self-explanatory and easily recognizable to you.

DEFINITION
This is where I break down the trope in detail, analyze it in depth, identify the core story type, and discuss any variations on the trope that are common.

DEFINITION of Forbidden Love
This is a trope of two people who are, for some reason, forbidden to love each other. There may be an excellent or deeply entrenched

reason why they're not supposed to be together, or it can be an altogether specious reason. Regardless, the act of ignoring this prohibition is fraught with danger and will exact a very high price upon the lovers if they are caught...which they inevitably will be in your story.

This story typically features distraught lovers, a great deal of drama, sneaking around, fear of getting caught, and angst galore. These people know they shouldn't love each other or be together, and yet they simply can't stop themselves. Their passion is too great to resist or even restrain.

It's also possible the lovers see some compelling reason why they should be together. They may think the reason they're forbidden from being together is stupid, ridiculous, outdated, or in need of reversal, and in this case, they may defiantly pursue their love and unconsciously—or consciously—hope to get caught. They may want to flaunt the rules and openly challenge them.

Either type of couple—the worried, secretive one or the openly defiantly one—is in for a rough road when they do finally get caught. They have their work cut out for them not coming to a tragic end.

At its core, this is a trope of rebellion and the price of that rebellion. The culture, system, or rules against which the hero and heroine are rebelling will set the tone for your story and its level of darkness, danger, fear, or its level of farce, silliness, and humor.

Unlike the Across the Tracks/Wrong Side of the Tracks or a Cross Cultural/Interracial/Interethnic tropes, in which the lovers *may* face strong disapproval, anger, and pushback, in the Forbidden Love trope, the lovers *will* face serious and inevitable legal consequences, punishment, or even death for disobeying a hard and fast rule, law, or taboo (along with the disapproval, disappointment, anger, and pushback of family and friends).

ADJACENT TROPES

If this particular trope is close to what you want to write, but not quite right, you might want to check out the trope write-ups for one or more of these similar,

but not exactly the same, tropes I've collected for you here.

Also, if you're looking for further inspiration or more things to think about while working with this trope (in this case, Forbidden Love), you can check out these similar tropes and find additional elements to add to your characters and plot.

ADJACENT TROPES of Forbidden Love
 -- Following Your Heart
 -- Feuding Families
 -- Rebellious Hero/Heroine
 -- Dangerous Secret
 -- Across the Tracks/Wrong Side of the Tracks
 -- Cross Cultural/Interracial/Interethnic Romance

WHY READERS/VIEWERS LOVE THIS TROPE

This is a deceptively useful little list. It's worth thinking seriously about the kind of experience you want to give your reader or viewer. This list will give you some starting insights as to why your audience is drawn to this particular story arc. This list will also give you some idea of what kind of experience you need to deliver to your readers or viewers if they're going to fall in love with your project.

This list is not meant to be exhaustive by any means. It's merely a jumping off point for you to consider what your audience wants from this trope and if you're delivering that experience.

WHY READERS/VIEWERS LOVE FORBIDDEN LOVE

- it's typically a highly charged trope that takes the audience on a roller coaster emotional journey

- we love to root for the underdog who's up against impossible odds
- your partner loves you enough to risk his/her *life* to be with you
- your partner will *die* for you
- we all like to think we would be heroic enough to defend our deepest values and/or true love with our lives

OBLIGATORY SCENES

As the title suggests, each trope has a traditional starting point, it develops in a predictable way, it reaches a crisis in a certain way, and it resolves predictably. This is where we explore in detail the archetypal requirements of telling this story in a satisfying way to your audience.

Keep in mind, your audience already KNOWS how every classic story trope should go. Deviate from some version of these obligatory scenes at your own risk...

OBLIGATORY SCENES of Forbidden Love
THE BEGINNING:

The hero and heroine are introduced to the audience, possibly separately or just before their paths cross. They may need to start the story apart while the writer establishes the forbidden-ness of any potential relationship between these two people. In this scenario, when the hero and heroine do meet, they know up front that any relationship between them is a very, very bad idea. Hence, their decision to pursue a relationship is probably driven by overwhelming attraction and informed by a shared sense of understood risk.

OR

The hero and heroine may meet without understanding who the other person is or that a relationship between them would be a terrible idea. They may enter into the early stages of a relationship before they find out who the other person is and how forbidden continuing with the relationship would be. In this scenario, they have a terrible choice to make right away—a choice they will have to make again and again as the story progresses—of whether to continue on with the relationship or call it quits before they get caught.

The consequences of getting caught may be spelled out right up front such that the audience is fully aware of the risk, or these consequences may only be hinted at, creating a sense of questioning and suspense in your audience. Of course, it's possible the hero and heroine don't yet know the full consequences of their actions, in which case the audience may not find out right away, either.

The early stages of the relationship may happen completely in secret, or the couple may enlist the aid of a few trusted confidantes. These confidantes will undoubtedly advise strongly against continuing the relationship and serve to heighten the tension and sense of risk. If you choose to add confidantes as accomplices to your story, the stakes are raised as the hero and heroine put other peoples' lives in danger, too.

Remember that, at its core, this is a trope of rebellion and the consequences of that rebellion...on steroids. The beginning typically introduces the system, rules, situation, or person(s) the lovers will spending most of the story rebelling against. The sky-high stakes these lovers are flirting with are almost always established early in the story for your audience, as well.

THE MIDDLE:

The hero and heroine begin to fall in love. Much of the action of the story revolves around arranging and pulling off their trysts, and on scenes with the hero and heroine in their separate worlds, living a lie where they pretend not to be in love with the forbidden person.

If the consequences of the hero and heroine getting caught

haven't been made clear before now, they definitely will be spelled out in the middle of the story.

The middle typically includes desperately romantic stolen moments, near misses with getting caught, and a rising sense of desperation in the hero and heroine the more they fall in love with each other.

It's not uncommon for lovers of this type to fall in love fast and for the relationship to move quickly. They probably have very limited time together for the relationship to develop, so each scene in which they're together is likely a significant scene with substance and that moves the relationship forward. There won't be many or any scenes where they just hang out together casually. Every moment is stolen, and every moment counts for these two.

The middle is characterized by increasing emotion, increasing stakes, and increasing risk. As the lovers continue to get away with spending time together, they may be emboldened to go for something bigger—consummating the relationship, eloping, getting married in secret, or the like. This bigger goal they try to pull off is often the one that will ultimately lead to a crisis and disaster.

BLACK MOMENT:

The lovers are caught. All is lost. They are pulled apart and the consequences of their ill-advised romance lands upon them (and possibly on anyone around them who helped them). Their gamble hasn't paid off. Not only have they lost their relationship, but they may now lose the person they love and face terrible repercussions themselves.

A black moment in this trope is bad. Really bad. As a writer, do not hold back on letting fly with all the terrible consequences you've promised earlier in the story. The devastation should be complete as you rake your characters and your audience over the coals.

THE END:

The hero and heroine are rescued, redeemed, or forgiven in the happy version of this trope. The lovers find a way to convince the authorities around them, those responsible for enforcing the rules, norms, customs, or taboos they've broken, to forgive them. The lovers snatch victory from the jaws of terrible defeat and are allowed to be together, after all. They may be forced to leave their home and go into exile, or they may flee to a place where they're safe or where nobody knows them.

Even though they end up together, in this trope they usually pay a great price before the story is over. It can be a price paid as punishment for their transgression, or a price levied upon them in return for their freedom. Often it is both.

Remember: this couple did break the rules. Depending on what that rule is, your audience may be angry if the lovers don't pay a price of some kind for their rebellion or infraction. If it was an unjust rule, your audience may cheer if the lovers find a way not only to escape but also to avoid retribution or punishment for their transgression.

KEY SCENES

Of course, it takes more than four major scenes to fill a novel, take up an entire movie, etc. Most tropes suggest other important events or moments between your main characters as their relationship and the story unfold in a way unique to this particular story arc.

The additional scenes in this list are not mandatory in the same way the obligatory scenes are. These are just a few typical scenes you might choose to include in your story as you flesh out the plot. They're meant to help you brainstorm and suggest things to consider doing next if you get stuck.

KEY SCENES of Forbidden Love

- the moment when the hero and heroine realize that their love is forbidden
- the moment when the real penalties for getting caught are made clear to the lovers and to the audience
- the moment when the hero and heroine (maybe together or maybe individually) have a crisis of doubt about their decision to pursue this forbidden relationship
- the moment when a friend, family member, or other supporter finds out about the forbidden and secret relationship and that person's reaction
- the hero and heroine's last moment together before they're torn apart forever
- the hero and heroine's moment of reunion at the end

THINGS TO THINK ABOUT WHEN WRITING THIS TROPE

This section is a detailed list of questions to guide your plot/character development and prompt thought about many of the major decisions you will need to make before you tackle writing your story or you'll want to ponder as you're discovering your way forward through your story.

Many writers tell me they come back to this list when they get stuck in the middle of drafting their project. Often, browsing through a bunch of questions like this can provoke a new idea or story direction. If you're REALLY stuck, you may also want to browse through the Things To Think About When Writing This Trope for one or more of the adjacent tropes listed earlier in this trope write-up.

You can also use this list as an editing/revision checklist. Have you included the major decisions and developments these questions cover, or are there areas

in your story that need fleshing out, beefing up, or further explanation?

THINGS TO THINK ABOUT WHEN WRITING FORBIDDEN LOVE

How do the hero and heroine meet? It is an accident or chance? Do they recognize each other immediately, or do they have no idea who the other one is?

Do the hero and heroine know a relationship between them is forbidden when they meet, or do they not learn that until later? If later, when and how?

Why is this relationship forbidden? Do the hero and heroine think this is a good, reasonable, or just reason *before* they meet each other? If so, how do they feel about the restriction on being in a relationship *after* they've met? Is it still a good rule?

Who enforces this prohibition on a relationship between the hero and heroine? Is this person the villain in your story? Is this person reasonable and right to enforce the prohibition? Does more or less everyone around this authority figure agree with the rule that makes the relationship forbidden? Are they right to agree or not?

What are the consequences to the lovers of being caught together in a relationship?

Who around them finds out about their relationship but keeps it secret or aids and abets the relationship? Why does this person help?

What will the consequences be to anyone who helps the lovers be together? Are the consequences less or the same as those faced by the lovers?

Who sends a warning shot across the bow to the hero and heroine that there will be bad consequences for anyone who breaks the rule(s) that the lovers are secretly flouting? How is this warning sent?

How will the hero and heroine sneak away for stolen moments and trysts together? They may use different tactics every time they meet, or they may repeat the same tactic.

How does each tryst get slightly more dangerous than the last one? What causes the stakes to go up each time?

Do the hero and heroine meet in a situation where they have to pretend not to know each other or to be in love with each other? How does that go? Does anyone around them pick up on something…off… between the lovers or get suspicious?

How far will they take their relationship in secret? Will they sleep together? Get married? Get pregnant?

What are they trying to do when they finally get caught? Is it just another tryst, or is this tryst special in some way?

How do the lovers get caught? Are they betrayed? Is it accidental? Do they make a mistake?

Who separates them, and how are they kept apart?

Are the full consequences promised earlier in the book leveled at the hero and heroine or not? If not, why not?

Are the consequences for the hero and heroine the same or different? Are they punished by the same person or by completely different people? For example, do their own individual families, clans, kingdoms, or governments punish them separately under different sets of rules? Or does the same official or person in authority punish them both under the same set of rules?

Does the hero or heroine own up to having done a bad thing by breaking the rules? Are they defiant about having broken the rules? Do they try to bargain with whoever's going to enforce their punishment?

Will the hero and heroine finish suffering the consequences before they get back together, or will they be pardoned, escape, or in some other way evade the full measure of the consequences? If they avoid some or all of their punishment, how do they do this? Do they do it together, or individually in separate pardons or escapes?

If the hero and heroine escape punishment, this may be the most difficult part of the story to pull off plausibly. Systems of control and punishment are typically designed to prevent escapes and are very hard to break free of. Also, your hero and heroine are probably separated, so two different escapes must be coordinated and timed simultaneously.

Where will they go after they're reunited? Can they stay home or will they have to leave? If they must leave, where do they go?

Are they known where they go or not?

What happens to their friends who helped them be together in secret? Are these people okay at the end of the story? How will the hero and heroine ensure these people are okay, assuming they're still alive?

TROPE TRAPS

While I make no claim to have thought of every trap you can fall into with any given trope, I've done my best to capture as many landmines lurking within each trope as I can. This is where they're listed.

This list is also useful to read through and use as a thought exercise as you plan your story. I'm told by many writers that they find it to be a source of ideas and inspirations as they plot, draft, or get unstuck.

TROPE TRAPS of Forbidden Love

Creating a hero and/or heroine who is more in love with the idea of love than their actual partner. Meaning, one or both of the characters gets so caught up in the tragic romance of it all that they lose sight of the very real risk and of the person they're actually in a relationship with.

Creating a couple that doesn't seem plausible for the long run. It may be all drama and danger now, but when all of that is gone, these two people are going to drive each other to distraction in a bad way and never survive as a couple for a happily ever after.

Creating a TSTL (too stupid to live) villain who enforces the rules even if they're silly or stupid rules.

Bonus trope trap: Failing to have the rule(s) the lovers are breaking make sense to the person(s) enforcing them. (although it's okay for the rules not necessarily to make sense to the lovers or your audience).

Not creating serious enough consequences for getting caught to sustain all the drama and secrecy the hero and heroine engage in. It's not enough for the hero and heroine to think the consequences would be horrible—the reader or viewer has to believe it, too.

Creating implausible situations where the hero and heroine get away with stealing a moment together but in which the audience knows they would normally be caught and should have been caught.

The lovers using the same tactics to be together over and over—when someone with an ounce of common sense around them would have caught on long ago to the tactic and caught them.

Not creating near enough misses with the lovers getting caught, which is to say, failing to keep your audience on the edge of its seats.

Creating a lame scenario in which the lovers are caught.

The lovers themselves create a lame or overcomplicated plan to be together that goes awry.

Failing to follow through on the consequences that were promised to the lovers and the audience at the beginning of the story.

Relying on a lame save to pull the hero and heroine out of the proverbial fire so they can be together at the end of the story.

Relying on an abrupt about face or change of heart in the person meting out punishment to relent and let the lovers be together out of the (brand new and heretofore unseen) goodness of his or her heart.

I can't tell you how many of my Asian friends loved the movie, Crazy Rich Asians right up to the moment where the dragon mother sees her son unhappy, has a change of heart, and gives him her engagement ring so he can go get the girl. That's when my friends universally groaned and said something to the effect of, "No Asian dragon mother would ever back down after having successfully chased off the woman she doesn't like or approve of for her son!" While I'm sure that's not universally the case, don't create a villain who suddenly acts completely out of character for no good reason to let the lovers be together in the end.

FORBIDDEN LOVERS TROPE IN ACTION

Last but not least, these are lists of movies, in some cases television shows, and books that use this particular trope. If you're looking for further inspiration for your story or want to see what this particular trope looks like in action, I've gone ahead and collected examples for you here.

Movies:

- Romeo and Juliet (the personification of the tragic version of this trope)
- The Thornbirds
- Dirty Dancing
- Titanic
- Guess Who's Coming to Dinner?
- Pride and Prejudice
- Clueless

Books:

- Birthday Girl by Penelope Douglas
- Twisted Games by Ana Huang
- Slammed by Colleen Hoover
- Matched by Allie Condy
- Daughter of Smoke & Bone by Laini Taylor
- Vampire Academy by Richelle Mead
- Delirium by Lauren Oliver
- The Sweetest Oblivion by Danielle Lori
- Red, White & Royal Blue by Casey McQuiston

The extended introductions of the other universal romance tropes have exercises in how to use tropes to find plot and character, advice on using tropes to revise edit your story, and suggestion for how to use tropes to package and market your story.

This is a guide, written by a working writer, for working writers. My intent was to create a useful tool that you can reach for any time you're stuck, need inspiration, or want to streamline and speed up your plotting, planning, writing, revision, or editing process. It's meant to help you brainstorm, think about a few things you might not have considered, and most of all to find your very best story.

That said, let's dive into the tropes themselves...

1
ARRANGED MARRIAGE

DEFINITION

Arranged marriages have been around since the institution of marriage was invented, and they still exist today, hence their classification as a universal trope. Marriages originally were more about political alliances and/or the transfer or property and wealth than about love, so it was perfectly logical that they would be arranged without any regard to the idea of love.

It was the norm for infants to be married to elderly partners, for couples who didn't speak the same language to marry, and even for close relatives to marry. However, for the purposes of fiction, most authors tend to shy away from these historical realities and choose two characters of compatible ages, backgrounds, and temperaments.

Indeed, fidelity in marriage wasn't introduced as a concept until the 13th century in response to women whose husbands who had died declaring that their eldest son was not the child of the deceased spouse and that she, not the son, should inherit the dead husband's estate. Dispossessed sons pressed church leaders and rulers to enforce a code of virginity before marriage and fidelity after marriage.

At any rate, in more recent times, arranged marriages have shifted to a system where parents or matchmakers choose spouses for their children partially based on wealth or earning potential, but partially or wholly on compatibility between the people to be married.

Although modern people tend to think of arranged marriages as historical in nature or old-fashioned, they do still happen today. Depending on the time period or world-building of your story, you may choose to base your arranged marriage on traditional reasons or something else altogether.

For the purposes of this trope, we're assuming that the couple getting married is not in love when they get married and may or may not know each other well or at all when they tie the knot.

It's the norm now in this type of story for the couple not to consummate the marriage until they have fallen in love, or at least in lust, with each other. Although in historical reality forced consummations happened, it was rape and very few readers want to read about that.

If you do go there, I would remind you to include clear trigger warnings in your marketing materials and expect the major book retailing sites to balk at selling your book.

At its core, this is traditional love story: the hero and heroine meet, get to know each other, fall in love, and live happily ever after. The only hitch to that arc is they're already married when it takes place.

In reality, if you stop there with plotting this trope, I would argue that there's no obstacle whatsoever to this couple ending up happy ever after together. They're already married—all they have to do is continue to live as a couple, just with love and sex added in when they're ready.

Hence, we need to find a source of conflict for this couple. Why shouldn't they fall in love? Why shouldn't they consummate the marriage? Why shouldn't they plan to stay married forever? Why shouldn't they have children together?

It's entirely possible that one or both of the spouses is simply infuriated at being forced to marry someone not of their choosing. This rage can sustain your story for a while, but eventually they're going to look whiny, immature, and petty if they refuse to admit that they've lucked into marrying a completely lovable partner. I encourage you to build in some other compelling reason why this couple shouldn't simply settle into their marriage and be happy.

This trope is often paired with some sort of external conflict that causes problems for the newly married couple: Feuding Families, Divided Loyalties, and Across the Tracks to name a few. Likewise, various internal tropes can cause conflict in the couple's relationship —Socially Awkward, Beauty and the Beast, Disabled Hero/Heroine, Nerdy/Geek/Genius, or even a Celibate Hero/Heroine.

ADJACENT TROPES

- Marriage Pact/Bargain Comes Due
- Marriage of Convenience
- No One Thinks It Will Work
- Forced Proximity
- Hate/Snark to Love
- Matchmaking/Matchmaker Gone Wrong

WHY READERS/VIEWERS LOVE THIS TROPE

- for anyone who's dating today and struggling to find love, the idea of having somebody else take care of it for you and find you the perfect mate without all the hassles and heartaches is wildly appealing
- for anyone who craves family or companionship, this is an instant family or companion
- we love the idea of finding love where we least expect it
- your life suddenly changes and your money problems/worries evaporate as you're swept into a world

or family that instantly provides safety/comfort and (possibly) wealth

OBLIGATORY SCENES

THE BEGINNING:

If the hero and heroine know each other before their marriage is arranged, typically, you'll begin by establishing what the relationship is between the hero and heroine, pre-marriage. If there's a compelling reason one or both of them wouldn't want to marry the other one, that's usually established early on, as well.

For some reason, other people around the hero and heroine think a marriage between these two would be a good match or would be beneficial to the families, clans, organizations, or nations they each come from.

A marriage is arranged between the hero and heroine. The two of them may or may not know about it, may or may not be asked what they think about it, and may or may not like the idea of marrying each other. At all.

Indeed, one or both of the pair may hate the idea of marrying the other one and may fight getting married tooth and nail.

If there's an external plot line or other tropes in your story, they're also introduced, and how they and the arranged marriage relate to one another is established.

The beginning of the story usually ends with the wedding between the hero and heroine, or possibly with their wedding night, specifically.

THE MIDDLE:

The hero and heroine commence living together as a married couple, and it doesn't go well. Their differences, conflicts, resentments of being forced to marry, and all the external pressures for having to stay married, like it or not, come roaring to the fore.

This is a story where you can feel free to let your hero and heroine bicker, argue, and generally drive each other to distraction. This couple is the opposite of a match made in heaven.

Into all this friction, one or both of the main characters starts to see a tiny spark of something attractive or likable about the other one. From this tiny spark, attraction and affection start to grow.

If the hero and heroine are forced into proximity with each other for some reason, or the two of them are forced to work together to solve some external plot problem, the more time they spend together, the more they get to know each other. And the more they get to know each other, the more they like each other. The more they like each other, the more they grow to love each other.

Alternately, this couple may have a passionate physical attraction to each other but may not intellectually like the idea of being married to this person or of having been forced into marriage at all. The dichotomy between their physical compatibility and their incompatibility in every other way may be a major source of conflict for your newlyweds.

The middle of the story ends with some sort of crisis in the relationship:

- An explosive secret is revealed.
- A simmering or unresolved conflict erupts into an intractable disagreement.
- The couple wasn't supposed to fall in love and gets caught.
- One of them breaks some aspect of the marriage bargain.
- They came together in an unconventional way; they weren't looking for love and didn't want it, but have found it anyway.
- The same forces who threw them together may be just as eager to tear them apart.

- The complicated dynamics of their relationship are too thorny for them to work out.

There are any number of other reasons this fragile new relationship might blow up in this couple's faces.

Typically, this couple faces both an external crisis—some threat to them or to their marriage—*and* they face an internal crisis—some personal crisis that one or both of them can't overcome, or some private conflict between them.

BLACK MOMENT:

Instead of working together, having each other's backs, and truly acting as a married couple, when faced with these insurmountable crises, the marriage—and their relationship—falls apart under the strain.

Individually they choose badly. They each fail to think of the other one first, or they each succumb to pressures from outside the marriage that are too great for them to resist on their own.

They each fail the ultimate test of the strength of their relationship. At the same time, they're each disappointed by their spouse's failure to pass his or her test in this marriage.

Their best effort at cobbling together a real marriage from their arranged marriage has failed. Both of them are stuck in what looks as if it's going to remain a loveless marriage forever.

OR

One or both of the newlyweds decides he or she does not want to continue on in this marriage at all. Whatever the blow-up was that ended the middle of the story, it was too much for one of the lovers, and he or she decides to leave the marriage altogether. The experiment in marriage was a total failure.

OR

The couple may not want the marriage to end, but it's ended for them. In the same way that a contract brought them together, a contract may tear them apart. There may be some sort of exit specified time period in which the couple was legally bound to stay together. When it expires, the relationship will end.

If the marriage was arranged to avoid hostilities between their families or nations, but war has broken out anyway, neither side may feel obliged to have their loved one continue on in this sham marriage.

The hero and heroine, who once craved getting out of this marriage, are now torn apart by others or by events—and neither one of them may like that outcome in the least. But breaking up is as out of their control as getting married in the first place was.

Regardless of how they get to it, the block moment for this couple is the failure of or dissolution of their relationship, if not their entire marriage.

Whatever external reasons caused others to arrange the marriage for them collapse. Whatever conditions were attached to the marriage contract in the event of the marriage's failure take effect. Or the terms of the contract were met that trigger dissolution of the marriage.

Any outcomes from breaking the contract or executing an exit clause take place. The alliance or treaty fails. Control of the company is not handed over as per the marriage contract.

Not only has their marriage failed but their relationship has failed. Their love has failed. Both of them have lost *everything*.

THE END:

Into their heartbreak, loneliness, misery, and sense of failure, the hero and heroine individually or together decide they'd like to give it one last go at making theirs a real and lasting marriage.

Externally, they may have to defeat a bad guy who has pulled them apart. They may have to change the marriage contract itself, navigate tricky politics, stop a war, or do something else dramatic to clear the way for the two of them to be married for real.

Internally, they may have to resolve an intractable disagreement between them. They may have to apologize to each other. One or both may have to prove that he or she has changed or grown or solved a difficult personal issue.

They may feel a need to prove to the other one just how much they love their partner. And they may each do this by making some sort of grand gesture of love or some great sacrifice to prove how big and real their love for the other person is.

The hero and heroine may have to work together to overcome the ultimate external obstacle to their love. The act of coming together as a team one last team shows them both that they do have what it takes to sustain and grow a forever marriage and that's exactly what they both want.

Finally, the hero and heroine's arranged marriage has evolved into a fully realized marriage partnership, complete with romantic love and their very own happily ever after.

KEY SCENES

- the hero and heroine, individually or together, are told about the marriage that has been arranged
- the hero and heroine find out why the other one has a compelling reason not to want to marry him or her and find out what that reason is
- the hero and heroine negotiate some deal between themselves that's separate from the official marriage agreement or contract
- the hero and heroine share a light or funny moment that breaks the tension between them…at least for a brief moment

- the hero and heroine find something that they vehemently and viscerally disagree about and it angers both of them or shakes both of them badly
- the first tender or romantic moment between the hero and heroine
- a big fight between them
- they act in the way their respective families expect them to act toward each other, (either acting happy or pretending to hate each other, for example) but it's not real
- the first moment they each think that they might like to remain married to their partner and have a real marriage
- someone else interferes in their relationship and causes a big problem between the hero and heroine
- one or both of the newlyweds betrays the other one in some way

THINGS TO THINK ABOUT WHEN WRITING THIS TROPE

Who are the hero and heroine? Where do they each come from? What are their backgrounds? Backstories? Who are their families?

Why can't they or don't they each find rule love on their own? Do either or both of them have the freedom to choose their own spouse or not? Why?

Is arranged marriage the norm in their family? In their culture? In their social circle?

Who first suggests an arrange marriage between this pair?

Who does the actually arranging, negotiating, contract signing, or whatever else happens as part of the arrangement?

What do the hero and heroine think of the idea of entering into an arranged marriage with each other?

Who do the hero and heroine candidly express their opinion of the arranged marriage to?

Do they hero and heroine tell each other candidly what they think of the idea of marrying the other one? If so, what do they say? If not, why not?

Are there any special conditions or terms to the marriage bargain? Is there a minimum time that, once they've stayed married that long, one or both of them may exit the marriage?

Is there a political or financial agreement, merger, peace treaty, or other formal agreement attached to this marriage? IF so, what is it? How is it important enough for these two people to agree to spend the rest of their lives together—or at least a lengthy period of time?

What happens to this agreement if the hero and heroine's marriage fails or ends?

Why do the hero and heroine agree to the arranged marriage? What's in it for each of them? What's in it for whoever arranged the marriage?

Why can't or doesn't the hero/heroine refuse to go through with the arranged marriage? Do they owe something to the person who arranged the wedding? If so, what?

Is one of them reluctant about this arrangement for personal reasons or some compelling, private reason? If so, why? What's the reason(s)?

What's their first impression of each other when the hero and heroine see each other for the first time after agreeing to the arranged marriage?

How quickly does the wedding happen?

How does the wedding night go?

Do the hero and heroine make some private arrangement regarding sleeping together and/or having sex? If so, what is it? How do they each feel about it? Does it chafe at either or both of them? If so, how?

What characteristics of the hero and heroine make them attractive to the other one?

What characteristics of the hero and heroine challenge or infuriate them about their partner? After all, no marriage is perfect.

What core values do the hero and heroine share that will make a strong and lasting marriage possible? How will they discover these shared values?

Why would these two people never have gotten together if left to their own devices, and how will they overcome those reasons and/or differences?

Why might these two people have fallen madly in love under other circumstances, and why didn't or couldn't those other circumstances come about on their own?

What external things happen or don't happen as a result of the wedding taking place?

Why do the hero and heroine feel trapped or pressured into staying in the marriage whether they like it or not?

How does married life go for these two? Do they argue all the time? Pretend to like each other in public but bicker constantly in private…or vice versa?

How are they forced to spend time together so they can get to know each other?

What do they discover they like about each other?

Do they make each other laugh?

Do they bring each other safety, security, or peace in some way?

How does their marriage transition from being a sham, or at least awkward and unnatural, to a more normal marital relationship? How do they grow into being married?

When do they each realize they're in love with their spouse? How do they feel about that? What do they do about it, if anything?

What external conflict from outside the two of them grows through your story that threatens to tear them apart?

What internal conflict in one or both of them grows through your story that threatens to tear them apart?

How do these conflicts explode and actually tear them apart?

What happens to the contractual, legal marriage when their relationship falls apart? Does fall the marriage fall apart, too? If so, why? If not, why not?

What makes the hero and heroine each realize they still love the other one and want to put the marriage back together?

What do they have to do—together or individually—to solve the crises that tore apart their marriage so they can put it back together?

Does either of them make some grand gesture of love or make some great sacrifice to prove to the other one just how much they love him or her? If so, what is it? Can you make it bigger? More dramatic? More romantic?

Who has to forgive whom? For what? Who apologizes for what?

What lesson(s) have they each learned from each other? What lessons have they each learned about themselves?

What do the hero and heroine know now that they didn't when they got married that will help make their marriage last?

Is an underlying theme of your story that any two people can, under the right circumstances, fall in love, or is there something special (and lucky) about this particular couple that allows them to find true love?

What does happily ever after look like for each character and how will they mesh their separate visions of happily ever after into a single reality?

TROPE TRAPS

These two people are so beautiful, rich, desirable, etc. that your audience doesn't buy for a second that he or she could find true love all on their own. This couple doesn't need an arranged marriage.

The person(s) arranging the marriage agree to something so ridiculous or so onerous that nobody would plausibly agree to such a deal.

Failing to create a compelling enough reason for the hero and heroine to enter into this arranged marriage.

Although marrying for money or to inherit an estate is INCREDIBLY cliché, it is also historically a very common reason for arranged marriages. The trap, then, is failing to create an interesting version of this dead—and fully mummified—horse of a reason for you couple's arranged marriage

Lack of conflict. It would seem at a glance that this trope is inherently packed with conflict, but at its core, it's simply two people meeting, spending time together, and falling in love. It's up to you to create enough interesting conflict to keep your audience interested and engaged.

Relying purely on superficial friction between strangers for conflict and failing to build in any of the real and deep conflicts that many marriages face.

Nobody meddles or interferes in this marriage…which is built entirely on formal meddling and interference into the natural course of true love.

The external conflict of entering into an arranged marriage for a specific reason that generates the plot of your story is not bolstered by strong internal conflict between and within the hero and heroine.

Creating a hero and heroine who are so fundamentally unalike or who have such opposing core values that they would never plausibly form a lasting and strong relationship on their own.

Creating an unlikable hero or heroine who never becomes likable to your audience.

The hero and/or heroine appear weak for agreeing to enter into an arranged marriage. While in a historical setting or certain cultural contexts this might not be a problem, the reader may bring a modern sensibility to how they view characters agreeing to an arranged marriage.

The hero and heroine bicker and argue so meanly or aggressively that they should hate each other's guts and never make any effort to build a real marriage with this hateful person.

Relying on great sex alone to save an otherwise completely incompatible relationship.

Neither spouse apologizes to the other spouse. Neither of them does anything to show the other one how they feel or how much they love the other one.

Instead of blending both of their lives and worlds, one spouse is forced to moved entirely into the other spouse's life/world and leave everything he or she was and knew behind in an unfair way that makes your audience doubt the equality and respect level of the relationship.

Failing to grow the relationship into a loving one that your audience buys.

ARRANGED MARRIAGE TROPE IN ACTION
Movies:

- Titanic
- The White Princess
- The Princess Bride
- Aladdin
- Sense and Sensibility

Books:

- A Princess in Theory by Alyssa Cole
- The Winter King by C.L. Wilson
- His Inherited Princess by Empi Baryeh
- A Bollywood Affair by Sonali Dev
- The Accidental Prince by Michelle Willingham
- Blame it on the Duke by Lenora Bell

2
BABY ON THE DOORSTEP

DEFINITION

In this story, an adult—either the hero or heroine—finds a baby on his or her doorstep. Traditionally, it's a literal doorstep the child is left on, but you could choose to leave the baby anywhere the hero or heroine might find the infant with the caveat that it must be somewhere the child is relatively safe. Don't ever leave a baby in the hero or heroine's car, for example, unless it's too cool to overheat the child and too warm for the child to get hypothermic.

It's worth noting that, although the baby on the doorstep is traditionally a newborn, you can write this trope with a child of any age. With older children or teens, they're often dumped on the doorstep of their non-custodial parent who has never had anything to do with them before now. Although I'll speak in terms of infants for the sake of ease in writing this trope entry, feel free to substitute in any age of child.

The hero or heroine is not prepared for a baby to drop into his or her life. This adult may have little or no experience with babies and certainly has none of the required gear with which to take care of a baby.

There's often a comic element to this story revolving around the ill-prepared instant parent scrambling to figure out what to do with a baby, how to care for it, improvising diapers, bottles, beds, clothing, and learning first-hand the joys of sleep deprivation.

This isn't solely a trope about becoming a parent, however. It's primarily a trope about romance. Typically the romance is introduced when the overwhelmed hero or heroine with the baby desperately seeks help from someone who knows something about the care and feeding of babies...or seeks help from a friend, neighbor, or other future romantic interest who can be recruited (or suckered) into helping out with the baby.

It's not uncommon to have neither the hero nor the heroine know a blessed thing about caring for babies and to let both of them flail as they get a crash course together on parenting.

It's not uncommon to pair this trope with some other trope that adds stress to the relationship—Grumpy-Sunshine, Opposites Attract, On the Run, or Nerdy/Geek/Genius to name a few.

Once the immediate crisis of how to keep the baby alive and safe is solved, the next problem is trying to figure out where the baby came from, who its parents are, and what the hero and heroine are going to do with this baby for the long term.

It's this journey of discovering where the child came from and raising the baby that forms the core of the plot in this story. The core romance between the hero and heroine develops as they come together as parents. It's in this context that they fall in love.

Furthermore, as the hero and heroine become a couple, all three of them—hero, heroine, and baby, become a family.

The baby's parent(s) are eventually found and cannot take baby back. Alternately, the birth parent(s) might take the baby back but ultimately cannot continue to the raise the baby and let the hero and heroine take over permanent custody of the child.

Wherever and whenever you set your story, you do have to resolve the legalities of how the hero and heroine are allowed to keep the child and raise it as their own, either by fostering the baby or adopting it.

Feel free to set up a temporary situation where the hero and heroine can't contact the proper authorities over the child or are given temporary permission to care for the baby. But the hero and heroine's long-term custody of the baby cannot be permanent until the legalities of it are fully settled.

This is because simply finding a baby and deciding to keep it is illegal pretty much everywhere, is wildly unheroic and selfish, and will freak out your audience. The parents in your audience, in particular, will panic at the idea of losing their child for some reason and whoever finds it just deciding to keep it and make no effort to return it home.

At its core this is a story of building a family. The hero and heroine may or may not evolve much over the course of the story. Rather, the transformation of the hero and heroine's relationship into not only true love but parents and family forms the core of this trope.

ADJACENT TROPES

- Single Parent
- Accidental Pregnancy
- Secret Baby
- Insta-Family
- Is the Baby Mine
- Raising Child Together

WHY READERS/VIEWERS LOVE THIS TROPE

- for audience members who wish for a family or children of their own, it's a dream come true to have a child simply appear in your life as if by magic
- many perceive a baby to be one of life's greatest gifts. To literally receive a baby as a gift would be an enormous blessing

- we all relate strongly to the idea of being needed. And who's more helpless and needy than a baby
- when the adult who finds the baby gets completely overwhelmed with its care, the love interest arrives to the rescue like a knight/dame in shining armor to rescue the main character in distress
- for those in your audience who lack a mother- or father-figure, the idea of being given to a loving mother- or father-figure to care for you, in the same way the baby is gifted with parents, may be deeply appealing
- having a person come into your life who belongs completely to you, depends wholly on you, and loves only you is deeply appealing

OBLIGATORY SCENES

THE BEGINNING:

The hero or heroine discovers a baby literally or metaphorically on the doorstep. There's a flurry of activity to make sure the baby is safe and its survival needs met, then there's a second flurry of activity to figure out where it came from, where the parent is, and to return the infant to its parents.

In the case of an older child, they can usually tell the main character where they came from and why. In this situation, you'll have to create a reason why this child has shown up at this adult's house and cannot immediately return to his or her custodial parent.

The main character gets overwhelmed and quickly calls in reinforcement in the form of the love interest. The love interest may be reluctant to get involved or may dive right into caring for the baby. Just be careful not to let the main character completely off the hook for the child's care and let him/her hand off all responsibility for the baby.

The beginning typically ends with the main character finding out he or she is unable to simply hand off the child to someone else for some reason and is stuck with the child.

OR

The first real threat to the child or to the child's presence in the main character's life happens. Particularly if the main character has already grown attached to the baby or feels responsible for the baby's safety, the beginning will end with a threat to remove the baby as opposed to a threat to make the main character keep the baby.

THE MIDDLE:
The hero and heroine have to come together to deal with this small alien who has entered their lives. Shenanigans, conflicts, and problems ensue as they care for the baby and try to figure out where he/she came from.

One or both of the adults may try to back out of having to care for the baby. Typically the other adult is having no part of that and this becomes a source of conflict between them.

Also typical is that the main character's pre-baby life, dating life, and/or career suffer as a result of the baby being in his/her life. The main character is forced to make hard choices between baby and work, baby and social life, baby and hobbies/personal time/travel/fun. These choices are important to include in your story because they illustrate a core truth of being a parent, which is the child's needs must come first before your wants.

If the search for the baby's birth parent(s) is ongoing, this becomes more complicated and more urgent through the middle of the story.

As the middle progresses, the main character finally begins to settle into a rhythm of parenting, finding his or her stride and getting the hang of it. This, too, is important to include in your story as an illustration of the message that anyone can learn to be a good parent if they try.

As the middle of the story concludes, the threesome moves closer and closer to becoming a true family.

The middle usually concludes with a threat to baby or to the custody of the baby or both. Just when the main character, love interest, and baby are figuring out how to be a family together, something comes along to rip it all apart.

While in many stories the middle includes a slow build toward the big crisis, it's entirely possible in this trope that the big crisis at the end of the middle comes as a surprise to everyone.

BLACK MOMENT:

The baby's real parent(s) returns to claim the child. The birth parent(s) may have a legitimate reason for having abandoned the child and may have an equally legitimate reason for returning to collect the child now. This may lead to a custody fight that the main character and love interest lose. Or the birth parent may simply take the child back and the hero and heroine of your story have no legal recourse to stop them.

The hero and heroine probably insist that the birth parent prove they're the parent of the baby...but the birth parent is able to do this.

OR

There's a very serious threat to the baby's safety. The big bad guy who's been hunting for this child to use it for some nefarious purpose finally catches up with the hero, heroine, and baby and successfully takes the baby away from the hero and heroine. This usually happens because the hero and heroine are unwilling to jeopardize the safety of the baby and are not willing to risk it dying in an effort to keep the baby away from the bad guy. The bad guy uses the hero and heroine's love for the baby against them to seize the child from them.

OR

In a less fraught black moment, the baby's presence in their lives costs the main character something huge—like his or her job or home—and the main character gets a huge reality check. What was he/she thinking, trying to raise a child when he/she wasn't ready and his/her life wasn't set up for parenthood at all?

OR

The main character makes some major parenting mistake that could have hurt the baby and freaks out, deciding that he or she isn't capable of being a good parent and isn't worthy of the baby.

The main character decides he or she isn't up to the task of rearing a child over the long term and backs out of the arrangement. Typically, other characters in the story have been trying to convince the main character of this the whole time, and the main character finally believes them after this near miss with disaster (it's a near miss because you never, ever kill a baby in a romance novel...or pretty much any genre of novel, for that matter).

On top of losing the baby, the brewing crisis in the romantic relationship between the hero and heroine explodes. The explosion is usually triggered by the main character losing or giving up the baby.

The main character has now lost everything and everyone who matters to him or her. The destruction of his/her life and happiness is complete.

THE END:
Depending on how your black moment goes, your ending will have to resolve the decision or event that took the baby away from the

main character and love interest. If the baby was stolen by a bad guy, the hero and heroine affect a rescue and recover the baby. If a birth parent got custody of the baby, something goes very wrong with the birth parent's life that makes him/her unable to keep the baby for the long-term. If there's a custody battle, some new evidence comes to light that tips the case in the hero and heroine's favor.

If the main character gave up the baby because the cost to his or her life was too high, he or she is so miserable in his/her restored "normal", babyless life that the main character reverses his or her decision and decides that he/she would rather give up his/her old life entirely and have the baby in it than live the old life without the baby.

If the main character's reason for giving up the baby was that he or she made a big mistake that almost harmed the baby, the love interest finally manages to talk the main character down off the guilt ledge and convince him or her that no parent is perfect, all parents make mistakes, and that good parenting is simply about doing your best. The baby wasn't ultimately harmed in the end and the main character has learned to be more careful and will never make that mistake again. He or she is no worse a parent than anyone else and is, in fact, a much better parent than most.

Whatever legalities haven't been worked out before now for the hero and heroine to keep the baby for the long-term get resolved.

Whatever romantic conflicts between the hero and heroine that have broken them up in the black moment get resolved, clearing the way for the little family to finally get back together and get on with living their lives together.

The hero, heroine, and baby have formed a permanent family together and the hero and heroine are committed to each other and to their new family in a long-term relationship.

In occasional stories, the baby may end up being safely returned to its birth parent(s), but the hero and heroine remain united in love and will start their own family together someday. Indeed, in this scenario it's common for the heroine to be pregnant by the end of the story.

KEY SCENES

- the first night alone with the main character and baby and *everything* goes wrong
- the main character tries to hand off complete responsibility for the baby to the love interest who isn't about to let that happen
- the main character expresses being overwhelmed by parenthood
- the main character gets something right—if unconventionally—about parenting
- the hero and heroine get some time away from the baby to be together and develop their romance
- the baby interrupts a romantic interlude between the hero and heroine
- the baby shows affection for the main character that melts his/her heart
- the birth parent(s) or the threat to the baby's safety shows up and the hero and heroine contemplate running away with the baby
- the hero and heroine love the baby enough to let it be taken away because it's best thing for the child

THINGS TO THINK ABOUT WHEN WRITING THIS TROPE

Who abandoned the baby? Why was the baby abandoned?

Why this doorstep? Was the hero or heroine chosen by the person abandoning the baby, or was it random?

How old is the child?

What does the main character do initially to try to find the baby's parent(s)? How does that go?

Is the baby in danger? If so, what kind? What does the main character do to protect the child?

Why and how do the hero and heroine initially retain possession of the baby? Why (plausibly) don't or can't they turn the child over to government childcare or protective services?

How much or how little experience do both the hero and heroine have with caring for babies?

Why does the main character recruit the love interest specifically to help him/her care for the baby? Does the main character have any reason to believe the love interest knows what to do with a baby? If so, why?

How reluctant is the main character to care for a baby? How does that affect the story?

How does a baby completely mess up some or all of the main character's regular life? Can you make this worse? Much worse? Catastrophic?

What investigation, and by whom, is undertaken to find out the identity of the child and why he/she was abandoned?

Who teaches the main character how to care for a baby?

Will finding the supplies to care for a baby be a challenge in this story? If so, how do the adults improvise?

What other obstacle to love besides a baby in the house do the hero and heroine face? (And yes, this is often an entire trope of its own)

What attracts the hero and heroine to each other?

Does watching the other one interacting with the baby show the hero and heroine some new side of the other adult they never saw before?

When does the love interest try to leave? Immediately after showing the main character the rudiments of baby care? After sticking around for a bit to make sure the main character has the hang of parenting a baby? Later? If later, why later?

When does the main character try to back out of caring for the child? We know he or she probably tries to back out of it immediately after finding the baby, but when else? When the baby messes up something in his/her personal life? When the love interest seems to be in love with the baby and could take over its care? Later? If later, why later? Why delay finding someone else to take over care of the baby?

If there's danger to the baby, what is it and how does it get worse over the course of the story? Who's the bad guy and what does he/she want with the baby?

If a parent or close relative of the child shows up to collect the child, will the hero and heroine voluntarily give the child back or not? Why or why not?

How will the birth parent prove that he/she is really the baby's parent to the main character?

What's the crisis that causes the main character to give up custody of the baby? How does he/she feel about it?

Does the main character consult with the love interest before relinquishing the baby? If so, how does that go? If not, why not?

How does the main character feel after the baby leaves?

How does the love interest feel after the baby leaves?

What event triggers the romantic black moment between the hero and heroine? How is the baby integral to that black moment?

Is your end goal in the story to return the baby to its family or to keep it permanently with the hero and heroine?

What changes happen that allow the main character to get back the baby?

How will you resolve the legalities that allow the main character to keep long-term or permanent custody of the baby?

How will you resolve the romantic relationship between the main character and love interest? How is the baby integral to that resolution?

. . .

TROPE TRAPS

A baby is not a football. It can't just be hauled around and tucked out of the way when it's inconvenient to have a baby around, for example, in love scenes and scenes with danger or violence. The trap here is not accounting for the practical and safety concerns of injecting a baby into the story.

The hero or heroine doesn't engage believably with the baby as they learn to be around a young child.

There's no plausible reason for the hero and heroine to keep the baby and not turn the child over to government or official authorities.

You give your audience a weak, implausible explanation or no explanation at all for the baby being abandoned in the first place.

You give your audience a weak, implausible explanation or no explanation at all for why the baby ended up with the main character specifically.

Unrealistic behavior of the baby based on its age. Example: infants scream when they hear a gunshot; they don't huddle quietly with the hero and heroine who are hiding. Also, stuffing a pacifier in said screaming infant's mouth won't immediately shut it up.

In the case of small children (particularly those who are talking), the child is *way* too wise or knowledgeable for their age.

There's no adult conflict in the hero and heroine's romantic relationship.

The only conflict revolves around how to raise the baby.

The main character's pre-baby life isn't messed up at all by the appearance of a baby in his/her world.

There are no rumors or innuendo about how the main character ended up with this baby.

Parenting is portrayed as nothing but an unrelenting nightmare with no sweet moments to make all the hard work worth it.

The main character doesn't catch on to parenting relatively quickly and comes across as dense or dimwitted.

If there's a threat to the baby, it's such a scary threat that your audience doesn't buy it (or hates it).

When faced with putting the baby in mortal danger or handing it over, the main character refuses to think of the baby's safety first.

The ways the baby interrupts romantic moments between the hero and heroine is cliché.

The hero and heroine could talk about all their problems if they just sat down and had an adult conversation...and they fail to do it for most of the story.

BABY ON THE DOORSTEP TROPE IN ACTION
Movies:

- Three Men and a Baby
- Rob-B-Hood
- Bundle of Joy
- Baby Boom
- How to Marry A Millionaire

Books:

- The Littlest Cowboy by Maggie Shayne
- Written With You by Aly Martinez
- The Baby Arrangement by Samantha Chase
- Contract Signed by Marie Harte
- Single Daddy by Stephanie Brother
- Baby on the Bad Boy's Doorstep by Victoria James
- Baby on the Doorstep by Lori Copeland, Cassie Edwards, Susan Kay Law

3
BOSS-EMPLOYEE

DEFINITION

In this workplace romance, one of the lovers is the boss of the other lover, the employee. While this has traditionally been a popular trope and workplace romances have been normalized in the past, this trope has become a potentially fraught one in recent years. As society has evolved and social conversations have changed, readers and viewers have become much more aware of unequal power dynamics in romantic relationships.

While boss-employee relationships have long been frowned upon or prohibited in public workspaces, they are so common in the homes of the very wealthy—having sex with maids, nannies, and pool boys—they have become cliché.

Today, it's generally considered wildly unethical for bosses to date their employees and vice versa. There's serious risk of the subordinate employee feeling coerced into engaging in a sexual or romantic relationship or else risking losing his or her job. There's also risk of an appearance of favoritism by the boss for the employee, especially if the employee gets promotions, raises, or some other form of special treatment by the boss.

Women, in particular, have fought against stereotypes and

accusations of sleeping their way to the top since the dawn of history, from Cleopatra to Anne Boleyn to Hollywood starlets, ever since women have been allowed to hold any wealth, job, or position of power. This stereotype is a close cousin of nepotism, hired for their looks, sexual extortion, and the infamous Hollywood casting couch.

The struggle by women to be taken seriously as equal work colleagues and valued for their skills or expertise is ongoing. It's important to keep this in mind any time you write a workplace romance where the boss is male and the employee is female. Your audience is going to be extremely sensitive to the potential for any subordinate female character you write being accused of any of the stereotypes I've listed.

Boss-Employee romances often are paired with a significant age difference between boss and employee, a power exchange dynamic, or one of the lovers (often the boss) already married and engaging in a workplace affair.

ADJACENT TROPES

- Dangerous Secret
- Right Under Your Nose
- Forbidden Love
- Rags to Riches
- Rivals/Work Enemies
- Nanny/Teacher-Single Parent

WHY READERS/VIEWERS LOVE THIS TROPE

- lots of people find power sexy, and a powerful boss is irresistible

- likewise, the idea of having a (forbidden) sex kitten or sex toy relationship is sexy to some, and either a boss or employee can fulfill this role, since the relationship is already forbidden, anyway
- the idea of engaging in a secret affair that would ruin not only your personal life but your career if you get caught adds a titillation that some audience members will find irresistible
- long hours, close quarters, and high stress in a workplace are a perfect recipe for explosive attraction and hot romance
- the titillation of imagining what it would be like to get into a romantic relationship with one's own boss or employee

OBLIGATORY SCENES

THE BEGINNING:

We meet the boss and employee separately or together. The employee may not even be hired yet or they may already have a long-standing work relationship. You can start at the very beginning of this relationship, or you can skip ahead and start at the part where it really gets interesting. This choice may depend on the length of story you're planning, what other tropes you combine it with and how complex a plot you're planning. The more space you have, the more likely you are to start closer to the beginning of the relationship.

It's not uncommon in this story for the employee to have an established crush on the boss, but for the boss never to have noticed the employee before now. In this scenario, the story usually begins with some sort of incident that thrusts the employee literally under the boss's nose and brings the employee strongly to the boss's attention.

Typically, the plot of the story throws the boss and employee together to work on a project, solve a work crisis, get stuck in an elevator or together on a work trip...anything to nudge the pair into continued proximity and need to interact with each other that allows them to form an attraction and eventually fall in love.

It's worth noting that this plot problem is an excellent source of potential conflict between the boss and employee, particularly if the plot problem in some way mirrors their relationship. For example, a much older boss and much younger employee might need to work together on an ad campaign targeting an audience much closer to the boss's age or to the employee's age, which highlights their generational differences and the large gap in their ages as they start to fall for each other.

Although there are sparks between the future lovers when they finally come into close contact with each other, the beginning also must establish the reasons why this relationship is forbidden. A few examples:

- company policy forbids dating other employees
- company policy specifically forbids boss-employee dating
- one or both of the lovers is already married to or in a serious relationship with someone else
- the power imbalance between the pair is wildly lopsided
- the age, status, or wealth difference between the lovers is so large it'll be difficult to overcome
- a romance would be a distraction one or both of the lovers can't afford right now
- they struggle to separate work from leisure or personal time and one interferes with the other

The beginning typically ends in one of three ways:

1. If you started the story at the beginning when they first meet, Act One usually ends with the first major

recognition of attraction between the boss and employee. It can be a kiss, a look, a touch, or something else depending on the heat level of your story.
2. The boss and employee are nearly caught in a romantic situation together that would ruin both of their careers and one or both of their personal lives if they were caught. This mini-crisis injects an element of suspense into their secret affair going forward in the story.
3. The boss and employee get close to having a romantic moment together (again, the sexiness of it will depend on your story's heat level). One or both of them pulls back, declaring this a terrible idea and something they must not do. This sets up a strong element of forbidden attraction to carry forward into the middle of your story.

THE MIDDLE:

The relationship develops whether or not the boss and employee think it's a good idea, and regardless of the risks to both of them if they get caught. If there's a spouse or partner to the boss or employee, the pair sneaks around behind that person's back.

The lovers sneak around behind the backs of the other employees they work with as well. There are snatched kisses in supply closets, empty conference rooms, and behind closed doors. They may flirt with each other secretly at work.

Others may sense the tensions between these two and misread it as negative tension. Rumors may float around that the boss is having an affair with someone as yet unknown (after all, secretaries and personal assistants spend more time with the boss than a spouse and know their boss nearly as well as the boss's spouse does).

The plot problem that throws the boss and employee into physical proximity has its ups and downs that set the rhythm of the middle of your story. This plot problem builds toward a deadline or some sort of crisis that may be a make-or-break moment for the company or for one or both of the lovers' careers.

The middle usually sees the boss or employee confide about the affair to a close friend who may or may not approve. Someone may try to sabotage the plot problem and/or the illicit relationship.

The secret office fling grows into a true romance as the boss and employee get to know each other much better, find common ground with each other, explore their mutual attraction, and fall in love.

If there's going to be a secret getaway, a tryst of some kind, or a business trip that's all about romance instead, that happens in the middle of the story. Just keep in mind that the happier they are, the worse the complication that happens next to puncture that balloon of happiness needs to be.

The closer the boss and employee become emotionally, the more strain this puts on their work relationship, however. They need to hide their feelings, focus on work, and above all not get caught, and the stresses of these take their toll on the relationship and on their job performance.

The middle usually ends with the plot problem of the story blowing up into a full-blown crisis. This crisis puts a tremendous strain on the relationship and stretches it right to the breaking point.

BLACK MOMENT:

The crisis goes against the boss and employee. They lose the marketing deal, they fail to stop the merger, they don't meet the critical deadline. At the same time their plot problem is falling apart, so does their relationship. All the conflicts and disconnects simmering between them through the middle of the story blow up in their faces, now.

If getting caught is the worst thing that can happen to this pair, then it happens now. Marriages or relationships may implode. They may get fired from their jobs; both of their careers ruined.

They gambled on a secret relationship that is forbidden for good reason, and they lost. They both knew better but did it anyway. They have no excuse, and all that's left to do now is face the music and clean up the mess as best they can.

THE END:

All of the dire consequences you warned of in the beginning if they got caught come to pass now. Don't hold back in making this pair pay a steep price for their folly. They both knew better but went ahead with this relationship anyway.

Typically the pair works together one last time to fix the mess they've made of the plot problem. It may be a last gesture before one or both of them leaves their job. Or, one of them may get the inspiration they've been searching for that solves the intractable problem they've been wrestling with.

A superior to the boss may order the boss to clean up his or her mess before being fired (or worse). A spouse may divorce one of the lovers and take the house, car, dog.

Of course, the boss and employee find a way to wrest success from the jaws of defeat at the last minute. By working together they find a way to reverse course and succeed at last at resolving the plot problem.

This last act of working together may also be just the moment they need to spend a little more time together so they can apologize to each other, confess that they miss the other one, and declare that nothing's been the same since everything blew up,

This may be the first time one or both of them actually declares their love for the other one, as well. Because this story revolves around an illicit affair that's strictly forbidden, it's likely that one or both of them has been very conservative about making any big declarations of everlasting love.

But once they've both lost everything, paid every price, and the dust settles, they may finally be free of all the constraints keeping them apart and be able to declare their true feelings for each other.

Because these two have been romancing each other in secret for most or all of the story, they will need to establish a new life together, now. You may want to give your audience a quick glance of them moving into a new place together, maybe starting a new company of their own, working together somewhere else, but openly together now...whatever makes sense for this couple and for your audience to want from this couple by way of a happily ever after.

KEY SCENES

- the boss has to pull the boss card and give the employee a work instruction or order that upsets the employee
- the employee is insubordinate to the boss in a way that would be okay in private in a personal relationship but isn't okay in a work environment
- a personal, romantic conflict spills over into the work problem
- the work problem spills over into their personal conflicts
- the lovers nearly get caught
- the lovers do get caught
- when faced with a choice, one or both of the lovers choose work over love and/or their regular life over their secret affair

THINGS TO THINK ABOUT WHEN WRITING THIS TROPE

Who's the boss and who's the employee in this relationship? Is there an age difference? Education, social status, or background difference?

How do the differences between these two people attract them to each other? How do their differences cause conflict between them?

Where do they work? How does their place of work provide an interesting backdrop for their romance? Will your audience find their workplace interesting?

What mood, tone, and atmosphere does this workplace bring to the boss and employee's romance?

Does the boss have a boss? If so, who is this person and what's his or her role in your story? Is this boss the villain? An obstacle to love? The personification of the consequences of the lovers getting caught? Something else?

If the boss has no boss at work, to whom is the boss accountable? If he or she is accountable to no one, where will the negative potential consequences of this workplace romance come from?

When in the lovers' relationship will you start your story? Will we see them meet? Will we see one of them get hired? Have they already worked together a long time?

Has one of them had a crush on or been infatuated with the other one for a while when your story starts? If so, has he or she tried and failed to get the other one's attention already, or has he or she merely admired the other one from afar? How will you show this to your audience (show them...not tell them)?

What inciting incident throws your boss and employee together in such a way that they notice each other sharply? How does this incident set the tone for the story going forward? Is it funny? Tense? Secretive? Sexy?

What problem, deadline, or crisis at work occurs that will keep your boss and employee interacting with each other frequently through your story so they have a chance to grow their attraction and fall in love?

How will this work problem mirror the lovers' relationship?

How can the work problem pose the largest possible threat to the lovers' relationship? Do they strongly disagree on how to handle the problem? Does the problem threaten to pit them against each other, cost one or both of them their job, reveal their secrets, tear them apart, or in some other way put unbearable pressure on their secret affair?

What's going on in their lives outside of work when they first start to notice each other romantically?

Is the boss or employee married or in a long-term/serious relationship with anyone else when your story begins?

What are the outside responsibilities and pressures upon the boss and employee that fill their lives outside of work before they get together? How will these things move aside, get neglected, get ditched, or suffer as the relationship begins to consume the lovers?

How will each of the lovers juggle their regular life and this new, secret relationship?

What kinds of stolen romantic moments will the boss and employee share at work?

When do they nearly get caught? Who nearly catches them?

Does anyone at work suspect they're involved with each other? If so, how does this person feel about it? Does this person do anything about his or her suspicions?

What are the consequences to each of the lovers if they get caught having this workplace romance? How will you show these potential consequences to your audience?

Will you give the lovers a warning shot across the bow before you hit them with the full consequences of their secret affair? If so, what is that?

What's the power dynamic in the boss and employee's romantic relationship? Are they equals? Is one of them in charge? Does the power dynamic shift over the course of your story?

What's a situation in which you can reverse the power dynamic or turn it on its head?

What's the worst-case scenario on the work problem (external plot problem) the boss and employee are working on? Can you make this worse? Much worse?

What's the worst-case scenario in the boss's personal life if he or she is caught being involved with his or her employee? Can you make this worse? Much worse?

What's the worst-case scenario in the employee's personal life if he or she is caught being involved with his or her boss? Can you make this worse? Much worse?

And the obvious question...how can you make all of these much worse scenarios happen in your story?

Do both of the lovers have some knowledge or skill specific to each of their jobs that they bring to solving the work problem? What's that thing each one knows that the other one doesn't?

How and why does one or both of the lovers choose job over love and trigger the black moment? How does the other lover feel about that? Do they each make this choice individually, or do they make this choice together?

How do they get caught having their secret affair? Who catches them?

How is their affair exposed to everyone? Who does it and how?

How does everyone around the lovers react to the news of their secret relationship?

Does the implosion of the work problem trigger the crisis in their romance, or does it happen the other way around...or does some outside event trigger both the crisis at work and the lovers' romantic crisis?

Once the work problem has gone as badly as it can go, how will the boss and employee ultimately reverse the disaster? Will they work together to fix it? Does one of them fix it for the other one? Does some outside force fix it? Or does it just stay bad?

Does fixing the work problem draw the lovers together one last time...so they can actually talk out their problems, apologize, or reconcile? If not, how will they come together again to work out their conflicts?

How do the boss and employee ultimately work out their personal conflicts? What lessons have they each learned that allow them to be together in the end?

How have these two people changed each other?

How do they rearrange their previous personal lives to be together now?

How do they rearrange their professional lives to be together now?

What does happily ever after look like for this couple?

TROPE TRAPS

The boss isn't accountable to anyone and there are no negative consequences for the boss and employee having whatever relationship they want, hence there's little to no conflict in your story.

The boss and employee have such a power imbalance because of their positions at work that a romance between them comes across as deeply squicky and wildly unethical.

The boss is unlikable for taking advantage of his or her position of power to get into this relationship.

The fact that the boss has totally failed to notice the hot employee for all this time, even as this ridiculously attractive person has worked right under the boss's nose, is totally unbelievable to your audience.

The employee comes across as pathetic or needy for pining after the unobtainable boss for so long before the boss finally noticed him or her.

Neither of these people have any personal life whatsoever outside of work that gets in the way of their workplace romance.

The boss and employee engage in—and get away with—romantic or sexual encounters at work that no sane person believes they'd get away with.

The couple *never* separates their romantic relationship from their work relationship.

The couple *always* successfully separates their romantic relationship from their work relationship.

The employee and boss don't each have specific areas of expertise that they bring to solving the work problem and only one of them does the heavy lifting on solving the problem…leaving the other one to look weak, ineffective, and not very useful in his or her job.

They don't get in enough trouble when they get caught for your audience to buy it as plausible.

Neither the boss nor the employee ever expresses ethical concerns about getting into this forbidden and possibly taboo workplace relationship, and they come across as selfish, narcissistic, and bad people.

This forbidden relationship magically doesn't hurt anybody else in your story and has no negative effect on their workplace.

You promise negative consequences if the couple gets caught but don't follow through on slamming them with the negative consequences when they finally do get caught.

Failing to force one or both of these people to leave their mutual workplace, or at least change positions to be out of each other's chain of command, so they can both resume ethical professional lives.

BOSS-EMPLOYEE TROPE IN ACTION
Movies:

- The Proposal
- Secretary
- Two Weeks Notice
- Long Shot
- Morning Glory
- The Newsroom (TV series)
- Superstore (TV series)
- Suits (TV series)

Books:

- Beautiful Bastard by Christina Lauren
- The Boss by Abigail Barnette

- Bared to You by Sylvia Day
- On Dublin Street by Samantha Young
- By a Thread by Lucy Score
- Bossman by Vi Keeland
- Managed by Kristen Callihan

4

BODYGUARD/PROTECTOR

DEFINITION

This is perhaps the most popular trope in the entire romance industry today, and it has endless variations.

If you watch the bestseller lists across the fiction publishing industry at large or the romance industry in particular, or you watch the top ten lists on streaming television, or you watch the top grossing films of the year, a significant portion of them are going to revolve around a woman in jeopardy and a strong male protagonist (insert one of dozens of flavors of protector here) taking care of the woman in danger and keeping her safe.

Books, dissertations, studies, and articles aplenty have been written on why this story trope is so popular but suffice it to say this is the 600-pound gorilla of romantic storytelling.

In this story, one of the main characters is in danger or for some reason needs protection. The other main character provides that protection. And yes, traditionally, it's a male bodyguard who protects a woman in jeopardy, and for the sake of this trope write-up, I'll talk about it in those terms.

Personally, I'm a big fan of turning gender roles and story roles on their heads, so please feel free to have fun with who plays what role in this story.

At any rate, the hero and heroine are a bodyguard and his or her protectee. While protecting the person in jeopardy, the bodyguard and protectee fall in love, ultimately face down and defeat the threat to the protectee, and they live happily ever after.

Where this theme gets its many, MANY variations is in the flavor of protector and protection the strong male figure brings to this story. To name just a few, all of the following character types traditionally act as protectors of a woman in need in romantic stories:

- billionaires
- SEALs
- soldiers
- cops
- cowboys
- dukes
- Scottish chieftains
- knights in shining armor
- superheroes
- vampires
- werewolves
- mafiosos
- bikers
- professional athletes

Some of these powerful male protectors are so popular and bring such individualized characteristics to how they protect the woman in jeopardy that I've actually broken them out into their own trope descriptions in this series of books.

But at the end of the day, they're all strong, protective heroes who fall in love with the heroine while keeping her safe from some sort of threat, danger, or jeopardy.

On the subject of actual bodyguards...

For the record, any real bodyguard worth his or her salt isn't about to be distracted by emotions or personal feelings while on the job. Professional bodyguards take their work extremely seriously and focus one-hundred-percent on threat assessment, threat abatement and avoidance, and protecting their "package."

The concentration, alertness, and situational awareness required to do actual protection work is intense, and topnotch bodyguards simply don't have the mental bandwidth to do anything besides the job when they're on duty. They wouldn't be topnotch bodyguards if they did spare any of their attention for anything besides the protection work.

This leaves you with several options in how to plausibly craft a love story between a bodyguard/protector and his or her protectee:

- The entire romance takes place when the bodyguard is off duty. In this scenario, there's more than one bodyguard or protector on the job. (This is the norm in true security details. They work in teams so one or more of the team members can rest while the others devote their full attention to the job.)
- The bodyguard/protector in your story isn't actually a trained professional bodyguard and acts more as a companion and deterrent to anyone trying to harm the protectee. This hero may know enough to take general protective measures, but he's there more to react to attempts to harm the heroine than he is to prevent attacks.
- The threat(s) to your protectee in your story is(are) intermittent enough that there's sufficient down time for the bodyguard to relax and breathe from time to time and to develop a romantic relationship with the protectee in the low-threat environments within your story.

This is, of course, a fictional story you're writing, so you can also ignore the realities of real bodyguards and have yours engage emotionally or even romantically with the protectee while on the job.

My purpose here is simply to make you aware of the need to choose how plausible or implausible a bodyguard you want to portray.

ADJACENT TROPES

- Billionaire
- Mafia Romance
- Boss-Employee

WHY READERS/VIEWERS LOVE THIS TROPE

- anyone who's ever felt unsafe loves the idea of someone taking care of him or her.
- Safety is one of the earliest and strongest urges all babies, all humans, experience. It's fundamental to who we are and our need to survive
- any person who's ever been threatened or felt threatened by someone bigger and stronger loves the idea of a very big, very strong protector swooping in to defend them
- alpha humans are sexy. People are wired to find the strongest, smartest, and most successful members of our species to be the most desirable parental material for our offspring
- when our own life gets hard, we love the idea of someone rescuing us from all our troubles and making them disappear

OBLIGATORY SCENES

THE BEGINNING:

You can introduce either the woman in jeopardy or the bodyguard/protector first, but the key is to establish the danger the woman is in and to recruit the big, strong, alpha male to protect her.

Sometimes we start by seeing danger come for a specific woman for a specific reason. She's his ex whom he's obsessed with. Her husband died and left information or something valuable behind that a bad guy thinks she might have. She witnessed a crime and the bad guy's going to try to kill her before she can identify him or testify against him. This woman successfully, but barely, gets away from the danger...this time. In the aftermath of this attack, she asks someone for help or someone offers her help.

Sometimes we start by seeing the bodyguard/protector stumble across a woman in jeopardy and jump in to intervene and protect her. Having saved her once and having really ticked off the threat against her, now he feels responsible for continuing to keep her safe.

Sometimes we start by establishing a threat to the woman in jeopardy, and the situation itself dictates that she be assigned some sort of protection. She's the daughter of a mob boss, she's running for political office, her family is very wealthy and she's a target of kidnapping...you get the idea.

The beginning section of this story not only sets up the threat but also the initial precautions the bodyguard/protector takes to safeguard the woman in jeopardy.

The beginning may end with the revelation or identification of the bad guy who's coming after her. Or it may end with revealing why the bad guy is coming after her. Or it may end with the first serious attack against the woman that the bodyguard/protector steps in to save her from.

. . .

THE MIDDLE:

This middle of this story typically involves the hero and heroine running or hiding from a bad guy while they search for a way to stop the bad guy.

The hero and heroine must find the thing the heroine didn't know she had that the bad guy wants.

The hero and heroine must draw out the villain and set a trap to catch or kill the villain once and for all.

The heroine must stay alive until a turf war ends, until she testifies in a trial, or until she inherits a title, takes possession of an inheritance, gets back home, or some other goal your external plot calls for.

The middle of this story type is typically quite active, with surveillance, break-ins, chase scenes, and outright attacks upon the heroine and her bodyguard. The middle is characterized by steadily growing threats and steadily increasing danger. The bodyguard is pushed to his or her limit to keep the protectee alive, let alone safe.

In the midst of all this growing danger, the hero and heroine realize they're attracted to each other and ultimately fall in love.

While I won't bore you with the nerdy details, many psychological studies have shown that when two people meet in a situation of heightened danger, they tend to feel attraction to each other much more quickly and powerfully.

You can use this to your advantage in this trope, particularly in the middle of your story where these poor, beleaguered souls are thrust together under a constant, looming threat.

Also worth noting, actual bodyguards have no compunction about invading the most private and personal aspects of your life in the name of keeping visual contact with you, staying in close enough proximity to protect you, and keeping you safe. This, too, is rich conflict fodder for the middle of your story.

If your protectee has little or no experience with being guarded, he or she is likely to find it deeply uncomfortable from time to time.

Indeed, this character may try to slip away from the bodyguard just to breathe and get a break from the extreme intensity bodyguards bring to their work.

The middle usually ends with a very serious threat to the protectee's safety. The situation has built to a crisis, and the degree of threat has risen so much that the bodyguard is in real danger of not being able to keep the woman in jeopardy safe.

Depending on the flavor of protector character you've chosen, the threat to the heroine may be a literal threat to her life or threat of a metaphorical death—she may be forced to marry the evil villain or she may risk losing her home or family to the big, bad corporation trying to buy her out, for example.

BLACK MOMENT:

The bodyguard or protector fails to protect the woman in jeopardy from the looming danger. The heroine is kidnapped. She's forced into going through with the wedding to the bad guy. She loses the thing she's trying to keep away from the bad guy.

This black moment can be tricky when the bad guy is out to kill your heroine. Once an attack is made upon her, the bad guy's success or failure at killing her is likely to be pretty straightforward. And, if your bad guy is truly scary, having the villain fail to kill the heroine when he or she finally gets a shot at doing it makes the villain seem weak or ineffective.

One way around this is to have an attack harm the heroine but fail to kill her. She ends up in a hospital, injured, or traumatized in some way but is still alive. The bodyguard feels he failed her (which he did). Worse, the bad guy will probably be back soon to finish off the job, and now the bodyguard isn't sure he's going to be able to keep the heroine alive, let alone safe.

OR

The black moment can revolve around the breakdown of the

romance between the bodyguard/protector and the heroine. Their relationship frictions and difficulties have built to a crisis and finally exploded into open conflict. The heroine may walk—or run—away from the bodyguard, leaving herself vulnerable to attack from the villain.

I'm personally skeptical of the bodyguard/protector type turning his back on the woman in jeopardy. These guys are the sort to set aside their personal feelings to do their job, and no matter how personally angry or devastated they are, I have a hard time buying that this type or person would abandon someone who's truly in danger.

At any rate, even if nobody runs away from the other person, the tensions in their personal relationship interfere enough with the bodyguard's ability to keep the heroine safe that something very bad happens to the woman in jeopardy.

Regardless of how you get there, the black moment in this story is defined by the collapse of the romantic relationship between the bodyguard/protector and protectee and by the villain getting most or all what he or she wants.

THE END:
The bodyguard/protector gathers himself and his resources for one last confrontation with the villain. The woman in jeopardy may or may not help, although the trend in today's fiction is for the woman in jeopardy to take action to help protect herself and claim agency over her own safety.

The villain is ultimately defeated.

The thing the heroine is trying to do, get to, or find is achieved.

Now that the heroine's jeopardy is resolved, the lovers can work out their remaining conflicts, apologize, make grand gestures of love, or whatever else you'd like to have them do to get back together and finally achieve their happily ever after.

KEY SCENES

- the bodyguard is reluctant to take on this particular woman in jeopardy…but he's the only one who can do this particular job
- we find out why the bad guy chose this woman to put in jeopardy
- the heroine resists doing something the hero is convinced is necessary to keep her safe
- the bodyguard does something to protect the heroine that puts his safety in grave danger, and she freaks out
- the heroine does something foolish, heroic, stupid or brave to protect the hero's safety and he freaks out
- the personal disagreements, frictions, or conflicts between the hero and heroine interfere with his ability to protect her and/or their combined ability to solve the external plot problem of stopping the bad guy
- the bodyguard doubts his ability to protect her
- the heroine distracts the bodyguard while he's on the job and it causes a nearly catastrophic incident that one or both of them barely escapes alive
- the heroine pushes the hero to express his feelings
- the hero pushes the heroine not to express her feelings

THINGS TO THINK ABOUT WHEN WRITING THIS TROPE

Who's your heroine and why is she in danger? Who's putting her in danger?

How does the bodyguard come to protect her? Does he have some prior connection to her or someone she knows?

Who is the bodyguard? What are his qualifications to protect the heroine from this particular danger?

What flavor of protector is your hero? How does this affect your story and what the hero is capable of doing to protect the heroine?

Is the hero part of a team or working alone? If he's part of a team, how big a team, what kind of resources does the team have, and how do the other team members feel about the attraction between the hero and heroine?

If the hero is working alone, how will he get rest now and then and still manage to keep the heroine safe during his down time?

What's the nature of the threat against the heroine? What must the hero do to protect her from it?

Can you make the threat worse? Much worse? So bad it's well beyond the hero's normal capabilities to protect the heroine from it?

Will this pair hide? Run? Be chased? Attacked? Followed? Surveilled? What will they actively do to avoid danger?

What must the hero and heroine do to stop the bad guy by the end of the story? What steps must they take to accomplish this? How does the threat grow with each new step they must take?

Do the hero and bad guy know each other or know of each other? If so, how? If not, what do they learn about each other and how do they learn it?

What attracts the hero to the heroine and vice versa?

What drives the hero and heroine crazy in a good way and in a bad way about the other one?

What about the heroine sparks the hero's strongest protective instincts?

How is the heroine strong in her own right, separate from the hero?

What measures does the heroine take to protect herself?

What special measures does the hero take to protect the heroine?

What does the heroine think of having a bodyguard/protector in her life? Does she feel smothered by it? Reassured by it? Both?

Is the bodyguard/protector with the heroine 24/7 or is his protection more from a distance and sporadic, intermittent, or hidden from the heroine to some degree?

At what point does the threat become serious enough that the hero must stick to the heroine like glue *all* the time? How does she feel about that?

How does the danger grow serious enough that the hero is stretched to the limit to protect the heroine? How is he stretched beyond his limit and skill set trying to protect her?

How does the hero fail to protect the heroine? What happens to her? Whose fault is it?

How does the hero feel when he realizes he has failed to protect the heroine? How does the heroine feel about it?

What will the hero do to collect himself, his remaining resources, and any outside help he calls in to protect or rescue the heroine?

Does the heroine help in her own rescue in some way? If so, how?

How is the bad guy ultimately stopped, defeated, killed, or permanently rendered not a threat to the heroine (and hero)?

How do the hero and heroine reconcile or work out their differences at the end of the story?

Does the hero keep doing dangerous work?

Does the hero return to his usual flavor of strong alpha maleness, or is he changed?

What lesson(s) do the hero and heroine learn about themselves and about each other by the end of the story that make happiness possible between them?

How will you demonstrate the hero and heroine putting these lessons into action?

What does happily ever after look like for this pair?

TROPE TRAPS

The heroine is so helpless she ticks off your audience.

The hero is so alpha and so overbearing that he comes across as unlikable or a bully.

The hero and heroine dislike each other so intensely or have so much friction initially that your audience doesn't buy that they would ever get along, let alone like each other.

The heroine is so colossally uncooperative with this person who's trying to keep her safe and help her with a terrifying problem that the audience hopes she dies.

The hero does a lousy job of explaining how his protection of her works and is brusque, invasive, and so scary to the heroine that she has more reason to fear him than the bad guy.

The bodyguard/protector allows himself to be distracted by the heroine when on the job. Moreover, neither of them pays a price for his lapse of focus.

You have your couple stop, drop, and make out (or have sex) in the midst of so much danger that it's completely implausible.

The hero never sleeps, eats, goes to the restroom or otherwise takes a mental break. While it's the norm to avoid bodily functions, it's a real problem for this hero and needs to be addressed at least in part in your story.

The heroine runs away from the bodyguard or sneaks away often enough or in such a way that she comes across as a brat.

The villain isn't dangerous enough or scary enough to really challenge the hero.

The villain is so overwhelming that any sensible person would call in a LOT more help than the hero does.

The hero doesn't take advantage of all the available resources at his disposal and seems implausible or dumb for not doing so.

The hero and heroine fight through the whole story but then magically end up passionately in love.

The hero and heroine's core values differ so much that they would never plausibly end up together.

Failing to address what the hero will do for a living after your story ends. Will he return to dangerous work and leave the heroine alone a lot? Will she still be safe in his absence? Is she okay with him putting himself in danger all the time?

BODYGAURD/PROTECTOR TROPE IN ACTION
Movies:

- The Bodyguard
- True Lies
- The Hitman's Bodyguard
- The Mummy
- Knight and Day
- Speed
- Romancing the Stone

Books:

- Naked in Death by J.D. Robb (Nora Roberts)
- Extreme Exposure by Pamela Clare
- Midnight Rainbow by Linda Howard
- The Unsung Hero by Suzanne Brockmann
- Protecting What's His by Tessa Bailey
- Fourth Wing by Rebecca Yarros
- Twisted Love by Ana Huang
- The Breakup Plan by Elle Kennedy

5

CELIBATE/UNCONSUMMATED MARRIAGE

DEFINITION

In this story the hero and heroine typically enter into a marriage relationship for some other reason than true love...at least to begin the story.

Of course, it is possible for a couple to be deeply in love but for some reason choose not to sleep together as part of their marriage. It's not, however a common version of most marriages in the romance genre. If you're writing a story in another genre where a marriage is a secondary plot, you may be more likely to create a story where this happens.

At any rate, one or both of the partners typically has a compelling reason wherein they NEED to be married but are not in love with anyone. Often the person in need of marriage has some sort of a deadline to meet and must marry NOW.

The main character finds someone who is willing to enter into a marriage in name only with him or her and may offer the full financial benefits of marriage...but without the obligation to sleep with him or her. In this case, the main character is the one who introduces celibacy to the marriage.

The love interest may also have taken a vow of celibacy of some kind or believe that consummating a relationship constitutes marrying for real, obligating him or her to spend the rest of his or her life with their partner who has also now become a mate. In this case, the love interest may insist on a celibate marriage before going through with a wedding ceremony.

Once they're living together as a married couple, attraction grows between the hero and heroine until they no longer want to maintain a celibate relationship. They eventually consummate the relationship, and the marriage becomes real.

Because the entire conceit of this trope is that the couple must not sleep together, the tendency is to delay this moment until the very end of the story. If you choose to do this, you'll need to come up with an extremely compelling reason why they should not sleep together. This couple has undoubtedly fallen in love well before the end of the story and they're going to need a compelling reason not to take their already married state and simply make it a complete marriage. In most cases, there's nothing legally or morally to stop a husband and wife from sleeping together and nobody else would disapprove of or interfere with such a thing.

If, however, you choose to have your couple sleep together somewhere in the middle of the story, you'll need to manufacture serious complications and consequences for this having happened.

A married couple consummating their marriage is pretty much the end of any tension in that relationship. They'll now move forward into their married life like pretty much every couple who's ever gotten married before…unless you create some special set of circumstances that make their sleeping together as a married couple a monumental problem for them, and possibly for others.

Your couple will have to resolve these complications and consequences by the end of the story if they're to go forward into the future as a happily married (and sleeping together) couple…or possibly as a couple at all.

. . .

ADJACENT TROPES

- Celibate Hero
- Commitment Phobia
- Only One Not Married
- Marriage Pact/Bargain Comes Due
- Drunk/Vegas Wedding
- Marriage of Convenience/Fake Marriage

WHY READERS/VIEWERS LOVE THIS TROPE

- enjoying the slow burn romance
- loving the idea that marriage is about more, much more, than sex
- the fantasy of getting right all the elements of a relationship that aren't physical and only then bringing that emotional closeness to a physical relationship
- the tension and anticipation of finally consummating the relationship has plenty of time to build to an unbearable level
- the fantasy of entering into a business/friendship arrangement but finding true love when and where it's least expected

OBLIGATORY SCENES

THE BEGINNING:
One of the main characters has a compelling reason to need to get married and it may have to happen NOW. This person does not have

the time, or possibly the desire, to go looking for a spouse the old-fashioned way by dating, getting to know someone, falling in love, and eventually proposing.

The main character approaches a friend, coworker, matchmaker, or total stranger in search of help. This can take the form of asking a favor, placing a want ad, hiring an escort, or making some sort of deal with the eventual love interest.

There is typically some sort of scenario in which a marriage proposition is put to the love interest. There may be negotiation of the terms of the deal, which may or may not be monetary.

If the hero or heroine has a compelling reason why the relationship needs to remain celibate, that's typically established up front. However, it is possible to neglect to share this tiny detail until after the couple is married, particularly if the reason is secret.

The couple may spend time together trading information about each other and preparing to convince others that they're married. Or they may throw together a hasty wedding that involves snagging a few witnesses and finding someone who will perform a wedding ceremony quickly.

The beginning of this story typically ends with the main character producing and introducing his or her spouse—be it to old friends at a class reunion, to an about-to-be boss who insists that the main character be married, or to an estate executor who's awarding the main character his or her inheritance now that he/she is married.

THE MIDDLE:

The middle of the story is where the couple must now engage in their business arrangement, celibate marriage. They may get tested by others to see how well they really know each other and if the marriage is real. They may end up in situations where they must share a single bedroom or bed. They have to act married—talking, eating, and laughing together, circulating at parties together, making social appearances together, and living in the same abode.

Situations occur that force the hero and heroine to notice their attraction to each other. Regardless of how good their intentions are, the pair cannot help but notice the other one, particularly given the close quarters they now find themselves living in.

One of the characters may have an excellent reason for wanting to consummate the marriage while the other one has a compelling reason to remain celibate. If this is the case, the partner set on consummating the marriage may launch a seduction campaign to convince the celibate partner to sleep with him or her.

The couple falls in love for real somewhere in the middle of the story. It may be gradual, or the realization that they've fallen in love may hit them like a lightning bolt. It may come before they consummate the relationship or afterward. But regardless of when it happens, it's a serious problem for the couple because people in love who are married tend to sleep together.

The couple often consummates their relationship as a dramatic midpoint reversal. In this case, some major complication ensues as a result of their sleeping together. The nature of their relationship often shifts dramatically, setting up a whole new set of doubts, fears, insecurities, misbeliefs, and misunderstandings between the lovers. The negative consequences of the celibate partner (if there is just one of them pursuing this goal) becoming not celibate occur, causing a whole new set of problems the couple must now deal with.

These consequences and the big plot problem that forced the couple into marrying in the first place intermingle to cause a crisis that will ultimately tear apart the couple's relationship.

BLACK MOMENT:

The marriage implodes and one or both of the lovers wants out of the marriage. The implosion may be a result of the big plot problem blowing up into a crisis. It may be caused by the negative consequences of having slept together. Other conflicts in their relationship may blow up as a result of the couple having made the relationship physical. External forces may tear the couple apart partially or wholly because they've slept together.

Which is to say, you have a lot of options as to how you want to destroy the marriage this couple has fought so hard to build an appearance of, fought so hard to keep from becoming real, and then fought hard to preserve and protect once it became real.

Regardless of how you do it, the all is lost moment for this couple is the loss/failure of both the marriage and the reason why they agreed to a celibate marriage.

THE END:

The couple is devastated at being apart and deeply unhappy without the person they've fallen in love with and want to spend the rest of their life with. No matter what the terrible consequences, the lovers are desperate to find a way to live as the married couple they legally are.

They may have to resolve the external plot problem before they can be together, and indeed, this may be how the lovers prove to each other just how much they want to remain married.

Lies or deceptions may have to be confessed to and the consequences of those dealt with.

The lovers may owe apologies to other people and to each other.

The lovers may have to overcome serious external obstacles to be together once more, but they'll both move heaven and earth to find a way to be together. Once back together, they must resolve and forgive any last conflicts or injuries inflicted between them so they can be together.

Finally, all the obstacles to love in their path are cleared away and they can marry each other for real or they can finally resume their marriage in every way.

It's not uncommon for the couple to reintroduce themselves to the world as a married couple at the very end of the story.

KEY SCENES

- the minutiae of living with another person causes humor, friction, or conflict
- other people question the marriage's authenticity
- the hero or heroine nearly slips up and gives away the fact that the marriage isn't consummated
- the first moment when they realize there's a real romantic spark between them
- the couple shares a passionate moment that could easily become sleeping together but at the last moment, one or both of them retreats from having sex
- the negative consequences are made clear of what would happen if the celibacy of the marriage were to be violated
- after they sleep together, the whole new set of problems presents itself and is worse than either of them anticipated
- after they're sleeping together in secret, someone nearly catches them
- the partner who demanded celibacy in the first place feel guilty for having had sex with his/her spouse
- one or both of the lovers resent having to feel shame or guilt for sleeping with their legal spouse
- the couple ends a disagreement or argument by sleeping together
- having started having regular sex, they can't stop even if they try

THINGS TO THINK ABOUT WHEN WRITING THIS TROPE

Why does the main character need an immediate or contracted marriage as opposed to waiting for a love match to come along?

Why doesn't the main character want to find a spouse the usual way?

Who does the main character ask to help him or her out with this crisis wedding he/she has to produce? How does that go?

How soon does the main character need to have a spouse? Is there a specific deadline?

What does the main character offer the love interest to engage in a celibate marriage with him or her? Does the love interest negotiate any terms of his/her own for the deal?

Who insists that there be no sex? Why? If it's just one of them, how does the other partner feel about that?

Does one partner have a compelling reason TO consummate the relationship while the other one has a compelling reason NOT TO?

What are the consequences to both partners if it's discovered they haven't had sex...or *have* had sex?

In the world you've created in your story, is the marriage valid and legal if the couple hasn't consummated it? What happens if they don't consummate their marriage and others discover they haven't done so?

Is there an interloper or third party who'd love to break up the marriage or prove it's unconsummated? If so, who is this person, why, and how will he/she go about breaking up the marriage?

Does anyone test the couple to see if they're really sleeping together? If so, how does that happen and how does it go? How can you make it a near miss with disaster that the couple barely avoids?

What do friends, family, and coworkers think of this marriage? Do they support it or try to sabotage it?

How are the celibate couple trapped or forced into acting as if they are sleeping together and have consummated the marriage?

What problems/conflicts/frictions will the couple encounter between them as they commence living together?

What about each other attracts the couple to each other?

What situations will you throw the couple into where their mutual attraction can grow—or explode—between them?

What social situations will you throw the couple into where they have to act married? How do those go?

Does one of the partners set out to seduce the other one? If so which one? How does that go? What are several increasingly seductive things he or she can do that will increasingly tempt the other partner to give in and sleep with him or her?

When and how do they each realize they've fallen in love?

When do they each tell the other one, "I love you?"

When do they consummate the relationship?

What happens in the immediate aftermath of their sleeping together? Can you make this worse? Much worse? Catastrophically bad?

What's the external plot problem that both forced them together and will eventually force them apart? How will it blow up into a crisis that destroys their marriage?

Does the implosion of the marriage cause the big plot crisis or vice versa? Or do they happen simultaneously?

What or who ultimately breaks up the marriage? How does this happen?

How do the hero and heroine feel about the destruction of their marriage?

How will the couple ultimately resolve the big plot problem?

How will the couple deal with the fallout from their breakup?

How will the couple physically get back together? This may involve overcoming obstacles to physically being in proximity, one may resist seeing the other, or some external force or person may be keeping them apart.

Who apologizes to whom and for what? Do the lovers owe any outsiders apologies?

What does "real" married life look like by the end of the story? How is it better, sweeter, and more honest than the arrangement they had before, and how will you show this to your audience?

. . .

TROPE TRAPS

The reason for entering into a celibate marriage is lame, dumb, or implausible to your audience.

Failing to establish sufficiently awful consequences for NOT marrying to convince your audience the main character is doing the right thing by entering into this celibate marriage.

The hero or heroine is unlikable and your audience roots for the marriage to fail.

There's another character in the story who would make a much better spouse for one of the main characters and your audience is mad that this character doesn't get the girl/guy in the end.

There's no compelling reason for the couple not to just sleep together and scratch that itch.

The couple gives in too soon to their lust or holds out way longer than is plausible.

There are no growing pains and adjustment to living with another person, particularly in a marital-style relationship.

The partner trying to seduce the celibate partner is being super disrespectful of a vow the celibate partner took or of the reason why the celibate partner made that a condition of the marriage.

Nobody's ever suspicious of this sudden wedding, and nobody ever challenges the veracity of the relationship or tests its veracity in any way.

If tested, the hero and heroine pass the "are you really married and sleeping together" tests with flying colors that are boring and don't add to the tension or suspense of the story.

The hero and heroine have no relationship problems or conflicts beyond the fact that they're not sleeping together.

Failure to add layers of complications to the marriage being consummated.

One of the partners could walk away from the marriage at any time with no negative consequences and has no good reason not to.

The couple falls in love too fast.

The couple falls into bed well before they start to fall in love.

The outcome of the big plot problem has little or nothing to do with whether or not they make the marriage real in every way.

The couple breaks up for a dumb reason.

Never explaining why, if they're so in love, the hero and heroine don't stay together to weather the storm when the consequences of their having slept together happen.

An honest, adult conversation and/or a simple apology would fix the whole breakup between the lovers, which is to say they don't have any really difficult or significant obstacles/conflicts to overcome.

Failing to make the hero and heroine face the consequences of their actions.

Neither the hero nor heroine learns any big lesson(s) or has any epiphany that makes them ready to have a healthy, real marriage by the end of the story.

Failing to show the couple engaged in a healthy, real marriage at the end.

CELIBATE/UNCONSUMMATED MARRIAGE TROPE IN ACTION
Movies:

- The Proposal
- Green Card
- Shadowlands
- What Happens in Vegas
- The Wedding Date
- Picture Perfect
- Loving Leah
- The Painted Veil
- Away From Her

Books:

- The Marriage Bargain by Jennifer Probst
- Roomies by Christina Lauren
- The Wall of Winnipeg and Me by Mariana Zapata
- Marrying Winterborne by Lisa Kleypas
- Marriage for One by Ella Maise
- A Kingdom of Dreams by Judith McNaught
- To Have and to Hoax by Martha Waters

- The Madness of Lord Ian Mackenzie by Jennifer Ashley
- Artistic License by Elle Pierson

6

COMING HOME

DEFINITION

In this trope, one of your main characters has left home at some point in the past. Now, for reasons that will drive the plot of your story, he or she has come home again. It may be a permanent move back home or it may be temporary.

What's unique about this trope is that backstory may play an outsized role in the telling of your story. You may need to use it to:

- reveal past events that drove the main character away from home
- reveal why the character has decided to come home again
- reveal past relationships that the main character resumes after he or she gets home
- reveal what has changed about the character in the interim that he or she has been gone from home
- reveal what the main character did after leaving home

A challenge of this trope, then, is making sure to keep the focus of your story on the here and now. Backstory is, by its very nature slower and less interesting than current events simply because we know more or less how the backstory turned out.

The main character is still alive, still here, other characters are still alive and here—there's not much suspense to most backstories unless you plan to reveal truly shocking secrets that your audience never saw coming.

Another challenge of this trope is seamlessly weaving in the backstory to the current events:

- You may choose to signal backstory scenes by italicizing them
- You may put a date and place stamp at the beginning of the scene (it's technically called an epigraph, in case you care)

Perhaps the biggest challenge of all in writing a backstory heavy story is finding the right balance of story spent in the past and story spent in the present. Each story is going have its own perfect balance, so I can't give you any rules or suggestions other than to be conscious of it.

The general wisdom on backstory is to keep it out of Chapter One, only tell your audience members what they absolutely need to know about the past not to get lost in the current story, and don't be in a rush to reveal your backstory. And, of course, when in doubt, leave it out.

Please note that I haven't called any of these "rules" of backstory. I'm a big believer that there are no hard and fast rules of writing, or at least none that can't be broken. Do whatever you need to do to tell your story in the most compelling way and that serves your story best.

Here are a few tricks I've learned over the years to sneak in bits of backstory without destroying the forward movement of your story:

- Characters in the present can talk about past events without you indulging in any explanations or lengthy narrative. A quick bit of reminiscence, a sidebar comment about a past event they all remember, can give your audience vital information about past relationships and past events. Who was the cool kid back then and who was the geek? Who knows about the big secret thing that happened in the past? Who has regrets about past events? All of this sort of detail can be revealed in very fast snippets of dialogue or internal monologue...and it's fine if your audience doesn't fully understand the references in the moment. Curiosity to fully understand a snarky or vaguely incomprehensible comment helps pull your readers forward into the story.

- **NOTE**: If the main character has something to say about past events to the audience, that's not actually backstory. That's his or her current perspective on past events and reflects his or her life experiences up to this moment. So, you can get away with a certain amount of commentary from the main character about past events without interrupting your audience's sense of still being in the present.
- Another trick is to have current events mirror past events. The homecoming game all those years ago that blew up the main character's life can be paralleled by the main character coming home to attend a homecoming game, or perhaps accidentally arriving home at homecoming season, for example. By going through the current event, the main character can remember or relive the past events seamlessly as the two similar experiences overlap in his or her mind.
- Use a current sensory stimulus to trigger a past memory—the main character smells something burned and it reminds him or her of the night of the fire and the horror of it. You give your audience a very brief snippet of

flashback and then jump right back to the present and continue on with your story. This works because it's how our brains all work, and your audience will very naturally follow the brief distraction and return to the present.

At any rate, your main character left home, went forth into the world and did things, and now is coming home again. This story arc explores why he or she did all three of these things. And of course, at the same time your main character is dealing with the emotional baggage left over from all three of these decisions, he or she is also falling in love.

It's worth noting that this trope focuses heavily on the character doing the coming home. It's easy for the love interest to become little more than an accessory to the main character's journey. Hence, this trope is often paired with a trope that focuses heavily on the love interest or a trope that involves the love interest—a second chance romance or a reunion story, for example. Often the love interest in this story is the girl or boy the main character left behind, never forgot, or fled from for some reason.

The love interest may be from the same place and share many past experiences with the main character.

OR

The love interest experienced the same past events but perceived them in a very different way from the main character.

OR

The love interest may have come to this place after the main character left, may have heard about the main character and past events the main character experienced, but has never met the main character.

OR

The love interest may have come to town after the main character left and knows nothing of the past events that shaped the main character's life and decisions to leave and eventually come home.

As the main character works out whatever traumas, memories, changes in self, or need to reconnect with something or someone from his/her past, the love interest is there to provide support, love, perspective, and possibly a swift kick in the pants to the main character as they fall in love and build or rebuild a romantic relationship.

ADJACENT TROPES

- Fresh Start
- Home for the Holiday/Vacation Fling
- Reconciliation/ Second Chance
- Reunion
- Right Under Your Nose
- Running Away from Home

WHY READERS/VIEWERS LOVE THIS TROPE

- there's real nostalgia in returning home and reliving old memories
- the fantasy of recapturing our relatively carefree, innocent, happy youth
- getting a chance to go back and fix past mistakes, to make things right, to put aside regrets that have haunted us
- we all love the idea of finding emotional healing at home, in a safe space surrounded by loved ones, family, friends, and familiar places and things

- when the world gets scary, we can go back to someplace we know, where we feel safe, and where we're unconditionally loved

OBLIGATORY SCENES

THE BEGINNING:

Usually, the opening scene is the actual moment of the main character coming home. We see him or her arrive in town—but do try to resist having the main character flooded in memories that leads to length flashbacks unless it's absolutely necessary to your story.

Typically in the very first scene or one of the very first scenes, the main character encounters the person who will ultimately become the love interest in your story. This trope is conducive to true meet cutes where the main character and love interest bump into each other and meet (or meet again) in some interesting or amusing way.

Even though it's called a "cute" meeting, it's probably more accurate to call it a memorable meeting that sets the tone for your whole story. But that's a big mouthful to remember, so it's generally referred to simply as a meet-cute. Just be aware there's no requirement for there to be anything cute about it if that's not the tone of story you plan to write.

We often see the main character physically return to his or her old home, meeting up with family, friends, and loved ones, and encountering people from his or her past. We'll learn a lot about who the main character is by the way all these secondary characters react to him or her without having to devolve into lengthy backstory narratives.

The beginning usually ends with the revelation of why the main character has chosen to return home and why now. Often this reason is a problem, dilemma, or trauma the main character has come home to deal with and resolve. You have a wide range of possibilities for what this problem is. It might be purely psychological—he or she has lost their mojo at doing something they used to do well here and they've come home to find it again. Or it might be terrifying and suspenseful—he or she has come home to expose an awful secret or solve the unsolved murder of a friend or loved one.

Have fun with why the main character has come back home. This will form the spine of your plot and be what makes it fresh, interesting, and unique to your audience.

THE MIDDLE:

We spend much of the middle with the main character going back to past places of significance to him or her, rehashing past events and experiences, reminiscing, perhaps investigating past events or trying to learn what others still in this place remember about past events...and of course, getting to know the love interest.

Even if the hero and heroine had a romantic relationship in the past, time has passed and they're different people than they were back then. They still have to go through the full getting to know you process again, even if they don't have to tell the other one much about their past in this place since they both lived it.

Note: very few people remember events and experiences in exactly the same way as anyone else. The details they noticed, the things that stuck out as memorable to them, what they thought of the event or experience, how they felt about it, all of that will color their recollection of the past. Hence, much of the middle of this story will revolve around your various characters comparing notes on how they remember past events and experiences, and potentially disagreeing on how things really happened.

The love interest gets sucked into the main character's reason for coming back home. If the main character is looking for some lost skill or lost confidence, the love interest is probably involved in that search in some way. If the main character is looking to heal a past trauma, the love interest is involved in that trauma in some way.

As the main character gets closer and closer to the core of the problem he or she has come home to fix, the more intense, stressful, or even dangerous the search for answers becomes. I'm not suggesting that this has to be a suspense story, merely that long-buried emotions get exposed, raw nerves get exposed, scabs get torn off wounds, and old traumas, conflicts, and bad memories get dredged up the more deeply the main character digs for answers.

If the hero and heroine have a shared past history, old conflicts from their past flare up to bite them again. Old conflicts may threaten to tear them apart. Old secrets fester between them.

If the hero and heroine have no shared past history, then the wounds from the main character's past and the love interest's frustration over those wounds or over the main character's failure to deal with those wounds probably serves as a major source of conflict between the lovers.

Whatever problem the main character has come to town to solve blows up into a crisis as the middle of the story ends.

BLACK MOMENT:

Whatever the main character has come home to try to do fails. He or she doesn't uncover the big secret or solve the old crime. He or she doesn't find the magical source of missing mojo. He or she doesn't find a way to heal the old trauma, wound, or pain that he or she was hoping to find.

Worse, in failing to put to bed old ghosts, the main character also blows up his or her relationship with the love interest. If they have a shared past, the problem(s) that broke them up before break them up again, now. The main character has failed to change the past and set things right. If they have no shared past, the main character fails to set aside the past to embrace the present...and the future...with the love interest. The long-suffering love interest has waited around patiently for the main character to get his or her act together, but the main character has failed (or refused) to do so, and the love interest is done waiting.

Everything is lost. The character coming home has failed to find what he or she was looking for. The main character briefly found love, but then lost it. He or she has made a mess of everything and ended up with nothing that he or she was searching for.

THE END:

Some new information comes to light, someone confesses something, or the hero and/or heroine puts together some piece of information that was right in front of them all along. Or the main character, in his or her moment of utter failure and loss learns something, has a revelation, or breaks through a mental or emotional block that finally allows him or her to succeed at solving the problem he or she has come home to face.

The main character and love interest make one last attempt to face the problems between them and find a way to come back together. They've lost their love once already and hated every minute of it, so they're willing to give it one more shot to get it right.

Apologies are made, grand gestures of love are made, serious talks and reconciliations happen, and the couple finds a way past their conflicts to be together.

In a perfect world, solving the plot problem leads to the lesson or breakthrough that allows the couple to resolve their personal conflicts and be together. But not all stories work out that way. It's okay to solve the big plot problem and, now that this all-consuming problem is off the lovers' plates, they can finally turn their attention to resolving their own relationship.

At any rate, the character who came home may choose to stay home permanently with his or her true love. Or the couple may leave home having resolved the thing that brought the main character back. Either is fine as long as you establish that home for the main character is wherever the love interest is and that home is the people you love and not the place where you hang your hat.

KEY SCENES

- the main character reveals why he or she left home (which may be totally innocent or can be a huge reveal)
- the main character reveals why he or she came back home (which is usually a big reveal)
- the main character and love interest have a major disagreement about their perception of the place the main character calls home
- family, friends, or loved ones from the main character's past have an unexpected, nuanced, complicated, or surprising reaction to seeing the main character again
- the main character decides to or tries to leave again
- the love interest accuses the main character of not facing his or her past

THINGS TO THINK ABOUT WHEN WRITING THIS TROPE

Where is "home" to your main character? Why did he or she leave there in the first place? Why is he or she coming home again? Why now?

Build the main character's backstory with a focus on the big events that shaped him or her as a person and made him or her who they are today. Now...be brutally selective in which pieces of this history your audience needs to know to understand the story.

Who's the love interest? Is he or she part of the main character's past? If so, how? Which is to say, you'll need to build this character's backstory as well.

If the hero and heroine are from the same place, what's their shared past? What did they think of each other before? Have they dated in the past? If so, what broke them up the first time?

If the love interest is from the hometown, why did he or she stay here…or has the love interest left and come back as well?

What unresolved traumas, problems, relationships, or secrets lurk in the main character's past in this place? Does the main character consciously intend to deal with this issue when he or she comes home or not? Why or why not?

How do the main character and love interest meet (or meet again) in your story? How does this meeting set the tone for the rest of your story?

How do the hero and heroine perceive the hometown and people in it differently?

How do they recall past events in this place differently?

Is there something from the main character's past in this place that he or she is terrified to face or deal with? What or who is it?

How will you force your main character to confront this person, thing, or event? Or more accurately, how will the love interest force the main character to face the terrifying person, thing, or event?

How do family, friends, and loved ones from this place react to the main character coming home? How is this a source of conflict in your story?

What does the main character want to achieve by coming home? Is this what he or she really needs…or is there something else he or she is actually searching for by coming home? If so, what is that?

How will he or she become aware of this need? How will he or she get what they need?

How is the love interest the key to your main character getting what he or she wants and needs from coming home?

What does the love interest want and need from this relationship?

Is the love interest going to have his or her own trope or development arc in this story? If so, how does it interact with, interfere with, and intertwine with the main character's growth arc and/or this trope?

What are the main conflicts between the hero and heroine that threaten to tear them apart? Are they old conflicts they failed to fix in the past? Are they new conflicts?

What are the layers of the conflict between the hero and heroine:

- What superficial thing do they disagree about?
- What important but external—relating to the story's plot—thing do they disagree about?
- What belief do they disagree about?
- What personal emotional issue do they disagree about?
- What about their relationship itself do they disagree about?
- What secret thing do they disagree about?

How will your hero and heroine resolve each of these conflicts?

What does your main character believe about his or her home, past events, or people in the hometown that's wrong? How will he or she figure out they've had it wrong all along?

What does your main character think or believe about himself or herself that's wrong? How will the love interest show him or her that this belief is wrong?

What lessons does the main character learn from having come home that are transformative and make him or her better able to face their life going forward? How is the love interest key to the main character learning this lesson?

What lessons do the main character learn from having come home that are transformative and make him or her able to have a healthy romantic relationship with the love interest? How is the love interest key to the main character learning this lesson?

Does the main character stay home for good at the end of the story, or do the hero and heroine ultimately leave this place?

. . .

TROPE TRAPS

The number one trap for this trope is that the love interest has no growth arc and no important role in the story other than being a prop for the main character's journey.

The main character has gotten "too big" for his or her hometown and comes across as a jerk.

The love interest is painfully cliché and uninteresting to your audience.

There are no emotional landmines lurking in the hometown for the main character to stumble upon and blow up.

The new conflicts in the story don't mirror old ones or at least make the old conflicts more interesting, understandable, and relevant.

Backstory overwhelms and buries the current-day story.

Too much backstory or the wrong backstory destroys the pacing of your story and slows it down too much or kills the suspense of what will happen next.

The main character remembers everything and everyone accurately.

Nobody has changed since the main character left.

The hometown is magically frozen in time in your story and nothing has changed.

There are no past secrets, scandals, or bad things lurking in this idyllically fake town.

The main character doesn't have a compelling reason for coming back home.

The love interest has had no life of his or her own since the main character left town and has no backstory and no baggage of his or her own.

Relying on nostalgia to fix all of the main character's problems.

Relying on the simple act of coming home to fix all of the main character's problems. He or she doesn't have to do any actual personal growth work to fix what's wrong inside himself or herself.

The main character is excessively, implausibly self-aware and knows exactly what he or she needs from the very beginning of your story.

The love interest plays no key role in the main character's growth arc.

The conflicts between the hero and heroine would be fully solved if they just sat down and had an honest, adult conversation with each other—a conversation they inexplicably refuse to have for the bulk of your story.

The main character doesn't learn any lessons by coming home, or the lesson he/she learns isn't relatable to your audience.

At the end of the day, coming home doesn't change anything for the main character.

COMING HOME TROPE IN ACTION
Movies:

- Sweet Home Alabama
- The Notebook
- Garden State
- Hope Floats
- One Fine Day
- The Judge
- Sweet November
- Grandma's Boy

Books:

- The Summer That Made Us by Robyn Carr
- Blue Heron by Kristan Higgins
- Sweet Magnolias by Sherryl Woods
- It Ends with Us by Colleen Hoover

- One Day in December by Josie Silver
- The Weekenders by Mary Alice Monroe
- Suddenly You by Lisa Kleypas
- Ain't She Sweet by Susan Elizabeth Phillips
- Coming Home by Rosamunde Pilcher
- The Summerhouse by Jude Deveraux
- The Girl Who Chased the Moon by Sarah Addison Allen

7
DEATHBED CONFESSION

DEFINITION

This story begins with a dying person revealing a secret of some kind. That secret sets off a chain of events that brings together the hero and heroine to deal with the aftermath of this big secret's revelation.

It's worth noting that certain mysteries and crime thrillers can end with a deathbed confession that solves the whodunnit...but this trope specifically *begins* with a deathbed confession that launches a search, problem, or crisis of some kind.

The secret can be as huge as the dying person having killed someone, as personal as the dying person having had a secret child, to something completely unexpected. Have fun cooking up something really imaginative for the dying person to confess to.

The word "confession" connotes a crime; however, this trope covers all secrets that are vitally important to the dying person not to take to the grave with himself or herself. As you cook up your dying person's confession, keep in mind that the information revealed will set the tone and mood for your whole story. It also will create the main problem or crisis of your plot, so make it big enough that it takes your entire story to resolve.

The hero and heroine may already know each other through the dying person, or they may never have met before. But they do both have some connection to the secret the dying person confessed to.

One or both of them may be present for the deathbed confession, or they may both be contacted after the death by someone who was present to hear the confession. Either way, the deathbed confession draws the hero and heroine together until the revelation can be dealt with.

Of course, along the way in solving the big plot problem, the hero and heroine fall in love and find their own happily ever after.

ADJACENT TROPES

- Dangerous Secret
- Forced Proximity
- Terms of the Will
- Treasure Hunt
- Matchmaker/Matchmaker Gone Wrong

WHY READERS/VIEWERS LOVE THIS TROPE

- who doesn't love a great, juicy secret being revealed? We're all naturally curious and desire to know hidden truths
- we'd all like to think that, at the end of our lives, we'll find closure and be able to release regrets and secrets and be forgiven by those who love us
- this trope causes us all to reflect on our own mortality and the secrets we may be carrying that we would hate to take to the grave with us

- we'd love to be torn out of our boring, mundane lives and sent on an exciting adventure that leads to something of great value at the end of it

OBLIGATORY SCENES

THE BEGINNING:

This story almost always begins with the deathbed confession itself. Not only is the moment of a human being's death dramatic and highly charged emotionally, but this moment reveals a secret so important that someone used his or her last breaths to reveal it. Your audience will desperately want to know more about a revelation this important.

We may or may not see the moment of the dying person's passing. It'll depend on the tone of your story, and it may depend on how the dying person dies.

You can, of course, choose to have the dying person make his or her confession and not die immediately. Instead, the dying person asks the hero and heroine to do something before he or she dies. In this scenario, you've set an urgent and short clock ticking down in your story that pushes the hero and heroine to frantic haste.

The hero and heroine, if not already drawn together to hear the deathbed confession are brought together because of their shared connection to the secret. And yes, this may actually be the dying person's plan all along. The confession can be the last machination of a matchmaker to force your hero and heroine together.

The hero's and heroine's motives for trying to resolve the problem revealed by the deathbed confession are usually not the same and may, in fact, stand in direct opposition to each other. The dying person may have put them into some sort of race against each other.

Or, one of them may have a vested interest in not letting the revealed secret become public knowledge.

This trope tends not to be particularly interesting if it's merely about two people working together in pleasant cooperation to solve a problem set for them by a dying person's confession. How much more interesting is this story if the hero and heroine are working at cross purposes, keeping secrets of their own from each other, or they dislike each other initially and struggle to cooperate even a little?

The beginning of your story usually sets up these cross purposes, secrets, and conflicts between the hero and heroine.

By the end of the beginning, the hero and heroine have come together and have launched upon the investigation, search, treasure hunt, or whatever other kind of journey the deathbed confession sets in front of them.

Because it's a good thing to end major sections of your book with some exciting revelation or major crisis, this story's beginning usually ends with some new revelation about the deathbed confession. Perhaps there was more to it than the dying person managed to express. Perhaps a somewhat incomprehensible dying confession has become clear, now, and the full story is even more shocking that the hero and heroine initially thought.

OR

You may end the beginning by the hero and heroine realizing that what they thought was going to be an easy or fast resolution is going to be much more complicated or difficult than they originally thought. Particularly in the case where they're racing against a clock of the dying person's death, this may constitute a rather large crisis.

THE MIDDLE:

The hero and heroine investigate, search, travel, or do what's necessary to pursue solving the problem the dying person has set for them. The cross purposes, secrets, and conflicts between the hero and heroine grow more complicated as we learn more details about them and we watch the hero and heroine spar and dance around each other like a pair of sword duelists, each trying to draw blood or disable their opponent.

It's against this backdrop of an urgent investigation and simmering conflict that the pair gets to know each other, experiences a spark of attraction, and begins to fall in love.

With each new discovery about the secret they're investigating, the urgency to get to the bottom of it increases. Each new piece of information you reveal to your audience should add a new twist to the truth the hero and heroine are trying to uncover.

Think in terms of surprises, twists, and changes of direction. Let your audience think the secret is one thing but then reveal something that makes your audience think it might be something else entirely. The more off balance you keep your main characters, the more off balance you'll keep your audience.

The conflict between the hero and heroine regarding their investigation will definitely spill over into their personal relationship as it develops. As personal conflicts, disagreements, and clashes of beliefs and values happen, these usually parallel the conflicts of the investigation or amplify the plot conflicts. Vice versa, the conflicts revolving around their investigation usually cause or amplify the relationship conflicts between the hero and heroine.

The middle ends with a big revelation in the investigation that triggers a crisis of some kind. This crisis is not only related to the plot but also spills over to become a crisis in the hero and heroine's romance.

If you've set up a ticking clock counting down to the dying person's death, the middle often ends with the hero and heroine running out of time. They get a call that they'd better get back to the dying person's side now to say their last goodbyes, the dying person has slipped into a coma, or something similar.

If the hero and heroine are going to solve the problem, they have to do it right now. If there's a big risk they've been avoiding taking, now is the moment they have no choice but to do it.

BLACK MOMENT:

The hero and heroine fail to find the thing they're searching for. The dying person may even die before they can return to his or her side and give the dying person the closure they both promised to deliver.

Furthermore, the conflicts in their relationship explode and they break up. By now, they may know the dying person forced them together in an act of matchmaking, and they've even failed the dying person in that way, too.

They've failed at the quest and they've failed at love. All is lost.

THE END:

The hero and heroine learn something new, see something they missed before, or make one last try to find the missing piece to the puzzle. And this time, they finally find a way to solve the mystery or reveal the last critical piece of the secret.

The couple may have to set aside their differences long enough to complete their quest with the understanding that once they've both honored their promise to the dying person, that'll be the end and they'll go their separate ways.

But once they come back together to finish the quest, they're reminded of why they actually love each other and of how much they've missed each other. At long last, they make apologies to each other, talk out their differences, and make grand gestures of love.

The act of uncovering the last of the secret, finding the MacGuffin, or solving the mystery is ultimately secondary to the couple figuring out how to be happy ever after together. Hence, you'll usually solve the mystery first and then resolve the couple romantic relationship.

If the dying person hasn't died already, the couple reports back to him or her with what they've found. If the dying person has already died, he or she may reach out from beyond the grave with a letter, will, recording (or in the case of a paranormal story, a dream or visitation by a ghost) to thank the hero and heroine for dealing with his or her deathbed confession.

It may be the act of going back to the dying person's side or memorial service that triggers the resolution of their personal conflicts.

Because this story begins with the dying person's deathbed confession, it's common to let the dead person have the last word in some way. It can be as simple as the hero and heroine remembering some prediction the now-passed person made or something that person said that has turned out to be accurate or true.

It could be a prediction that the hero and heroine are perfect for each other, or it could be some pithy life lesson that the pair has learned over the course of their investigation, or it could be a statement of the theme of your story.

The story ends with the hero and heroine having found true love and heading off into their happily ever after together.

KEY SCENES

- the hero and/or heroine don't want to do whatever the dying person has asked of them. Individually or together, they try to refuse to accept the quest or to dodge doing it
- the hero and heroine blame the dying person for forcing them together (in what turns into a shared moment of commiseration)
- the hero and heroine's conflicting purposes for doing this investigation come into direct and open conflict
- conflict between the hero and heroine threatens to or does derail their investigation

- if there's danger involved in their investigation, conflict between the hero and heroine nearly gets one or both of them harmed or killed
- the dying person leaves some sort of communication for them for after he or she is gone or, if still alive, communicates with them during the investigation, revealing something that changes everything about their investigation

THINGS TO THINK ABOUT WHEN WRITING THIS TROPE

Who's the dying person and what's his or her deathbed confession going to be? What's the whole backstory of the deathbed confession?

How will you reveal the whole truth in bits and pieces? Can you make the reveals of information more surprising, more twisty, more misleading, and more prone to changing or reversing everything the hero, heroine, and audience think they know about the big secret, problem, or crisis?

What makes the thing confessed about urgent enough to force two people to drop everything and go on a hunt for a resolution? Can you make it more urgent? Much more urgent?

When does the dying person actually expire in your story? Why then?

How does the dying person feel about the thing he or she is confessing? How will you show this?

What is the dying person's relationship with and to the hero and heroine, individually and/or together? What does the dying person think of each of them and feel about each of them?

Does the dying person have an ulterior motive for making this confession now?

Who does the dying person make his or her confession to? Who hears it directly? Why that person(s)? Is it a matter of running out of time and telling whoever's there to listen, or is the dying person intentional in who he or she confesses to?

Do the hero and heroine know each other before the deathbed confession? If so, how? What's their past history together? What's their relationship like now?

If the hero and heroine are strangers when the story begins, how are they each connected to the deathbed confession or the dying person making it?

Is the hero or heroine an expert in investigating the thing they've been sent to find?

Does the hero or heroine have any special skills or expertise they bring to the investigation?

What do the hero and heroine think of each other when the story begins? How do they feel about each other?

Why are the hero and heroine each reluctant to do the thing that's been asked of them in the dying person's deathbed confession?

Why do each of them ultimately agree to resolve the thing revealed in the deathbed confession?

What do the hero and heroine have to do to research, investigate, and resolve the problem caused by the deathbed confession?

How will their investigation force the hero and heroine into continued proximity with each other throughout the story?

Why doesn't just one of them investigate the problem? Why do both of them have to do it together?

What motives for doing the investigation do the hero and heroine have individually? How are these motives in conflict with each other?

What do the hero and heroine each hope to gain from the investigation? How are these goals in conflict with each other?

How does the hero and heroine's romantic relationship mirror their investigation in terms of conflicts, friction points, and cross purposes?

What do the hero and heroine each find attractive about each other? Fascinating? Irresistible?

What drives them crazy about each other in a good way and in a bad way?

Is there an element of danger to their investigation? If so, what is it and how does the danger grow throughout the story?

How does the hero and heroine's romantic relationship interfere with their investigation? How does the investigation interfere with their romantic relationship?

How does conflict between the hero and heroine nearly derail the entire investigation?

How do they work together very well to avoid a difficult or dangerous situation?

How do they fail to achieve what the dying person asked of them, or fail to achieve it in time?

How do they feel about this?

What changes that convinces them to give solving the problem one last try?

How will they eventually resolve the problem caused by the deathbed confession?

Do they make it back to the dying person in time to tell him or her the outcome of their investigation, or do they have the satisfaction of keeping their promise to the now deceased person?

Do they attend a memorial service of some kind for the deceased confessor or in some way celebrate that person's life?

What legacy do they fulfill that was asked of them?

Did the deceased person actually throw them together intentionally? If so, when do the hero and heroine figure that out? How do they figure it out?

What lesson(s) do the hero and heroine learn over the course of this investigation? How does it make each of them a better person, heal a wound, or make them capable of healthy love (or all of the above)?

How do the hero and heroine ultimately resolve their personal disagreements, differences, and conflicts to be able to be together happily in the long term?

What does happily ever after look like for this pair?

TROPE TRAPS

The dying person gives away too many details in his or her deathbed confession that wrecks the suspense and surprise of revealing the full details of the thing he or she is confessing to.

The big secret revealed isn't big enough or complicated enough to sustain a good plot all the way through your story.

The hero and heroine don't make sense to be the ones asked to resolve the big problem.

The hero and heroine magically develop specialized skills necessary to complete their investigation without any actual training or explanation of how they know how to do something that takes a long time to learn.

The hero and heroine are so fundamentally different that your audience doesn't find a romance between them plausible.

One or both of your main characters is deeply unlikable and turns off your audience.

The hidden motives the hero and/or heroine has for doing this investigation makes one or both of them seem selfish, greedy, sneaky, and wholly unheroic.

There are no big surprises along the way in the investigation.

Failing to create any sense of urgency or ticking clock to the investigation to give it some sort of reason for needing to move at anything other than a leisurely, boring pace.

There are no real conflicts between the hero and heroine that threaten their long-term romantic relationship.

Their investigation never affects their romantic relationship and vice versa.

Their investigation in no way mirrors or has anything to do with their romantic relationship and vice versa.

The hero and heroine bicker so much or so meanly that your audience doesn't buy them ever falling in love.

Failing to have the hero and heroine actually grieve for the person who died.

Surprise! The dying person isn't really dying. (If you're going to pull this tired, old rabbit out of the hat, try to find a way to make it actually surprising, actually interesting, and actually necessary to your plot.)

Failing to ever memorialize or celebrate the life of the person who died.

DEATHBED CONFESSION TROPE IN ACTION
Movies:

- Big Fish
- The Usual Suspects
- The Notebook
- Citizen Kane
- P.S. I Love You
- Letters to Juliet

Books:

- The Best Man by Kristan Higgins
- The Sweetest Thing by Jill Shalvis
- The Marriage Bargain by Jennifer Probst
- The Secret Life of Violet Grant by Beatriz Williams
- The Last Letter from Your Lover by Jojo Moyes
- The Truth About Forever by Sarah Dessen
- The Summer Guest by Emma Hannigan
- The Matchmaker's List by Sonya Lalli
- The Last Promise by Richard Paul Evans

8
DISGUISED AS MALE/FEMALE

DEFINITION

In this story, one of your main characters disguises himself or herself as the opposite of their chosen gender for some reason. Doing this as a one-time occurrence in a story doesn't rise to the level of a trope. What turns this cross-dressing into a trope is when the character sustains the disguise through a significant portion of the story for a specific reason.

This is a common trope in historical romances where women were excluded from many places, and the only way to gain entrance was to masquerade as a man. For example, visiting gentlemen's clubs, crewing on a ship, or attending classes at a university would have been men only activities.

Likewise, women have a long history of not being allowed to act in theaters or perform in public. It's not uncommon in historical fiction to see men dress as women to perform on stage or even to see women pretending to be men pretending to be women.

There are, of course, many other reasons your main character might choose to masquerade as the opposite of their identified gender that range from silly to lethal. Indeed, the reason a character decides to gender switch will determine the entire tone and mood of your story. This compelling reason probably forms the core of your story's plot, as well...which is to say, give serious thought to why your main character disguises himself or herself in another gender.

In one version of this story, the hero and heroine meet while presenting the genders to which they usually identify and are attracted to each other. Then one or the other chooses or is forced into presenting as another gender, and they meet again with one of them disguised. Complications, misunderstandings, and attraction ensue.

The love interest is torn between the two people he or she is simultaneously attracted to while the disguised main character must figure out how to reveal the ruse without alienating the love interest and without causing a crisis in the plot problem that's causing him or her to disguise himself/herself.

OR

Vice versa, the lovers may first meet with one of them disguised in a gender in which he or she doesn't usually identify. In this scenario, they become friends or are attracted to each other, and complications ensue.

It's common in this version of the story for the love interest to dislike the main character when he or she is not in disguise, effectively trapping the main character in his or her disguise to romance the love interest, while unable to admit to the love interest who he or she really is. In this version, it's the main character caught on the horns of a dilemma. Does he or she reveal their true identity and risk losing the person he or she loves?

Regardless of how you set up the disguise and what the love interest thinks of the two versions of the main character, the love interest ultimately sees through the disguise and is drawn into the main character's jeopardy.

The entire world typically finds out about the disguise eventually, and the main character has to face the consequences of his or her masquerade. But with the love and support of the love interest, they find a way through to the other side and to happily ever after.

ADJACENT TROPES

- Dangerous Secret
- False Identity
- Secret Identity
- Hero/Heroine in Hiding
- Hero/Heroine in Disguise
- On the Run

WHY READERS/VIEWERS LOVE THIS TROPE

- who isn't curious from time to time to wonder what it would be like to live in another gender
- getting a glimpse at the secret world of another gender
- being invisible and able to move through the world without anyone knowing who you are
- exploring one's feminine or masculine side, particularly in a time and place where it might otherwise be difficult to do

OBLIGATORY SCENES

THE BEGINNING:

The hero and heroine may meet first and then one of them encounters a problem whose only solution is for him or her to assume another gender identity. Or these two events may occur in the opposite order.

Likewise, the main character may first meet the love interest while in disguise or while not in disguise. In either case, fairly early in your story, the love interest encounters the main character again, but this time in disguise.

The beginning is often taken up by the decision to assume another gender identity and figuring out how to do it. It's common for at least one other person to be in on the secret, a trusted confidante or relative who can help pull off the disguise.

The beginning usually ends with the first big test of the disguise. Can the heroine attend a medical lecture as a man and get away with it? Can the hero enter a harem dressed as a woman to search for or rescue a female target and convince the women there that he is actually a she?

THE MIDDLE:

Once the main character has shown proof of concept—that he or she can get away with masquerading under a different gender identity—he or she can get on with the business of solving the big plot problem that has required him or her to disguise himself or herself.

But the real meat of the middle of your story will be taken up by the developing romance between the main character and love interest…and between the disguised main character and the love interest. The main character is clear in his or her feelings and is unequivocally attracted to the love interest.

However, the love interest's feeling are anything but clear. Either the love interest is simultaneously attracted to two very different people, or the love interest is deeply attracted to the disguised main character and deeply dislikes the undisguised main character. In this scenario, the love-struck main character must deal with a dilemma of whether or not to admit that he or she is both the person the love interest is falling for and the also the person the love interest dislikes or even actively despises.

The middle also contains near misses with the disguise being discovered, with the main character having to make quick changes from one persona to the other, and with the character himself or herself experiencing confusion and making mistakes about which persona he or she is supposed to be projecting.

The plot problem that caused the main character to assume the disguise continues to get worse until it finally boils over into some sort of crisis.

Meanwhile, the love interest, whose emotions are becoming increasingly more torn, finally has to choose only one person to pursue romantically. And possibly, the main character is having to weight the love interest's potential reaction if and when the main character decides to reveal his or her true identity. These strains stretch the romantic relationship to the breaking point.

BLACK MOMENT:

The main character's true identity is revealed. This may be an accident, the plot problem may end up revealing the truth, or revealing the truth may be necessary for the main character to solve the plot problem. This revelation blows up the plot problem completely, and the main character's efforts to solve it by subterfuge are all for naught. It's a catastrophe. In addition, the main character has lied to the love interest and to others in the story, and the consequences of that deception land squarely upon his or her head. Often these consequences include dealing with scandal related to the assumption of the alternate gender disguise.

Regardless of how the truth is revealed, it devastates (or infuriates) the love interest, who breaks up with the main character.

All is truly lost for both of the lovers.

. . .

THE END:

Now that his or her true identity has been revealed, the main character (with the love, support, and help of the love interest if they've made up already, possibly with the love interest's grudging support if they haven't) can confront the problem directly and solve it outright. There's no longer a need for a disguise and the main character can step into his or her true identity.

This baring of true self, literally and metaphorically, finally allows the lovers to work out their own conflicts. The main character apologizes for the deception, the love interest accepts the apology.

The main character integrates the lessons he or she has learned while living in the alternate persona with his or her regular persona and becomes both personas in one. This integrated persona is finally the complete package for the love interest. Instead of loving two halves of a whole split between two people, he or she now can love one person who is all the things he or she loves.

At long last, after many trials and tribulations, these two people get their happily ever after.

KEY SCENES

- the main character sees himself or herself for the first time in the alternate identity
- the main character, hanging out with people of the assumed identity, hears a frank conversation about people of his or her undisguised gender identity that is revelatory to him or her
- the love interest is surprised or confused by his or her attraction to someone of the assumed gender identity, which may not be the norm for him or her
- the main interest is nearly caught making the shift from one identity to the other (by the love interest or by someone who would blow the secret wide open)

- the consequences for getting caught and his or her true identity revealed are made clear to the main character
- the disguised main character and love interest have a romantic encounter that troubles the love interest, who may also be attracted to the main character in his or her other persona
- the love interest feels deeply torn between attraction to the main character and his or her alternate persona
- the main character tries to tell the love interest the truth but chickens out or is stopped from doing so

THINGS TO THINK ABOUT WHEN WRITING THIS TROPE

Why is your main character going to assume an alternate gender identity in your story? Why is this the only way for him or her to solve the problem that's driving him/her to do this risky and drastic thing?

How will your main character pull off assuming another gender identity in this disguise?

Who, if anyone, helps the main character disguise himself or herself?

Will the main character maintain this disguise all the time, or will the main character continue to live life in his or her usual identity as well?

Who is the love interest?

Do the main character and love interest already know each other when your story starts or do they meet after it starts?

In which persona will the main character first meet the love interest? What does the love interest think of him or her?

What about the love interest attracts the main character romantically to him or her?

Does the main character also romance the love interest in his or her usual identity or only in his/her disguised identity?

How do the parallel relationships between the love interest and the main character's two personas progress? You may want to map them out side by side to compare them.

How does each of the parallel relationships affect the other? Meaning, what's the cause and effect between the two relationships? For example, if the love interest has an argument with the main character in his or her usual persona, does the love interest run to the alternate persona to complain about the main character?

How does the love interest feel after the first romantic encounter with the main character in his/her disguise?

Does the love interest dislike one persona and fall in love with the other? Does the love interest fall for both personas? In either case, what does the love interest feel and do about his/her dilemma?

What's the main character's big dilemma regarding the love interest? Will the love interest dump him or her when she finds out he/she is also the person the love interest despises? Or is the dilemma purely about the love interest feeling lied to, tricked, and betrayed when he/she finds out the main character is both people the love interest has fallen for?

What does the main character learn about being a different gender that he/she didn't know before?

What does the main character learn about his/her own gender that he/she didn't know before?

Why can't the main character reveal to the love interest who he/she really is?

How does the situation get ever more complicated for the main character while juggling the two personas?

How, when, and why does the main character get "stuck" in the disguise?

Is there a moment when the main character has to be both personas at the same time? How will he/she handle it? Does the main character get help from someone or have to do a quick switch back and forth between the two personas?

How does the plot problem the main character is trying to solve with his/her disguise get worse over the course of the story? Much worse?

How does the plot problem get more complicated the deeper the main character gets into being the alternate persona?

How do the main character's two lives both blow up into crises? Does one cause the other or does this happen in parallel in your story?

When does the love interest find out about the disguise? How does he/she react?

When do the other characters in the story find out about the disguise? How do they react?

How does the main character use the lessons he/she has learned in the course of pretending to be another gender to solve the plot problem?

Does the love interest help solve the plot problem? If so, how does he/she feel about doing it and why does he/she do it?

How will the main character apologize to the love interest?

Does the main character make a grand gesture of love to the love interest? If so, what is it and can it be bigger?

Why does the love interest ultimately forgive the main character?

Do the other characters in the story (and society at large) forgive the main character for the deception or not? Why?

Will the couple start their relationship over or will they continue on from where they broke up?

What does this couple's happily ever after look like?

TROPE TRAPS

The reason the main character is attempting this difficult-to-pull-off gambit isn't big enough or sound enough to justify taking the risk.

The main character is so hyper-masculine or -feminine in his/her usual appearance that your audience doesn't buy that he/she can pull off pretending to be the opposite gender.

The rest of the characters in the story totally buy the (lame) disguise and look dimwitted for doing so.

The main character never messes up or makes mistakes in the disguise.

You never put the main character in any excruciatingly uncomfortable situations while being in disguise.

The love interest is never conflicted about having feelings for two people at once, or for feeling attraction to someone he/she wouldn't usually be attracted to.

The main character should trust the love interest enough and sooner to reveal the disguise to him/her well before it actually happens in your story.

The main character owes it to the love interest to tell him/her the truth but looks like a jerk for not doing it.

The main character never struggles to juggle his/her two personas and lives.

The main character doesn't learn anything from living in another gender.

What the main character does learn about living in another gender is cliché and obvious.

The conversations people of the assumed gender have around the main character are cliché and obvious.

The two personas of the main character have no external effect on each other over the course of the story, meaning what the main character does or says as one character never affects the other character in any way.

The main character never even tries to confess the truth to the love interest before the truth is finally revealed and comes across as dishonorable or selfish.

The love interest is too mad or not mad enough when the main character finally reveals the truth to him or her.

The main character never tells the love interest the truth but lets him or her find out when everyone else in the story does or find out by accident.

The main character never properly apologizes to the love interest or apologizes for the wrong thing.

The love interest has no reason whatsoever to forgive this person who lied to him/her yet forgives the main character quickly and easily.

There are no negative consequences for the main character's ruse.

Failing to follow through on the promised negative consequences when the main character does get caught.

The other characters in the story forgive the main character far too easily.

The plot problem solves itself in the end...making the entire disguise unnecessary.

The solution to the big plot problem is simple enough that the main character could have dropped the disguise much earlier in the story and just solved the problem.

DISGUISED AS MALE/FEMALE TROPE IN ACTION
Movies:

- Shakespeare in Love
- Mulan
- Mrs. Doubtfire
- Tootsie
- Some Like It Hot
- Yentl
- Victor/Victoria
- She's the Man

Books:

- Twelfth Night by William Shakespeare
- The Masqueraders by Georgette Heyer
- The Nobleman's Guide to Scandal and Shipwrecks by Mackenzi Lee
- Silk and Steel by Ariana Nash
- Romancing the Inventor by Gail Carriger
- The Lady's Secret by Joanna Chambers
- A Lady Never Tells by Lynn Winchester

9
DRUNK/VEGAS WEDDING

DEFINITION

The drunk wedding or quickie, on-a-whim Las Vegas wedding is often a plot device to add a complication in the middle of a story or a funny midpoint reversal in a romantic comedy.

For those of you unfamiliar with "Vegas weddings", the city of Las Vegas, Nevada is famous for its all-night wedding chapels, drive-through wedding chapels, and wedding chapels where you can walk in with no prior planning and get married in a few minutes.

The British historical version of this would have been eloping to Gretna Green, just over the border into Scotland, where anyone could obtain a fast wedding without lengthy posting of bans and marriage contracts.

But when it's used as an entire trope, this wedding typically opens the story or happens very early in the story, then the remainder of the story is taken up with the complications and getting-to-know-you portion of the relationship.

Often some other trope leads to this drunk or quickie wedding. Only One Not Married, Commitment Phobia, Rebellious Hero/Heroine, and Left At the Altar/Jilted are a few examples of a trope whose opening might result in the drunk or Vegas Wedding that launches this trope.

Because the wedding happens first and true love comes later, this trope turns the typical sequence of love on its head. Two people meet, barely know each other, or are not romantically involved. But for some reason, they decide in a moment of temporary insanity to get married. When they sober up or wake up the next morning, they're faced with the stark reality of having gotten married (and in most cases, having consummated the relationship).

In pretty much every case, the couple is horrified by what they've done. They typically have to face friends and family and admit what they've done, and this is usually embarrassing at best and humiliating at worst. Of course, they could also keep the wedding secret and introduce yet another trope to your story.

At any rate, you'll have to answer the immediate question of why they don't just annul the wedding and go back to their regularly scheduled lives. This reason is likely to form the plot problem that drives the remainder of your story forward. The tone of this problem —be it comic, suspenseful, or dramatic—will set the tone and mood for your story.

For some reason, this couple decides to stay married for a little while or they have no choice but to stay married for a little while—or at least long enough to solve the plot problem that prevented them from getting an immediate annulment or quickie divorce.

As they work together to solve the plot problem, they get to know each other better. In fact, they fall in love and eventually realize they've married exactly the right person after all. What started as a joke, whim, or wild night of partying leads to true love and happily ever after.

ADJACENT TROPES
Marriage of Convenience/Fake Marriage
Arranged Marriage

Marriage Pact/Bargain Comes Due
Tricked Into Marriage
One Night Stand/Fling

WHY READERS/VIEWERS LOVE THIS TROPE

- we all wish to be more spontaneous and have the courage to do wild and crazy things
- rather than go through all the bad dates, bad relationships, and bad break-ups, how cool would it be to just jump off a romantic cliff and end up finding true love
- for anyone who's gotten married and then wondered if they made the right decision, seeing this relationship work out gives them hope
- at least we didn't end up with our (questionable) spouse in this embarrassing way
- some people enjoy turning socially acceptable behavior on its head, and this type of wedding definitely does that

OBLIGATORY SCENES

THE BEGINNING:

This story may be begin with a little set-up about who the hero and heroine are, why they're each not married (which may introduce another trope or two to your story), and how they come to be in a place together where they're both drunk, desperate, despondent, in Las Vegas, or all of the above.

Your audience probably does need to see the headspace or emotional state the hero and heroine are in before they decided to get married so your audience can appreciate what a wild, crazy, or impulsive idea it is to get married.

We see the wedding, and depending on the heat level of your story, we see the wedding night. Which is to say, you show your audience that they really did this crazy thing together.

The beginning usually ends with the waking up the morning after and the mutually horrified refrain of, "What did we do?"

THE MIDDLE:

It may be as late as the beginning of the middle of the story before you introduce the plot problem that prevents the hero and heroine from immediately annulling the divorce or getting a quickie divorce on the spot.

The middle is where the aftermath of the impulsive wedding really gets rolling. They have to face family, friends, coworkers and anyone else whom they know and who might judge them. If one of them is very wealthy, the absence of pre-nuptial agreement may cause legal problems. If one of them had a specific reason for having to marry—to inherit an estate or get a job, for example—the couple may need to stay married while the problem is sorted out.

At a minimum, there needs to be some delay in the pair getting an immediate annulment or divorce so they have time in your story to get to know each other and fall in love.

Immediately after their drunken wedding night, they may revert to a celibate relationship. But, if you throw them together in close quarters or living together, you can use this to your advantage to create sexual tension galore.

Once they've agreed that the wedding was a mistake and they need to get out of it as soon as possible, you've just thrown both of them into the territory of forbidden partners, which makes them all the more tantalizing to each other as the story progresses.

Complications to the plot problem that are slowing or stopping their divorce get worse and grow into a crisis by the end of the middle.

The middle is also where they'll discover things they love and hate about each other, where they learn how to live together, how to be friends, and eventually how to be lovers. In this respect, the romance in the middle of the story will progress pretty normally. The only difference is they're already married and have already agreed to exit the marriage as soon as possible. (In the arranged marriage, the couple has no exit ramp from the marriage visible in their near future. But this drunk wedding couple does.)

The middle typically ends with simultaneous or nearly simultaneous declarations of love with the divorce finally coming through or the condition being met so they can divorce now. The timing couldn't be any worse.

BLACK MOMENT:

Just when the couple has finally realized they're in love, they're torn apart by the plot problem coming to a head or delivering the divorce they wanted so desperately not long ago.

They've gotten it wrong *again*. In the beginning, they've each given up on finding the right forever person and engage in a drunk or quickie wedding that's meant to be a joke. But now, they've each found the one person they'd be happy with forever just in time to lose him or her.

The plot problem may not only make divorce possible but may make it necessary or may deliver the divorce as a fait accompli whether they want it or not at this point.

The couple, having made grand declarations of wanting out of the marriage in the past may not feel as if the other partner wants to stay married and may go through with the divorce on the mistaken assumption that the other partner wants out.

While I'm generally not a fan of conflicts or misunderstandings that could be readily solved with a simple, honest adult conversation, this is one trope that can get away with such failures to communicate. This is still a relatively new couple who don't know each other all that well and can be forgiven for misreading each other and misreading the situation.

There may actually be a serious romantic conflict at work between the hero and heroine that also leads to their breakup. If there is one, it explodes and tears them apart in the black moment.

The couple may or may not go through with the divorce (yet), but that's certainly the plan by the end of the black moment.

THE END:

The plot problem is finally resolved. The hero and heroine may have to do something actively to resolve it, or the act of getting separated or divorced may be sufficient to resolve the problem.

One or both of the characters, typically in a farewell conversation, may casually express their sorrow that they ended up breaking up, or some other catalyst may spur the pair to finally talk honestly with each other. Imagine their mutual surprise when they each discover that the other wanted to stay married the whole time.

If the couple never officially divorced, they can now resume their marriage for real this time. If the couple did legally divorce, they may commence planning another wedding, they may run off to Las Vegas to marry again, or they may decide to reset all the way to the beginning and start dating again.

The promise to your audience, however, is that this couple is definitely going to end up together and happily ever after even if they don't end this story properly married, yet. It's important to make it clear in this scenario that they have, in fact, found their soulmate and are going to salvage the relationship.

It's not uncommon in this trope to see an epilogue or time jump forward where we get to see the couple getting married or experiencing happy marriage together.

. . .

KEY SCENES

- the hero or heroine first brings up the idea of getting married
- the hero and heroine don't think the wedding was real... and then find out it was
- one or both of the newlyweds tell someone about the wedding
- they find out that getting an annulment or divorce isn't going to be anywhere as fast and easy as getting married was
- the consequences for the impulsive wedding hit
- the hero and heroine blame each other for the wedding happening
- one or both of them is highly attracted to the other one but must keep his or her hands off the spouse
- one or both of them meets somebody who's exactly what they were looking for in a spouse...but now they're married and can't pursue this perfect specimen
- the hero and heroine, in spite of their agreement to exit the marriage as soon as possible, share a romantic interlude
- there's a crisis and the hero and heroine work well together as a team to handle it and support each other throughout it

THINGS TO THINK ABOUT WHEN WRITING THIS TROPE

Why is the hero single?

Why is the heroine single?

Why is each of them cynical, despairing, desperate, or hopeless about the idea of finding the perfect mate?

Why does each of them think in the moment that getting married is a fabulous idea?

Do they have fun at their wedding?

Do they consummate the relationship afterward? Do they remember that?

Do they remember their wedding and/or wedding night the next morning?

What's their first reaction to waking up and realizing what they've done?

How do they react to each other the morning after?

Why can't they get an immediate annulment or divorce? How do they learn of this?

How will you force the pair into proximity repeatedly over the course of the story so they have time together to fall in love?

How do their friends, family, and coworkers react to their drunk/Vegas wedding?

Do they get in trouble with anyone over their impulsive wedding? If so, who? How?

What bad thing will happen if they don't end the marriage?

What bad thing will happen if they do end the marriage?

How will you force them to live together or at least spend a lot of time together in close quarters?

What about their spouse drives each of them crazy in a good way?

What about their spouse drives each of them crazy in a bad way?

What fundamental qualities (morals, beliefs, values) do they share in common?

What stupid or trivial thing do they disagree about sharply and bicker about?

Does one of them have any other possible romantic relationships developing or waiting in the wings when they get married? If so, what happens to those relationships after they get married?

Do the hero and heroine trust each other? If so, why?

If the hero and heroine don't trust each other, how will they learn to trust each other?

How does the plot problem keeping them from divorcing get worse or more complicated over the course of the story? Can you make it worse? Much worse?

Does one or both of them ever declare loving the other one before the black moment? If so, when?

Does the other spouse believe the declaration of love? Why or why not?

What blows up that tears the couple apart?

What's the plot element to this blow-up?

What's the romantic relationship element to this blow-up?

How do they each feel about breaking up? Do they tell someone how they feel? Do they tell their spouse how they feel?

What do they have to do, individually or together, to solve the plot problem?

Does solving the plot problem clear the path to divorcing or clear the path to being together?

Do they legally divorce before they resolve their relationship and realize they want to be together for real and forever?

Who apologizes to whom? Who makes a grand gesture of love to whom?

Do the hero and heroine only have to talk out their difference or feelings, or does one of them have to learn something, do something, or change something so they can be together? If so, what is that and how does he/she do it?

Will they remarry or do another marriage ceremony with friends and family present before the end of the story?

How will you give your audience at least a glimpse of this couple being happily ever after before the end of your story?

TROPE TRAPS

This couple is too sensible to do something as crazy as drunk marrying or quickie marrying in Vegas.

It's too easy to get a divorce or annulment and they would surely have done so the next morning.

The reason they don't immediately annul the wedding or divorce is lame or implausible.

They're not horrified enough by what they've done.

Neither of them seems to have any attraction for the other one that would explain their crazy, drunken, impulsive decision.

The couple's morals, values, and beliefs are so different there's no plausible way for these two people to be happy together in the long term.

The consequences for them doing something this crazy aren't serious enough or are too serious.

The couple doesn't have a plausible reason to spend much time together and it makes no sense that they keep seeing each other.

The hero and heroine don't even like each other, let alone love each other, and your audience doesn't buy that these two could ever fall in love.

The hero and heroine fight all the time. It's a terrible foundation for a long-term relationship.

The hero and heroine are mean, disrespectful, or denigrating of each other—also a terrible foundation for a long-term relationship.

The reason someone forces them to stay married is lame or implausible and your audience doesn't buy it.

The conflicts and disagreements between the hero and heroine can easily be talked out in a single honest, adult conversation that the audience is frustrated that they seem incapable of having.

The way the hero and heroine make up is sophomoric, immature, or lame and makes the audience think their marriage won't last for the long term.

We see the couple happy for now but fail to see any proof of a happily ever after.

. . .

DRUNK/VEGAS WEDDING TROPE IN ACTION
Movies:

- The Hangover
- What Happens in Vegas
- Knocked Up
- Fools Rush In
- Love Vegas

Books:

- Waking Up Married by Mira Lyn Kelly
- Married in Vegas by Sariah Wilson
- Accidentally Married on Purpose by Rachel Harris
- What Happens in Vegas by Kathy Lyons
- Hitched by Kendall Ryan
- The Gambler by Denise Grover Swank
- Married in Montana by Jane Porter
- The Wedding Pact by Katee Robert

10

FAKE FIANCE/BOYFRIEND/GIRLFRIEND

DEFINITION

Who hasn't gotten the dreaded invitation to a wedding, family-, or class-reunion where everyone they know will be there, and everyone will be checking up to see if they've finally gotten around to getting involved in a serious relationship? That's usually the start of this story.

The fake fiancé, fake boyfriend, and fake girlfriend tropes tell the classic tale of the hero/heroine convincing someone to help them out and pretend for a short period of time to be their significant other. But lo and behold, over the course of the story, the romance becomes real.

Although this is traditionally a comic trope, it works in any type of romantic fiction, hence its inclusion in the volumes on universal romance tropes.

In most cases, the fake fiancé, boyfriend, or girlfriend has volunteered or been hired to pretend to be in a romantic relationship with the main character. The significant other is typically a friend, neighbor, or coworker—someone the main character already knows at least in passing. This person may or may not be someone the main character has fantasized about having a relationship with.

Now and then, the main character makes up a fake significant other based on someone he or she knows. They describe the fiancé/boyfriend/girlfriend, may send pictures of that person, or may create fake pictures, voice messages, text chains, and more. Then, somebody comes to town or invites the main character to an event the main character cannot avoid and is invited to produce the fake fiancé/boyfriend/girlfriend. Faced with his or her lie being exposed, the main character (sheepishly) approaches the person whom they've based the fake significant other on and asks for a favor. Could he or she, just this once, pretend to be romantically involved with him or her for a few hours?

In either case, complications ensue as the main character and fake significant other pretend to be in a romantic relationship. They may spend some time preparing to pretend—getting a crash course in each other's lives, likes, dislikes, and more. They're faced with quizzes about a past together that doesn't exist, they're forced into uncomfortable displays of affection, and the fake relationship causes problems in one or both of their real lives.

How the other person in the pair handles the complications that pop up may be one of the endearing things that makes the other person fall in love with him or her.

Particularly in the case where the significant other is hired to play the role, you will have to figure out how this pair is going to spend enough time together for a romantic spark to ignite between them and why they're going to continue seeing each other after the wedding, reunion, or family event is over.

ADJACENT TROPES

- Only One Not Married
- Marriage of Convenience/Fake Marriage
- Forced Proximity
- Friends to Lovers

- Pretend/Celibate Marriage
- Spinster/Bluestocking/On the Shelf

WHY READERS/VIEWERS LOVE THIS TROPE

- who hasn't cringed in embarrassment at the idea of having to face old friends, classmates, or family and feeling as if they're judging you, pitying you, or laughing at you
- we all enjoy the tension of will they-won't they
- most of us have fantasized about what it would be like to be in a romantic relationship with someone we know or know of and would love to find out for real
- do we know anyone who would do this for us if we were in the same situation, and would we do it for a friend if asked
- if only it were this easy for a friendship to grow into true love

OBLIGATORY SCENES

THE BEGINNING:

Need for a fake fiancé/boyfriend/girlfriend must be established before the main character asks anyone to play the role.

Typically, the single hero or heroine is invited (or ordered) to attend an event or be seen in a specific public situation and he or she is embarrassed not to have a significant other to bring along.

Alternately, the main character may be asked to bring a plus-one or the main character may simply feel a compelling need to bring along a fiancé, boyfriend, or girlfriend because of family or social pressure.

Frequently, this event is a wedding. Class reunions and family reunions are other typical events to start this story.

But it could also be some sort of party, business, or charitable event—anything that's public where the main character will be highly visible and where he or she expects to be negatively judged for not having a romantic companion.

In response, the single hero or heroine must obtain a fake fiancé, boyfriend, or girlfriend.

The main character may ask a friend, hire an escort or actor, place an advertisement, or may ask someone whom he/she barely knows—a neighbor, coworker, boss, someone he/she sees across a bar —to play the part.

There's usually some preparation before they're seen together in public. The main character may want to clean up or dress up the fake significant other. They may tell each other about their pasts, things they like to do, favorite things.

The beginning may end with the couple's first appearance at the big event…or it may end with something going wrong at the big event that threatens to expose the ruse.

THE MIDDLE:

By the skin of their teeth, the couple manages to get past threats to expose the ruse. They probably have to improvise on the fly. Mistakes get made and shenanigans ensue as they try to keep up the pretense of being a couple. Often, they're forced into displays of affection that make one or both of them uncomfortable and that are extremely awkward.

The couple bonds to some extent over having to work together to keep up the pretense. Every time they're forced into close proximity or an awkwardly intimate situation, they become more aware of each other.

They may also spend a lot of time chatting with each other and actually getting to know each other over the course of the big event. If your event is a single, several hour long appearance—an office party or awards ceremony, for example—you'll need to establish a strong attraction between the pair very quickly. If, however, the event is a multi-day or multi-party affair like a wedding or weekend-long family reunion, you can slow roll the building attraction between the pair.

The event ends, and the main character and fake love interest go back to their regularly scheduled lives.

Your main character has already plucked up his or her courage to ask for a big favor. He/she may not feel as if they have a right to ask the fake love interest out on a real date. Hence, it typically falls to the fake fiancé/boyfriend/girlfriend to approach the main character to ask if they'd like to go out for real.

OR

Unforeseen complications from being seen out in public together force the couple back into proximity with each other. A picture in a newspaper or gossip column forces the fake fiancé/boyfriend/girlfriend to produce their new significant other. The shoe's on the other foot. Now the fake love interest needs the main character to return the favor and to pretend to be in a relationship with him or her.

OR

Trouble ensues from being seen together at the big event from the beginning. The fake significant other's real love interest is angry. The fake fiancé/boyfriend/girlfriend needs the main character to tell someone it was just a fake appearance. Or the actor will get a big role if he/she has cleaned up their act and settled down with one person at last. In this scenario, the main character and fake love interest are thrown back together to deal with a crisis that's going to take both of them to solve.

In each of these scenarios, the initial attraction grows into real feelings for each other. The more time they spend together, the more they get to know each other, and the more they find they have in common, the more there is to like.

Of course, into every romantic ointment, a fly must land. In the middle of the story, a complication (or several) has to threaten the relationship. This complication can be someone from the original event figuring out the main character and fake love interest weren't really a couple at that time.

It can be a threat to expose their ruse by someone who was aware of it from the beginning or who figured it out but agreed not to expose the main character's deception at the time.

The complication can be some other threat to their relationship—another romantic interest interferes, work interferes, family members set some expectation for the couple or ask the couple to do something they're not ready to do—appear in public again, marry before a dying relative passes away, fix the fake love interest's terrible romantic reputation.

This external plot complication puts a ton of pressure on the new romantic relationship. Plus, any personal conflicts, disagreements, or friction points you've developed (and any other tropes you're running) also are aggravated by the external plot pressures and also grow toward a crisis.

Any doubts one or both partners have about just how genuine the relationship really is may come to a head as well as the middle builds to a crisis.

The middle typically ends with the ruse turning into a full-blown crisis.

BLACK MOMENT:

Pretty commonly, the black moment revolves around the ruse being exposed. This can be a moment of personal embarrassment or humiliation, or the ruse can have grown through the story into something much larger than a fake date or one-time fake fiancé/boyfriend/girlfriend appearance. In this case, its exposure could be a scandal, involve public embarrassment or humiliation, and affect reputations, jobs, and entire lives.

If there's some sort of external plot reason the ruse was continued through the story, that reason blows up in the couple's faces and goes worse than they could have possibly imagined.

One or both of the lovers may be pressured—or forced outright—to break off the relationship.

If one of the lovers has inadvertently, or even intentionally, revealed the ruse, the other partner is likely to feel betrayed and attacked and break off the relationship as a result. Even if the revealer had an excellent reason for doing so, the other lover may not feel very forgiving in the initial aftermath of the big, embarrassing revelation.

The relationship is blown apart and all is personally (and possibly professionally) lost for these two unlucky people.

THE END:

Whatever external plot problem has ripped the lovers apart must be solved. One or both of the lovers may work to fix this problem, together or separately.

Once the big plot problem is finally solved, it's time for big apologies. One or both lovers may owe the other one an apology. One or both of them may also owe other people whom they lied to initially about their relationship being real.

Apologies may be combined with or followed by grand gestures of love by one or both lovers. This relationship was started dishonestly, and it may need to end with some specific gestures of honest emotion to cement the realness of the relationship now.

This couple has come full circle, from faking true love to finally having it for real.

. . .

KEY SCENES

- the main character asks the future fake love interest to help him/her out
- someone questions the veracity of the fake love interest
- someone questions whether the main character could land someone as hot as the fake fiancé/boyfriend/girlfriend
- the first real date between the main characters
- the first real romantic moment between the main characters
- one or both main characters' real lives interferes with or is interfered with by their new relationship
- the couple's first big fight
- one or both main characters question how "real" their real relationship is
- one or both characters isn't fully honest with the other one about something, casting the whole relationship into doubt
- one character betrays the other in some way

THINGS TO THINK ABOUT WHEN WRITING THIS TROPE

What specific event does the hero or heroine need a fake fiancé, boyfriend, or girlfriend for?

Does the main character have to bring a date, or does he or she merely feel heavily pressured into bringing a date? Why?

How will the hero or heroine obtain the fake fiancé/boyfriend/girlfriend?

Does the main character already know the person recruited to be the fake love interest? If so, how? How well do they know each other already? Are they already friends? Coworkers? Neighbors? Something else?

Will they prepare in some way before making their fake appearance as a couple? If so, what kind of preparation? How extensive is it? Is there a spark of attraction between them by the time this preparation is done or not yet?

What do they miss in their preparations that ultimately trips them up during their appearance as a couple? How do they cover it up? Does the cover-up lead them into some awkward situation?

What do they learn about each other that they didn't know before or that they find fascinating about each other as they first get to know each other or prepare for their appearance?

What awkward situations are the couple thrown into while they fake being a couple?

Is the event they're going to a one-off event that only lasts a few hours or does it involve multiple parties, events, or appearances?

How do other people at the event(s) react to the existence and presence of the fake fiancé/boyfriend/girlfriend?

Is the main character pleased with other people's reaction to the fake love interest? If so, why? If not, why not?

What complication ensues at the event that throws the couple into a more intimate situation than either of them bargained for? How do they react to it?

What's the status of the main character's and fake love interest's relationship after the event(s) end and they go back to their regularly scheduled lives?

What plot complication, problem, or additional event(s) will bring them back together again?

How will you force some degree of ongoing proximity between these two people, or will they choose to be together for real fairly quickly after the fake event together?

Who asks to see the other one again? How?

Why is it a problem for these two to date each other for real?

Will they keep their real relationship secret or go public with it once they're dating for real? Why?

As they continue to spend time together, what do they learn about each other, how will they learn it, and why will it draw them together?

What do they learn about each other that they dislike?

Does one or both of them doubt how real their relationship is at some point?

Is one of them dishonest with the other one? How does the person who was lied to react when he or she finds out?

Does one of them betray the other? If so, how? How does the person betrayed react? Why?

What problem or conflict will force them apart? What obstacles stand in the way of them getting together for real?

How will their deception be revealed? How do other people react to finding out they were initially faking a relationship?

What plot problem tears them apart? Does it have to do with their deception? If so, how?

How does the plot problem exacerbate or blow up the conflicts or problems in their romantic relationship?

What are the consequences for their having lied initially about being in a relationship?

Will there be an apology to the people they deceived?

Is there an apology by one of the lovers to the other one? What for? How is it delivered? How is it received?

Does one or both of them make a big gesture of love to the other? If so, what is it?

How will you show the reader that all is well in the end with this couple, that they've been forgiven, and that their very real relationship is fully accepted by the people around them?

TROPE TRAPS

Failing to give this character a compelling enough reason for resorting to a fake relationship that the reader will forgive him or her for doing it.

Failing to give the fake love interest a compelling reason for going along with the ruse, one that readers will accept and forgive.

The main character is so insecure, so self-conscious, so status conscious that your audience dislikes him or her.

The main character is so wrapped up in what other people will think of him or her that he or she is unlikable to your audience.

The fake love interest takes advantage of fake intimate situations to act a little creepy toward the main character and your audience dislikes him or her.

There's no compelling problem with the couple getting caught in their deception.

Nobody in your story has any reason to care if the main character faked having a love interest.

Your audience doesn't buy that it's a big scandal to have faked a romantic relationship.

There are no questions or doubts about the honesty or realness of their relationship after the couple starts dating for real...after they've both deceived a bunch of people.

There's no compelling problem that poses an obstacle to the couple getting together for real.

People wildly overreact or under react when the deception is eventually revealed.

The reason the couple's romantic relationship implodes is lame or contrived.

There are no consequences for the deception the couple has perpetrated.

The couple never apologizes to anyone for their deception.

The lovers never apologize to each other for any doubts, dishonesty, or betrayal.

. . .

FAKE FIANCE/BOYFRIEND/GIRLFRIEND TROPE IN ACTION
Movies

- While You Were Sleeping
- The Proposal
- One Small Hitch
- The Decoy Bride
- My Fake Fiancé

Books

- The Marriage Bargain by Jennifer Probst
- The Hunger Games by Suzanne Collins
- Sliding Home by Kathy Lyons
- The Wall of Winnipeg and Me by Mariana Zapata
- A Week to be Wicked by Tessa Dare
- The Duke and I by Julia Quinn
- Kiss an Angel by Susan Elizabeth Phillips
- The Cinderella Deal by Jennifer Crusie

11
FALSE IDENTITY

DEFINITION

In this story the protagonist has a secret identity or is living under a false identity that causes a serious problem he or she must ultimately admit to the love interest while dealing with a big plot problem. The false identity may be a reaction to a big problem, or it may be a tactic for dealing with a big problem.

The main character may live entirely under a false identity, or the main character may switch back and forth between his/her real identity and the false one. If he/she is living solely under a false identity, the story follows his or her efforts to retain the false identity while threats to the truth being exposed grow.

The love interest falling in love with the false identity greatly complicates the main character's quandary. Does he or she dare reveal the truth, or will doing so cost him/her the love and trust of the love interest? Worse, would revealing the truth endanger the main character and/or love interest?

OR

The main character spends part of the time in his/her true identity and part of it in the false identity. The two lives come into increasing conflict over the course of the story, each of them experiencing their own crises. Worse, the love interest may meet both personas. The love interest may like the false identity but despise the real one, which puts the main character into quite a dilemma of whether to and when to reveal the truth to the love interest.

Likewise, if the love interest falls for both identities, he or she may find himself/herself in quite a dilemma. Which one should he/she choose? Is he or she wrong to fall for two people at the same time?

In both scenarios, the false identity must be maintained for some important reason. Into this backdrop, something happens to threaten its secrecy. The main character must fix the problem or stop the uncovering of the false identity, all the while falling in love with the love interest and juggling the love interest's growing feelings for him or her.

The first thing that comes to most people's minds when they hear this trope is a superhero who must keep his or her identity secret, or perhaps an undercover cop living a double life. There are many other reasons someone might assume a false identity, however, or might need or want to keep his or her real identity secret.

A woman might be hiding from a violent ex. A witness against a dangerous criminal has been given a new identity. A spy is working under an assumed identity. A person is leaving behind a traumatic, troubled, or criminal past and changes his or her name.

Have fun coming up with your own reason why someone has a false identity and the problems caused when this identity collides with a big problem and love.

ADJACENT TROPES

- Dangerous Secret
- Hero/Heroine in Disguise

- Disguised as Male/Female
- Secret Identity
- Hero/Heroine in Hiding
- Dangerous Past

WHY READERS/VIEWERS LOVE THIS TROPE

- what would it be like to shed your old life completely and assume a new one
- could I leave behind my entire life, never look back, and start over
- getting two lovers for the price of one
- being in on the secret that nobody else in the story knows
- we can all relate to having to make choices between the competing priorities in our lives and how difficult those choices can be

OBLIGATORY SCENES

THE BEGINNING:

We meet the main character going about his or her life, and the audience may not know right away that he or she is living in a false identity. Rather, you may choose to let that revelation come to your audience along with the love interest.

The main character and love interest meet. This meeting will set the tone and mood of your story, be it comic, emotional, suspenseful, or something else. Attraction happens immediately and a relationship starts to unfold between them.

During the beginning, we see a threat to the main character or he/she acts unusually cautious, suspicious, or paranoid. We may not know why he or she is acting this way, but we have an inkling that something is up with this character.

A serious problem unfolds that threatens the safety of the main character or puts him/her at serious risk of discovery.

If the main character spends some time in his/her real identity in your story, we get a glimpse of that in the beginning, as well. This is when your audience catches on to the fake and real identities...but this is probably not when your love interest figures it out. You'll need to choose the identity the main character spends the most time in, but whichever one makes the most sense for your story or gives you the best opening is fine.

Into this tension, a mini-crisis occurs to end the beginning of your story. Somebody recognizes the protagonist from his or her other life. Someone from the other life threatens him or her. Someone threatens to reveal his or her other identity. Something dangerous happens to the protagonist in one identity that threatens to upend, expose, or harm his or her other identity.

THE MIDDLE:

This is when complications resulting from whatever drove the main character into a false identity happen. These complications also pose a complication to the budding romance between the main character and love interest.

The main character may have a near miss with the love interest discovering the truth. For example, a letter addressed to the protagonist's real name arrives at his or her house. He or she must hastily hide the letter from the love interest. The main character may be alarmed that someone knows his or her real name and knows where he or she lives, as well.

The stakes are spiraling out of control in the false identity (and possibly in his/her real identity) as he or she tries to maintain the false identity (while also juggling his/her real identity).

The love interest may also be put into danger, if for no other reason than proximity to the main character. Threats come at the couple thick and fast as the main character tries to keep up the false identity and simultaneously protect the love interest. If the main character has a family, loved ones, or friends in his or her false identity, they're also threatened by whatever or whoever is coming after him or her.

Threats are now coming at the lovers from every direction, and the main character scrambles to contain them while maintaining the false identity, managing the problems happening in his or her real identity, and while trying to solve a huge problem that's rapidly spinning out of control.

The love interest, who may be very confused, very conflicted, very suspicious, wants answers the main character isn't prepared to give, leading to a crisis in their romantic relationship.

BLACK MOMENT:

The plot crisis explodes, forcing the main character to take a huge risk. As the main character's plan goes terribly wrong, the love interest may find out by accident that the main character is living a false identity, or the main character may have no choice but to confess the truth to the love interest as danger erupts around the couple.

The main character fails to vanquish the problem or the bad guy associated with the big problem. Worse, the love interest feels betrayed, lied to, tricked, disappointed, angry, or whatever else he/she feels in response to the revelation that the person he/she loves isn't who they said they were and lied about their identity the whole time.

If the main character has been living part-time in his/her real identity and part-time in the false identity, the love interest is likely even angrier that all of his/her internal conflict, angsting over being attracted to two people, or loving one and hating the other was all for naught.

The love interest breaks up with the main character.

They've failed to solve the big plot problem, the main character's true identity has been revealed, he or she has no cover from his/her enemies and is exposed, vulnerable, and visible to anyone out to harm him or her.

Worst of all, the couple has broken off their relationship.

All is lost.

THE END:

Typically, in the ending of this trope, the bad guy represents the big plot problem, or who's out to get the main character, comes after him or her. Everyone knows who the main character really is now and knows where to find him or her. The consequences of failing to maintain the false identity land on the main character and may land on the love interest as well.

The main character has no chance to run, hide, or create another new identity. His or her only option is to stand and fight. Like it or not, the main character finds himself or herself in a climactic confrontation with the bad guy.

The love interest may help the main character confront the bad guy, or the main character may go it alone. This works in a romance because the main character is, in effect, doing penance for his/her lie by having to take on the bad guy alone. He or she must prove worthiness to earn back the love of the love interest.

The main character, bruised, bloodied, but still standing after defeating the bad guy, finally gets a chance to apologize to the love interest and make amends for deceiving him or her. This apology is often accompanied by a grand gesture of love. After all, this love interest has a lot to forgive.

At long last, the protagonist gets a chance to be himself/herself (or be both sides of himself/herself) openly and honestly with the love interest. The love interest's misgivings, confusion, or suspicions are finally allayed and he or she finally feels free to love the main character without reservations.

The lovers finally get their happily ever after together.

KEY SCENES

- the main character realizes someone has recognized him or her
- the main character gets stuck in one identity or the other and for some reason *really* needs to shift over into the other identity but can't
- the love interest nearly realizes the main character is living a false identity or nearly catches the main character switching identities
- the brewing crisis in the protagonist's false identity bubbles over into his or her real identity, or vice versa, and causes big trouble
- the main character does something to fix or contain the crisis in one identity but accidentally makes things a lot worse in his or her other identity
- the love interest gets really frustrated with his/her own confusion, suspicions, or inexplicable lack of trust in the main character
- as the main character's worlds collide more and more, even the main character gets confused sometimes about who he or she is supposed to be
- the main character lies to the love interest or betrays the love interest in some way
- the love interest finds out the main character has lied to or betrayed him or her
- a loved one confesses that he or she has known for a while about the secret/false identity and has been waiting for the main character to tell him or her about it

THINGS TO THINK ABOUT WHEN WRITING THIS TROPE

Who's your protagonist? What's his or her original backstory? What did his/her life look like before assuming the false identity?

Why does the main character assume a false identity? Is it in response to a threat or problem or is it assumed to solve a problem?

Who or what has put the main character into danger?

How does he or she assumed a secret/false identity? What does it look like?

Is the main character recognizable to those who know him or her while in the disguise? Which is to say, does he/she need to avoid those who know him/her in real life?

What are the details of the false identity? What's the name? What does it look like? What's its story?

What's the purpose of the false identity?

In what identity does the protagonist spend most of his or her time—the real one or the false one?

Does anybody from his or her real life know about his or her false identity? If so, who? Why does the main character trust this person(s)?

Does anybody from the protagonist's false identity know about his or her real life? How did this person find out? How does the protagonist feel about them knowing? Why does this person keep the protagonist's secret for him or her?

Which identity does the protagonist consider to be his or her "real" life, now? Has he or she completely abandoned his or her original identity to live full-time in a new one? Or does the protagonist temporarily assume a false identity part-time to do something that has nothing to do with his or her real life?

What does the main character do while living in his or her false identity?

How do the main character and love interest meet?

Which persona is the main character living in when he/she meets the love interest?

Is the love interest part of the world the main character is moving into in his/her false identity? If so, how?

Does the love interest meet the main character in his/her real life as well? If so, when and how?

Does the love interest recognize the main character in his/her false identity and real identity or not? If not, how does the main character alter his/her appearance so the love interest (and others) doesn't recognize him/her?

What does the love interest think of the false identity version of the main character?

What attracts the main character and love interest to each other?

What's the big plot problem that endangers the main character?

How does the love interest become entangled in the big plot problem, too?

Does the main character try to keep the love interest out of the big problem? If so, how? Why doesn't it work?

How does the big problem threaten one or both of the protagonist's identities? How does it threaten the love interest?

What is the human face of this big problem, meaning who's the bad guy? How does he or she know the protagonist, and in which identity?

How does the big bad guy threaten the main character's other identity?

Does the big bad guy threaten loved ones, family, or friends from one or both of the protagonist's identities? If so, who and how?

How will this problem grow until it threatens to completely destroy one of the main character's identities? How will it grow to threaten to destroy both identities? How will it threaten to kill the main character and/or his/her loved ones?

At what point does the protagonist confess to the love interest about his or her real or false identity (the one the love interest doesn't know about or only knows a little about)?

What does the main character tell the love interest in this confession? Does he or she tell the whole truth? If not, what does he or she omit and why?

How does the love interest react to finding out the truth?

Does the love interest help the main character with his or her crisis going forward, or does the love interest get out of the way, flee to safety, or watch from the sidelines?

What does the main character do to try to stop the big crisis? How and why does he or she fail?

What change happens that makes it possible for the main character to win the next time he or she tangles with the big bad guy?

At what point, how, and why is the protagonist's false identity (or real identity) unmasked? How many people find out about it? Who are they? Will they keep the secret after this story ends or not?

What does the climactic fight with the big bad guy look like? What's different about it from the last time these two fought?

How does the main character win? Does he or she have any help? If so, who from?

Does the love interest help the main character in the climactic battle? If so, how? If not, why not?

What happens to the bad guy? Does he or she live? Flee? Go to jail?

How do the main character and love interest reconcile?

What does the main character need to say for the love interest to trust him or her going forward?

Who does the main character apologize to for the deception, if anyone? What does he/she say?

How does the love interest feel about knowing both sides of the main character now?

When the main character reconciles with the love interest at the end of the story, what does life look like for them? Do they live in the world the love interest comes from or the world the main character comes from?

How does the main character react? Is he or she relieved to be done with the ruse? Worried about how the love interest is going to keep the secret? Delighted to finally be able to be himself/herself all the time and to stop lying and obfuscating to the love interest?

Will the couple stay in the place where they met or leave this place and go somewhere new where nobody knows either of them?

TROPE TRAPS

The protagonist doesn't have a compelling reason for having assumed a false identity.

The main character's real and false identities are so similar as to be nearly indistinguishable to your audience and are confusing.

The bad guy in your story doesn't know the main character in either of his or her identities, meaning he or she is just some random bad guy who wanders into your story to cause trouble for the main character...which feels disjointed and incongruous.

The big problem the bad guy causes only ever affects one of the main character's identities. There's never any overlap...which is thematically weak and will disappoint your audience.

The main character has no friends within the false identity...who lives an entire life and never develops any friendships or at least acquaintances?

The main character's friends, family, and loved ones in the identity he or she considers to be his or her real life know everything about the false identity to begin your story—and you give away a huge potential source of stress, tension, and conflict for your story by choosing this.

The big plot problem in your story has no personal stakes for the main character—he or she isn't in direct danger nor is the love interest ever in serious danger.

When the big problem finally explodes into a big crisis, it's so big the protagonist by himself or herself isn't able to stop it. Moreover, he/she fails to recognize this or fails to call for help from the appropriate people quickly enough, thereby looking stupid, slow, or inattentive.

Nothing changes between the big fight at the end of the middle and the bigger fight to end the story that would help the main character win the second time around.

The love interest doesn't help the main character in the final big fight and looks petty for sitting it out and not helping the person he/she loves but is mad with.

The bad guy's fate at the end of the story isn't commensurate with the bad things he or she did and your audience is dissatisfied.

The main character's relationship with the love interest isn't changed in any way by him or her now knowing everything about both of the main character's identities.

We and the love interest never see the main character as one integrated, whole person who contains both identities.

FALSE IDENTITY TROPE IN ACTION
Movies:

- While You Were Sleeping
- The Wedding Planner
- Never Been Kissed
- How to Lose A Guy In 10 Days
- Pillow Talk
- Miss Congeniality
- True Lies

Books:

- The Scarlet Pimpernel by Baroness Emmuska Orczy
- The Liar by Nora Roberts

- The Highwayman by Kerrigan Byrn
- Hot Pursuit by Suzanne Brockmann
- The Spymaster's Lady by Joanna Bourne
- Naked in Death by J.D. Robb
- A Kingdom of Dreams by Judith McNaught
- Dream Man by Linda Howard
- The Duke and I by Julia Quinn
- To Catch a Pirate by Jade Parker
- Extreme Exposure by Pamela Clare
- The Madness of Lord Ian Mackenzie by Jennifer Ashley

12

FATED MATES/SOUL MATES

DEFINITION

This trope is based on the premise that the hero and heroine are meant to be together by fate or by soul, and this is the story of how they find each other, realize they're meant to be together, and overcome the obstacles to the two of them being together happily forever.

Some writers choose to make the fated-ness of the hero and heroine a biological fact. For example, werewolves may each have one and only one fated mate in the whole world. They must search until they find their fated partner, and only then can they find happiness and true love.

It's not uncommon for only one of the fated mates to understand that he/she has a fated mate out there in the world somewhere.

The other mate may not be aware that there even is such a thing, let alone that he or she is possibly the fated mate of someone in particular.

It's also not uncommon in the fated mates story that some negative effect accumulates the longer the hero and heroine don't find each other. They may steadily become more aggressive, may lose their sanity, or may even die if they don't find their fated mate.

In this scenario, the story's suspense and forward momentum are driven by this ticking clock counting down to disaster if the hero and heroine don't find each other before one of them suffers the terrible consequences.

In the soul mates version of this story, when the hero and heroine meet, they quickly realize they are in complete simpatico with each other. It may feel as if they've found the other half of their heart or soul and are finally whole now that they've found their soul mate.

While it's a topic of debate in the real world whether there is such a thing as a singular soul mate for each one of us, in the romance fiction space, this concept is generally held to be true. That said, you may certainly choose to explore the argument of free will versus destiny in your story.

It's not uncommon that one of the lovers may resist the idea of being fated to be with the other lover or soul mates with someone at all.

But as the attraction between them becomes more and more irresistible, the reluctant lover gradually or finally gives in to the inevitability of a romance with the other lover.

ADJACENT TROPES

- Oblivious to Love/Belated Epiphany
- Following Your Heart
- Quest/Search for the MacGuffin
- Lone Wolf Tamed

WHY READERS/VIEWERS LOVE THIS TROPE

- this is one of the most romantic of all romance tropes—the idea that there's one perfect person for you and that you can find him or her and have perfect, true love

- the idea of being destined for a person is both comforting and exciting to most people
- given how hard real-life relationships are, who wouldn't love the notion of finding himself/herself in an absolutely simpatico relationship with the person who's perfect for you
- the fantasy of being absolutely certain of your romantic relationship and that your partner will never leave you, never betray you, and never want anyone but you
- most of us will never experience love at first sight, but it remains a widely held wish for many people

OBLIGATORY SCENES

THE BEGINNING:

We typically meet the main character first who's in the most urgent need of finding his or her fated mate. This urgency may come from a biological negative effect that's starting to happen. Or it may come from a cultural, social, or political need (or requirement) to connect with his/her fated mated or soul mate.

For example, if a shapeshifter cannot assume leadership of his/her clan until he/she is mated, and the current leader is ill, dying, or in danger, it may become an emergency for the number two in command to find his/her fated mate or soul mate as soon as possible.

As for the love interest, we often meet him or her going about their regular life oblivious to the fact that their fated mate/soul mate is searching desperately for him or her. Indeed, this person may not be looking for love at all.

The main character may be coming out of a bad relationship (obviously...because it wasn't with his/her fated mate or soul mate).

Or the love interest may simply not be interested in romance or finding a life partner at this point in his or her life.

It's not uncommon to see this trope combined with another one that provides a sharp obstacle to the couple being together. One of them may be engaged to marry someone else. They can come from feuding families or opposite sides of the track, or one of them may have divided loyalties. If this is the case in your story, this trope providing the main obstacle to love is always introduced in the beginning, as well.

The main character, who urgently needs to find his/her fated mate, may not make exactly the most tactful, thoughtful, or appealing introductory approach to the future love interest while in the state of agitation, physical pain, or high stress that the main character is in. Which is to say, this couple's first meeting rarely goes smoothly or well.

Particularly for the love interest who's never heard of the concept of a fated mate or who doesn't believe in the idea of soul mates, he or she probably responds pretty badly to a very forceful, assertive, or desperate initial interaction with the main character. The love interest may be angry, put off, or even afraid of the main character.

The beginning may end with the main character announcing to the (disinterested or downright hostile) future love interest that they are going to be together forever and there's nothing the love interest can do about it.

Of course, our feisty, independent, strong love interest is having no part of being forced into anything, and the personal conflict is on.

OR

The beginning may end with both the hero and heroine aware that they've met someone very special who may be The One, but the big obstacle to their being together rears its ugly head and throws a huge and apparently insurmountable roadblock in front of the couple to end Act One. Cue the plot conflict...

. . .

THE MIDDLE:

This is where the big plot conflict preventing the hero and heroine from being together gets more and more complicated and more and more impossible to overcome.

The partner pressing the relationship forward may have to regroup and take another approach to wooing and winning over the love interest after his/her initial approach fails spectacularly.

For his or her part, the love interest will undoubtedly start to feel the attraction of their fate or souls, but he or she may fight the feeling with everything he or she has.

The main character may be an enemy, outsider, or stranger with whom the love interest has no desire to be in any relationship with let alone a happily ever after as his/her true love. Which is to say, the main character may have his/her work cut out for him or her to convince the love interest to give a relationship between them a chance.

People around the couple may know that the pair is fated to be together but may not care.

Enemies of the main character may actively try to keep him/her away from the love interest to weaken, harm, or kill the main character or to keep him/her out of a position of influence or power.

People around the couple may have no idea that fated mates or soul mates exist and may think it's insane of the main character or love interest to even consider getting into a serious romantic relationship with the other lover. These people may try to talk the lovers out of pursuing a relationship or may actively interfere with the development of a romance between the main character and love interest.

One or both of the lovers may have family, close friends, or allies who do understand the concept of fated mates/soul mates and who do want the couple to find a way to be together. These people help the hero and heroine find a way to be together.

These secondary characters opposing and supporting the fated romance may provide significant plot complications as conflict erupts between the factions.

The middle of the story is where this pair gets to know each other and falls in love. The attraction between them is undeniable no matter how hard one or both of them tries to resist it.

Bit by bit, they give in to the inevitability of their match.

The more time they spend together and the better they get to know each other, the more they realize how perfectly matched they are and how perfectly they fit together, forming the two halves of a whole.

That said, if there's some internal, personal conflict brewing between them, it simmers through the middle, heating up toward a crisis.

The big plot problem threatening to keep the lovers apart or to tear them apart also builds to a crisis.

BLACK MOMENT:

The main character may try to handle the crisis threatening his/her ability to be with his/her fated mate/soul mate but fails.

The external plot problem not only goes terribly, but it also triggers or helps along the personal implosion of the lovers' relationship. The lovers are torn apart.

If there are negative physical, mental, or external consequences to the lovers being apart, those hit.

This time it may be both the main character and love interest who experience strong negative reactions to being separated.

Debilitated by grief, rage, loss, and any other negative emotions you'd like to heap upon this pair, the lovers not only are apart but may not have the means or ability to find a way back together.

All is lost for this pair. The worst possible disaster external to them has happened, and the worst personal disaster has happened—they've lost their true love.

. . .

THE END:

Something changes that makes the lovers think there might be a chance to get back together.

An ally might arrive. Secondary characters (from both sides of the relationship) who support them being together may do something to help them try to get back to their fated mate/soul mate.

The lovers gather themselves for one last, all or nothing, live-or-die-trying effort to get back to their mate. They may have to go through the big bad guy or solve the plot problem they've failed to solve prior to now.

But now they know exactly what's at stake and are willing to go to any length to get back to the person they love or, literally, die trying. Life has no value to either of them without the other one in their life.

The lovers (and their allies) confront the external plot problem and whoever is the personification of it, and empowered by their love for each other, the lovers finally defeat the bad guy and resolve the big, external obstacle standing between them and being together forever.

The lovers resolve any remaining conflicts between them. It may be as simple as, now that they've been apart after finding each other, they both understand how empty their lives would be without the other one.

It may make compromising or stepping off of hills they were previously willing to die on much easier now that they've experienced being separated.

Regardless of how they go about it, the lovers resolve their differences, forgiving each other for any transgressions, mistakes, or stubbornness that have been a past problem.

They are finally joined together once and for all as a fated couple and soul mates and will never allow themselves to be separated again. They look ahead to their future together and step into it side by side.

. . .

KEY SCENES

- if one of them is unaware of the existence of fated mates or soul mates, he or she hears about it for the first time and thinks it's ridiculous
- the fated mate/soul mate introduces himself or herself to the future love interest and it goes terribly
- the love interest feels attraction to the main character but doesn't admit it
- the main character protects the love interest from some real or perceived threat
- the love interest reacts protectively toward the main character and is shocked by it
- the negative consequences of the couple getting together are explained to the lovers (together or separately)
- the negative consequences of the couple NOT getting together are explained to the lovers (together or separately)
- the lovers are apart for a short time in a foreshadowing of the big separation at the end
- each of the lovers does something out of character or really hard for each of them to bring themselves to do for the other one
- the main character betrays the love interest in some way, or the love interest believes the main character has betrayed him/her
- the main character confesses that he/she can't live without the love interest
- the love interest finally admits that he or she believes in (or at least accepts) the idea of being fated mates or soul mates

THINGS TO THINK ABOUT WHEN WRITING THIS TROPE

How does being fated mates or soul mates work in your world building?

What are the consequences for the lovers NOT finding each other at some point in your story? How can you make these worse? How can you make them much worse?

Who is the main character?

Who is the future love interest?

Do either or both of them know about the concept of fated mates or soul mates? If so, who? If not, why not?

Is one of both of your lovers experiencing any negative consequences of having not found their fated mate/soul mate? If so, what is it?

How do your future lovers meet? Does this meeting set the tone and mood for the rest of your story?

Does the main character mess up their first meeting in some way, or does he/she get it exactly right?

How does the love interest react to their first meeting? Is he/she startled by the main character? Confused? Impressed? Infuriated? Afraid?

Is the love interest at all attracted to the main character when they first meet? If so, does that bother him/her? If not—is that complete lack of attraction real, or is the love interest denying having any attraction to himself/herself and not being entirely honest with himself/herself?

What external plot obstacle stands in the way of this couple ending up together? Can you make it bigger? Worse? More impossible to get around or overcome?

Will you use another trope to create a major obstacle to this couple ending up together? If so, which one(s)? What obligatory scenes from this trope can you tie in to this trope or layer with this trope in some way?

What do the people around the lovers think of their fated

mate/soulmate? Are they delighted at who the love interest turns out to be or appalled?

Who questions whether the lovers are actually each other's' fated mates/soul mates? Why?

Who tries to interfere with their romance?

Who helps along their romance?

What personal conflicts, disagreements, differences of beliefs and values do the lovers have when they meet? How will these cause problems in their relationship?

Can you make the personal conflicts between the lovers worse? Much worse? Nigh impossible to overcome?

Does one or both of the lovers refuse to believe the idea of fated mates or soul mates existing? If so, how do they react to meeting their future mate? Does it confuse them, anger them, upset them, shock them, or something else?

How do the main character and love interest know the other one is actually their fated mate or soul mate? Is there a specific mechanism for this in your world building, or do they just recognize each other at some deep level?

If your main character and love interest are relying on their instincts or recognition of their fated mate/soul mate deep inside themselves, how will they convince other people that they've found The One?

How will they convince each other they've found The One?

What will one of them do to try to talk the other out of the belief that they're fated mates or soul mates? How does that go over with the lover who's sure they are?

Will one of the lovers do something to fight the inevitability of their being together? If so, who and what will he/she do? How does the other partner react?

What changes do they each have to make in their own lives to be with the other one? Does one or both of them fight making any of these changes? If so, which ones?

How does the external plot problem ultimately break them apart or trigger their break-up?

How do their personal disagreements and conflicts come to a head? How do these contribute to their failure to resolve the external plot problem?

What happens to each of the lovers when they separate in the black moment? Do they experience negative physical, mental, emotional, or other effects? If so, what are they? Can you make them worse? Much worse?

At what point and why do both of the lovers ultimately accept the inevitability of their romance? What do they do about it, if anything?

What changes that allows the lovers (and their allies) to take on the big bad guy or big external plot problem after the black moment and win this time?

How do the lovers resolve their last (and most difficult) personal conflicts in the end?

What does happily ever after look like for this pair? Will you give us a glimpse of it?

TROPE TRAPS

You don't adequately explain how fated mates/soul mates work in your world and your audience doesn't buy that it's a real thing.

Failing to explain one or both of the lovers isn't aware of the concept of fated mates/soul mates...particularly if they're susceptible to this phenomenon.

There's no negative consequence built into your world for never finding your fated mate/soul mate, which disappoints your audience and gives away a chance to develop great tension and suspense.

There's no ticking clock on one or both main characters finding their soul mate, giving away another great chance to develop tension and suspense.

Neither of the lovers does anything that's hard for him or her for the other one—they never sacrifice anything for their fated mate/soul mate.

The way the lovers meet doesn't match the mood and tone of the rest of the story and is jarring to your audience.

You rely solely on biological or chemical attraction to bring the lovers together and they have nothing else in common on which to build a solid and lasting relationship.

The main character comes on so strong to the future love interest that your audience is put off by him/her and doesn't like him or her.

The love interest is so stubbornly opposed to even considering the idea of being destined to end up with the main character that he/she comes across as unlikable.

One or both of the lovers is so sure they're destined to be together that they don't bother to actually romance each other. At all. Making your story deeply unromantic.

The lovers spend so much time fighting they never have time to plausibly fall in love...or even learn to like each other.

The plot problem keeping the lovers apart is lame or not serious enough to justify keeping this couple apart and miserable forever.

The personal conflicts between lovers are petty, mean, sophomoric, or not worthy of two people who are so clearly meant to be together and allegedly are perfect for each other.

Nothing changes from the failures of the black moment to the triumphs of the final, climactic conflict, and your audience wonders why the good guys couldn't beat the bad guys earlier.

Just because these characters are destined to be together doesn't mean your audience will be happy if they end up together but continue to fight all the time, bicker, have friction, and don't find peace and joy together.

Failing to convince your audience that everyone around the couple accepts their relationship and isn't going to cause problems for them remaining together going forward.

. . .

FATED MATES/SOUL MATES TROPE IN ACTION
Movies:

- Serendipity
- The Notebook
- Eternal Sunshine of the Spotless Mind
- Slumdog Millionaire
- The Time Traveler's Wife
- Lady Hawke
- Somewhere in Time
- Made in Heaven
- One Day

Books:

- Outlander by Diana Gabaldon
- Pride and Prejudice by Jane Austen
- Twilight by Stephanie Meyer
- A Court of Thorns and Roses by Sarah J. Maas
- Slave to Sensation by Nalini Singh
- Dragon Bound by Thea Harrison
- Moon Called by Patricia Briggs
- Dark Lover by J.R. Ward
- Fated by Rebecca Zanetti
- Acheron by Sherrilyn Kenyon

13
FLING/ONE NIGHT STAND

DEFINITION

In this story, your hero and heroine meet casually—very casually. They each, for reasons of their own, engage in a one-night stand or short fling with each other. Neither of them expect anything to come of the short encounter. Indeed, both of them may immediately return to their regularly scheduled lives after their one night or few nights together.

NOTE: in a book with low heat, the fling may be something short of sex together. In this case, the couple shares a deep emotional connection while they're together. Particularly if one of the emotional lovers is involved with someone else, this fling may amount to an emotional affair.

A variation on this theme is for one of the emotional lovers to be celibate for some reason. Even this much emotional, persona contact with the other person comes dangerously close to a betrayal of his/her vow of celibacy.

It's worth taking a close look at why each of these people indulges in a one-night-stand or brief fling. It will tell your audience a lot about each of these people, their wounds, weaknesses, insecurities, and motivations in life. Your audience will definitely be examining why each of these characters jumped into a one-night-stand or fling—and with that particular partner especially.

Something happens to bring this couple back together again. They may encounter each other at work or somewhere else they both live, work, or spend time. They may be introduced by someone else who doesn't know they've met (and slept together) before. One of them may be unable to forget the other and track down the other lover.

It's also possible to introduce a second trope that brings this couple back together—an unexpected pregnancy is the classic trope many writers reach for to bring this couple back together.

While a surprise baby is a perfectly fine way to force this couple back together, I encourage you to think creatively and come up with a fun, innovative, interesting, or unique means of bringing these two people back into each other's lives. Doing so will set your story apart from the crowd—a lot—in the arena of this particular trope.

At any rate, the couple is brought back together or forced back together and now must build a relationship with this virtual stranger. Moreover, the pair may be under a great deal of pressure while they try to build a relationship out of nothing but a passing attraction or chance encounter.

While an external plot problem poses an increasingly insurmountable obstacle to this couple ending up happily ever after together, the couple nonetheless perseveres in trying to build a lasting relationship.

In the end, the couple resolves all their conflicts, resolves the big plot problem, and discovers they've found their true love, after all.

ADJACENT TROPES

- Accidental Pregnancy

- Home for the Holiday/Vacation Fling
- Is the Baby Mine
- Rebound Romance
- Drunk/Vegas Wedding

WHY READERS/VIEWERS LOVE THIS TROPE

- we would all love to have someone who meets us be instantly attracted to us
- a no strings attached would take a lot of pressure off of us in a new relationship and make it a lot more relaxing and enjoyable
- how cool would it be if a chance encounter led to true love
- cutting through all the hassles, heartache, and failures of dating to find my true love and skipping all the lengthy and difficult dating and getting to know you stuff
- being spontaneous and jumping into bed with a stranger sounds like a terrific escape from the mundane struggles of everyday life

OBLIGATORY SCENES

THE BEGINNING:

In most cases, this story begins with the main characters meeting each other and heading straight into their one-night-stand or fling. It is, indeed, the hook for this entire story.

A hookup, two ships passing in the night, together in grand (emotional) isolation, random strangers comfort each other...these are other names for this trope that you might have heard before.

The key to this trope is that the initial encounter between the hero and heroine is understood by both of them to be a no strings attached affair...or at least both of them should understand this.

Complications may definitely ensue if one of them hasn't gotten this memo and expects more from this non-relationship.

You may choose to slip in a little backstory or character set-up before the pair meets and rapidly progresses to their romantic encounter. But unless it's absolutely vital to know something about one or both of the characters before they jump into the sack together, it's generally best to skip the backstory and head straight into the one-night stand or fling. You can catch up later with revealing the backstory that makes your audience react with interest, surprise, or shock.

The beginning typically ends with the BIG COMPLICATION that forces the couple back together. They may discover they work for the same company or they're attending the same conference or live in the same building. Or it may be something more challenging—she's pregnant. He needs something back from her that she inadvertently picked up and carried away from their tryst. Somebody's not amused that they had a romantic encounter and is out to harm or kill one or both of them.

THE MIDDLE:

The problem is big enough that they need to work together to deal with it. At least temporarily, they're forced into proximity by this problem.

This is when the couple starts to actually get to know each other. They may know very little about each other until this moment—they may not even know each other's names prior to being thrown back into proximity.

The one thing these two people do know about each other is that they had great romantic chemistry together.

This chemistry will ultimately go well beyond physical compatibility as they get to know each other and find all the other things they have in common and genuinely like about each other.

Initially, one or both of them may resent being forced into proximity with the other. But they both have to take responsibility for participating in the one-night stand/fling in the first place, whether they like it or not. Whatever downstream repercussions result from that night or fling—it's on each of their heads.

As adults, they both step up to deal with the big plot problem. And, in the meantime, they start getting to know each other as humans.

They may repeat their romantic encounter fairly quickly. More frequently, they take their time and choose to get to know each other the second time around before they end up back in each other's arms. They may both think a lot about repeating their one-night-stand or fling, but this serves to add an element of sexual tension to the relationship and build anticipation in the characters and in your audience.

Complications from the big plot problem continue to build and the couple scrambles to stay ahead of the burgeoning problem.

The more they get to know each other, the more they like each other, and the more they're attracted to each other, the more likely they are to discover each other's flaws and areas of friction and conflict between them. These also begin to build up as the tensions and stress of dealing with the big problem stretch both of these characters to the limit.

Meanwhile, any doubts or fears they've had about trying to build a long-term relationship out of one that started so frivolously, so casually, so without thought, blow up in their faces.

The middle usually ends with a big crisis in their relationship. The big plot problem and the big relationship problem exacerbate each other and provoke each other into crises that ultimately tear apart the lovers.

. . .

BLACK MOMENT:

The flimsiness of the foundation of this relationship (or at least the couple's perception of how flimsy it is) has caused it to collapse. There seems to be no way back from this breakup. And furthermore, there's no way back from the big plot problem that has torn them apart.

All is lost for both of them.

THE END:

In the aftermath of losing each other and failing to resolve the external problem tearing them apart, the hero and heroine realize they truly miss each other and that their feelings for each other really are genuine.

Regardless of how they met and how unconventional it might have been, they nonetheless have forged a real relationship that can last for the long term...if they can only find a way to put it back together.

The hero and heroine typically work together (whether or not they've reconciled personally) to deal with the big plot problem that now threatens them both. Something has changed since they failed to solve the problem at the end of the middle of the story—they've learned something new, found some new resolve, some greater reason to fight through to a victory, or they've gained a new ally—and now they have the necessary resources to win.

It's still a dramatic conflict and the hero and heroine barely pull it out, but they resolve the big problem by working together and/or working with others.

In the aftermath, they can finally resolve any lingering personal conflicts they have yet to resolve. When faced with the prospect of losing the person they love forever or to death, their previous problems may seem petty and small. Or they may have finally learned the lessons they needed to build a lasting and healthy relationship with each other.

KEY SCENES

- the morning after…when they wake up and/or sober up and realize what they've done
- first time the hero and heroine see each other after they've separated from their tryst
- one of them asks the other one out again
- friends put together that this is the person their friend had the one-night-stand or fling with and give them heck for it
- the hero or heroine resents being forced back into a relationship with this near stranger
- one or both of the main characters feel lonely even though they're with the other person
- the hero and heroine share a moment of truce or commiseration that's the beginning of friendship and getting to know each other
- the hero and heroine have an epic argument
- one or both of the lovers doubts the relationship's veracity given the flimsy premise upon which it is based
- the hero and heroine fail to work together when put under a bunch of pressure by the big plot problem, confirming their worst fears about their inability to become a couple
- the hero and heroine miss each other terribly after they break up
- the hero and heroine realize they've learned lessons that change their outlook or approach to love

THINGS TO THINK ABOUT WHEN WRITING THIS TROPE

How do the hero and heroine end up in the same place at the same time?

How do they meet?

How do they hook up?

Why does each of them decide a one-night stand or fling is just the thing for them right now?

What's the hero's backstory before this moment?

What complications stem from his backstory that will interfere with this relationship going forward?

What's the heroine's backstory before this moment?

What complications stem from her backstory that will interfere with this relationship going forward?

Do the hero and heroine remember their one-night-stand or fling or not? If not, why not? If so, what do they remember most?

How do the hero and heroine feel the morning after? What do they think of what they've done?

Did they have fun? How did they connect? What was special or fantastic about their one-night-stand/fling that makes it memorable to both of them?

How and where do the hero and heroine see each other again?

Are they surprised to see each other? If so, why? If not, why not?

How awkward is it seeing each other again? Can you make it more awkward? A lot more awkward?

What plot problem forces the hero and heroine to spend time together going forward in your story? How does this problem set the mood and tone of the rest of the story?

Is it a permanent problem or a temporary one that, once fixed, will let them go their separate ways and live their own lives without ever seeing each other again?

If it's a permanent problem, how do the hero and heroine feel about potentially having a connection for a very long time or the rest of their lives? Does one or both of them fight the idea or look for other alternatives?

How much time do the hero and heroine spend together as a result of the big plot problem? Is it enough for them to get to know each other and eventually fall in love?

Why do they each doubt the relationship as it begins to develop?

Does either lover have any other personal relationships or romantic entanglements they must get out of before they can be with the other main character? If so, how will they do it?

How does the big plot problem get worse over the course of the story? Can you make it worse? Much worse?

How do the hero and heroine each feel about being forced to spend time with the other one initially?

What attracts them to each other besides the hot one-night-stand they spent together or the fling they had?

What drives them crazy about each other in a bad way?

How do the people around them react to their renewed relationship? Who helps it along and why? Who sabotages it and why?

Does either of them have another trope at work that might prevent them from forming a lasting relationship with the other one or might pose an obstacle to that character finding and grasping love? If so, what trope is it?

How does the growing plot problem exacerbate the conflicts in their personal relationship and vice versa?

What conflict between them grows or deepens until it threatens to tear apart their relationship?

What does ultimately tear them apart?

How is their conflict meaningful, relatable, and serious (as opposed to shallow, sophomoric, and irritating to your audience)?

How will they resolve the big plot problem?

What lessons do they learn about themselves or about each other that allow them to move toward resolution of their issues?

How will they resolve their personal conflict?

Who apologizes to whom and for what?

Who makes a grand gesture of love? What is it? How does the other lover receive it?

TROPE TRAPS

The hero and heroine were so drunk that neither of them remembers what happened in the one-night-stand or fling, making them seem immature.

One or both of the main characters have no decent reason for thinking a one-night-stand is a good idea...but do it anyways.

The backstory that leads each of the main characters to a one-night-stand or fling is lame or nonexistent.

There is no backstory for these characters. They just step onto the screen or page fully formed and jump in the sack together without any plausible explanation for doing so.

The hero and heroine have so little in common that they would never plausibly form a lasting and healthy romantic relationship.

The reason the hero and heroine are forced back together is lame or very cliché.

The one-night-stand or fling isn't memorable enough to make a big impression on either character.

The big plot problem only affects one of the main characters and never has any impact on the other one.

There's another potential solution to the big plot problem that doesn't force the hero and heroine to be together a lot or permanently going forward...and the couple fails to take this way out when it's what they would logically do.

The hero and heroine have nothing in common and would never plausibly be attracted to each other.

The hero and heroine bicker or argue all the time and don't seem as if they even like each other let alone love each other.

The hero and heroine never find anything they have in common that's solid enough to build a relationship on.

Although the hero and heroine end up together, they never

resolve their personal conflicts in a way that makes your audience think they have any chance of being happy for the long-term.

The hero and heroine fail to work together to solve the big plot problem.

The hero and heroine never learn anything new about themselves or each other and remain the same shallow, wounded, lonely people they were when the story started.

The personal problems between the hero and heroine could be solved with a single honest, mature conversation between them...and yet they never have that adult conversation with each other.

The audience is convinced this couple will break up shortly after the story ends.

FLING/ONE NIGHT STAND TROPE IN ACTION
Movies:

- One Day
- No Strings Attached
- Knocked Up
- Love and Other Drugs
- Fools Rush In
- Two Night Stand
- Friends With Benefits
- Nine Months
- Love, Rosie

Books:

- Beautiful Stranger by Christina Lauren
- The Proposition by Katie Ashley
- Red, White & Royal Blue by Casey McQuiston

- One Night with a Hero by Laura Kaye
- After Hours by Cara McKenna
- Secrets of a Summer Night by Lisa Kleypas
- The CEO's Little Surprise by Jennifer Faye
- The Pregnancy Plot by Paula Roe
- The Consequence of Falling by Claire Contreras
- The Two Week Arrangement by Kendall Ryan

14
FORCED PROXIMITY

DEFINITION

As the title suggests, the hero and heroine in this story are forced together by some event (usually) outside of their control. It is possible that one or both of the main characters machinates to end up stranded somewhere with the other main character. It's also possible that another character in the story—frequently a meddling mama looking to arrange a marriage in an unconventional way—schemes for the hero and heroine to end up forced into proximity together.

The ultimate expression of being forced into proximity is the two main characters becoming stranded together in a survival situation where they must work together to live. A milder expression of forced proximity might be a work project or office setting where the hero and heroine must work together or a situation where they're forced into co-parenting, volunteering on the same project, or planning an event, for example.

The key to this trope is that the hero and heroine must spend time together for some reason. They may not know each other beforehand, may only know each other in passing, or may dislike each other enough that they would never usually choose to spend time together, let alone concentrated time alone together.

It's not enough that these two characters forced together, however. The circumstances must isolate just the two of them together with plenty of privacy and no outside interference for long enough that they have plenty of opportunity to get to know each other, work out past arguments, and fall in love or fall in love again, or at least fall into each other's arms.

Common devices for actually stranding the couple together include broken down elevators, accidental lock-ins, power blackouts, snowstorms, car breakdowns, road closures, floods, hurricanes, wildfires, or any other natural disaster you can use to trap two people in the same place for a while.

Your stranded lovers may or may not have communications with the outside world—whatever best serves your story. They typically have a stash of food, water, firewood, blankets, candles, and other supplies conveniently available and sure to make the lover's time together romantic and/or sexy.

This isn't usually a trope of literal suffering and fighting to survive, although it certainly can be. Instead, this is usually a trope of a cozy, relatively comfortable getaway that neither the hero nor heroine planned nor anticipated. Often, it's the act of escaping the real world, getting away from the noise and distractions, that allows these two people to finally notice someone else romantically.

This trope is frequently combined with another trope that explains why this pair has never explored a romantic relationship before. A boss and employee may end up locked in the office or stranded in an elevator and finally really see each other. The girl next door and her emotionally distant neighbor may finally be thrown together by a blizzard and get to know each other. A Grumpy-Sunshine couple or May-December couple who wouldn't have otherwise considered exploring a relationship may suddenly find attraction when thrown together.

And, of course, all the tropes of reconciliation are ideal to pair with this trope.

At its core, this is a classical Cupid's arrow story in which a chance meeting and surprise tryst lead to true love like a bolt out of the blue.

ADJACENT TROPES

- Oblivious to Love
- Estranged Spouses
- Reconciliation/Second Chance
- Right Under Your Nose
- Everyone Else Can See It
- Arranged Marriage

WHY READERS/VIEWERS LOVE THIS TROPE

- these two people focus entirely on each other while they're together, and who doesn't want their own romantic interest to do that when with us
- we all like and need the idea of being safe in the midst of a storm or in the midst of a crisis. Indeed, for someone whose life is in crisis, this story is a welcome escape to safety
- we love the idea of the meant-to-be encounter, of being fated to find this person and have true love with him or her
- we crave being able to break down emotional barriers between us and our coworkers, neighbors, or ex-lovers— for them to really see us as we are and see us as people with whom they can find common ground

OBLIGATORY SCENES

THE BEGINNING:

This story typically begins just before the event that forces the hero and heroine together. There's a storm coming but it's not here, yet. There have been power flickers for a while, but the power hasn't gone out, yet. One or both characters is driving in bad weather conditions but hasn't been forced off the road, yet.

In this slice of life before the crisis, we see that one or both characters is busy, distracted, overworked, and not looking for love.

The crisis or event happens that throws the hero and heroine together. The elevator stops, the motel only has one room left, the car (or horse-drawn carriage for the historical writers out there) hits a patch of ice and goes into a ditch.

If the couple has past history together and they know each other, sparks fly. This is the *last* person he or she wants to have to deal with. They may not want to cooperate, let alone work together to get out of the situation. Sparks fly and they argue instead of figuring out how to get out of here. They may work individually to get out of this place, or they may reluctantly pool their resources and work together to try to get out of wherever they're stuck.

The hero and heroine may expend a fair bit of time and effort trying to get themselves out of their fix. After all, they've got nothing better to do until they're out of here. Their efforts to escape are all to no avail, however. They're well and truly stranded together until help comes or until weather conditions improve.

It's not uncommon that one of the characters has some sort of perceived crisis that he or she must deal with—a meeting he or she must get to, a work deadline that has to be met, perhaps a date he or she is supposed to go to. This character is agitated and upset that he or she is missing the "important" thing. The beginning often ends with the pronouncement by the other character that they might as well get comfortable because they're not going anywhere for a while.

It's also possible that it's scandalous that they're stranded together like this and one character is upset and agitated at being alone with the other person. In a historical context, this could ruin a young lady's reputation. In a modern context, one character may have a jealous boyfriend or girlfriend who's going to freak out...particularly if this pair has a past romantic history together.

You get the idea. Have fun coming up with a reason why one or both of your characters is freaked out at being stuck with the other person. The realization that there's nothing to be done about it is usually the climax of the beginning of this type of story.

THE MIDDLE:

Your hero and heroine go about the business of taking care of their physical needs—finding food, water, warmth (or cool), a comfortable place to sleep. This may be the first time the pair works together without fighting. They declare a temporary truce to make sure they're going to be safe for the duration of their stranding.

Typically, this couple has limited access to the outside world. You may choose to give them working phones, a television, Internet, or a radio. But you'll want to give the hero and heroine the bare minimum of communication ability that's necessary to advance your story. After all, the idea is to force this couple to do nothing but spend time together, getting to know each other.

The couple usually engages in conversation, for lack of anything else to do, and talk about whatever these two people might reasonably talk about. They typically start by talking about superficial things and gradually work their way into talking about more personal and intimate topics.

In a high heat-level story, they may go for some boredom making out or boredom sex for lack of anything else to do. But this, too, gradually shifts from superficial to more personal and intimate.

If there actually is a crisis brewing for one or both characters elsewhere because of their failure to be somewhere or to do something, that crisis grows through the middle of the story. A boyfriend's or girlfriend's texts may grow increasingly jealous and angry. A board meeting to fight off a hostile takeover may be going very badly without the stranded CEO there to fight for his or her company. The pressure to get out of here may grow…but there's still nothing this character can do about it. That pressure may translate into friction and bickering…or an intense, reckless romantic encounter.

In the situation where the hero and heroine are completely cut off from the outside world, a sense of being suspended from reality may envelop this couple. This is a magical getaway, a complete escape from their real lives. Into this complete removal from the rest of the world, this pair may find themselves falling into a romantic fog, a fantasy relationship that can only exist here in this bubble of suspended reality. They may both throw themselves headlong into the moment and indulge in a passionate romance.

By the end of the middle, this couple has thrown themselves headlong into this instant romance…

…and then reality intrudes to end the middle of the story. A repairman goes to work on unlocking the door to let them out. A snowplow starts working on the roads that have been closed. A tow truck arrives to pull the stranded character's car out of the ditch.

BLACK MOMENT:

The fantasy tryst is over. They have to return to the real world and resume their normal lives, their real-world jobs and roles, their other relationships, responsibilities, and distractions.

They almost got to happily ever after, but they didn't have quite enough time to make the relationship permanent. They never got around to talking about what would happen when they left their bubble of suspended reality. They might have set aside their differences for the duration of being stranded, but they never fully worked out their differences.

And now the magical time together is over. The magical veil has been ripped away and they've been ripped apart by real life. They almost had it all, but they let it slip through their grasp, and they're both devastated and heartbroken.

THE END:

Unable to forget or get over the memory of their magical time together, both the hero and heroine realize they're in love with the other person and must find a way back to him or her. This may involve one of them breaking off a relationship with someone else, giving up a high-powered job, walking away from the fourteen-hour workdays, or in some other way upending their life, first. This character sets about doing what's necessary so he or she can be with the other person.

If a crisis got badly complicated by the hero or heroine's absence while stranded, that character has to work out the crisis before he or she can go after the person he or she truly loves.

If you're a fan of double black moments, you can give these characters a second set of black moments when they both do something to be with the other person that works at cross-purposes. For example, without telling each other, they each arrange a job transfer to be close to the other person—he moves to where she has just left, and she moves to where he has just left. If you pull a stunt like this, obviously, the hero and heroine will have to sort it out before they can finally be together forever.

The characters finally overcome all the obstacles to being together and can be together at last, never to be separated again.

KEY SCENES

- they worry about each other's safety. They set aside past bad history or the discomfort of being strangers for long enough to ensure the other person is okay

- one or both characters refuse to believe that they're going to be here for a while and there's no way to leave
- once they know they're safe, they individually notice the other one's attractiveness
- the sleeping arrangements have to get sorted out, and the only logical arrangement is uncomfortably intimate
- the hero and heroine argue about something that devolves into laughter
- the hero and heroine each confess something to the other person that, under normal circumstances, they would never tell the other one
- they create a sense of magical detachment from reality for themselves...and lose themselves in it
- the aftermath of a romantic scene appropriate to the heat level of your story, where it dawns on one or both of them that what they just did is probably a mistake
- the hero and heroine are physically pulled apart by their real lives when they emerge from their tryst
- one of the lovers contacts the other one to say that he or she misses the other one (To which, the other lover may or may not respond or may respond badly)

THINGS TO THINK ABOUT WHEN WRITING THIS TROPE

Do your hero and heroine know each other before they're stranded together or not? If so, what's their past history together? Why aren't they together now?

How do the hero and heroine end up stranded together?

What do they do to try to get out of their predicament? Why doesn't it work?

How do they each feel about being stranded with this person?

Where are they actually stuck together?

What's the physical setting?

What supplies do they have?

What are the sleeping arrangements going to be?

Has someone machinated to throw this pair together, or are they stranded together by random chance?

If this isn't random chance, when and how in your story will you reveal who threw them together and how?

What entertainments do they have to occupy themselves? Can these things force them to interact, for example, a deck of cards or a board game?

Does one or both characters have a crisis of some kind brewing outside of where they're stranded? If so, what is it?

Why is it vital that the hero or heroine be present in person to deal with this crisis (or to get out of here as soon as (possible)?

How, later in the story, will the hero or heroine realize that what he or she thought was a crisis at the beginning of the story really isn't that important to him or her? How will the time stranded with the other person teach him or her this?

Do these characters bicker, disagree, argue, or have friction about certain topics? If so, what topics?

Do they argue about why they broke up, why one of them is a rotten boss, which sports team is better, or something else?

What happens to affect their situation that draws them closer together?

Does the natural disaster get worse?

Does the power go out?

Do they run short on firewood and have to gather or chop more?

Will the worsening of the situation force them to spend more time together than they anticipated? If so, how do they each feel about that?

How do their interactions progress from superficial to personal to intimate to never-told-anyone-else (or never-done-with-anyone-else)?

How will you create an atmosphere of being in a magical space or bubble completely separate from reality? What physical setting elements will help this sense? What emotional or atmospheric elements will help this sense?

How physically intimate will this pair get? Is this abnormal for one or both of them?

How does any external, real-life crisis worsen over the course of the story? How do your stranded characters find out about this worsening of this crisis? Why is that character unable to do anything to make it better or deal with it while still stranded?

What aspects of each other do the hero and heroine find fascinating, unexpected, attractive, and irresistible?

What are the rational reasons why these two should not get together romantically? Why do they each ignore these reasons? How do they each rationalize having a romantic tryst with the other person?

What from the real world intrudes upon their tryst? Do they ignore it or deal with it?

How does their tryst come to an end? How do they feel about it ending?

What does returning to their individual real lives look like?

How is each of them different in the wake of their tryst together? How does it mess up their real lives?

Do the people around them notice differences? What do the people around them think of the tryst the hero and heroine have shared? How does the tryst cause problems between the hero/heroine and loved ones, friends, coworkers, and other major characters?

Do they get in contact with each other after their tryst? If so, how? Is it done in secret or not? If not, why not?

How do they feel about being in contact or not being in contact?

What happens to force each of them to acknowledge to themselves what their feelings are for the other person?

What will each of them do about their feelings?

How does acting on their feelings precipitate a crisis in each of their real lives? What's that crisis? How much havoc does it cause?

What final obstacle do they have to overcome before they can be together? How will they overcome it? Do they act individually to overcome it or do they work together to overcome it?

How do they finally get back together? Where do they reunite?

How do the people around them feel about their relationship in the end? Do the lovers care?

What lessons have they learned from their experience of being stranded together? How will this change their real lives going forward?

What does happily ever after look like for this pair?

TROPE TRAPS

The hero and heroine have a plausible way to get out of being stranded together but don't think of it and seem dumb to your audience.

The hero and heroine fight like crazy when they first get together and act so unlikable that your audience doesn't buy them liking each other, let alone loving each other.

Survival supplies are shockingly plentiful in the right place at the right time, and they implausibly lack for *nothing*.

The hero and heroine fail to make use of readily available resources to rescue themselves.

One or both characters is so preoccupied with his or her real life that it's not plausible when they abruptly shift into romantic tryst mode.

The hero and heroine are so dissimilar they would never get together in real life.

The hero and heroine's lives, careers, or social statuses are so dissimilar they would never get together in real life.

The hero and heroine go straight from strangers to telling each other all their most intimate secrets and your audience doesn't buy it.

The hero and heroine jump straight into each other's arms without getting to know each other at all.

The hero and heroine are so passionately in love by the time they leave their tryst that it makes no sense for them to go their separate ways the minute they get out of being stranded.

Nothing stands in the way of their being together when they get out of being stuck together.

The hero and heroine return to snobbish, prejudiced, or bad behavior that keeps them apart the minute they leave the tryst, and you never justify how or why they overcome these unlovable beliefs to end up together.

Neither character learns anything about himself or herself during the tryst that changes his or her outlook on their real life once they return to it.

Your audience doesn't buy that this couple would end up together after the tryst ends. They're too different or from too different worlds.

If someone machinated to throw this couple together, he or she never confesses to it, and is never reviled and later thanked for doing so.

FORCED PROXIMITY TROPE IN ACTION
Movies:

- The African Queen
- Six Days, Seven Nights
- The Blue Lagoon
- Overboard
- Romancing the Stone
- The Bounty Hunter
- The Mountain Between Us
- Speed
- The Proposal

Books:

- The Unhoneymooners by Christina Lauren
- Swept Away by Robyn Carr
- The Flatshare by Beth O'Leary
- Beauty and the Beast by Hannah Howell
- The River of No Return by Bee Ridgway
- The Wall of Winnipeg and Me by Mariana Zapata
- The Wreck by Landon Beach
- Whiteout by Adriana Anders

15

GRUMPY-SUNSHINE

DEFINITION

In this trope one of the lovers in your story is grumpy to the point of being a full-time grouch and the other lover is cheerful to the point of possibly being annoyingly happy.

This is a classic story of opposites attract.

The grumpy character typically is an introvert or fully anti-social and uses his/her grouchiness to keep other people away from him or her. The grumpy character may also be a hard-headed realist who sees clearly the worst of the world around him or her.

This pragmatic person prepares for the worst and isn't surprised by much of anything negative that happens around him or her. He or she may be deeply surprised when anything goes well around him or her.

He or she isn't hurt by others very often because the grump holds most people at arm's length, is slow to trust anyone, and doesn't form deep relationships with anyone he/she doesn't trust completely.

The sunshine character is more likely to be an extrovert and outgoing, highly social, friendly, and have a large social circle of friends and family.

This character may also be unrealistically optimistic and idealistic about the world and everyone around him or her and assumes that everything will always turn out great. He or she may be deeply surprised when events don't go well around him or her.

The sunshine character is emotionally open, vulnerable to hurt, and is often taken advantage of or disappointed by friends and family from whom the sunshine person always expects the best of.

Typically the sunshine character sets out to cheer up the grumpy character and draw him or her out of their shell of grumpy isolation. Of course, the grumpy character wants no part of cheering up, becoming social, making friends, or otherwise changing his/her grumpy attitude.

For his or her part, the grumpy character may try to prepare or protect the sunshine character from the harsh realities of the big bad world. The grump may also try to get the sunshine character to see the people around him or her more clearly, to stop being taken advantage of by friends and family, and protect himself/herself from being hurt.

It's up to you to decide if one character changes the other to be more like him/her or if the pair meets in the middle somewhere between pragmatism and idealism, openness and caution, trusting and untrusting, grumpy and cheerful, pessimistic and optimistic.

ADJACENT TROPES

- Cold/Serious/Uptight Hero/Heroine
- Bad Boy/Girl Reformed
- Goody Two Shoes
- Reclusive Hero/Heroine
- Socially Awkward Hero/Heroine
- Lone Wolf Tamed

WHY READERS/VIEWERS LOVE THIS TROPE

- many of us relate strongly to one or the other of these characters personally
- it would be nice to have a life partner who balances out our more extreme personality tendencies and protects us from our own weaknesses and vulnerabilities
- many people get deep satisfaction from fixing a fixer-upper, be it a sofa, house, or person...and both of these characters can be perceived as fixer-uppers depending on which one you believe most needs "fixing"
- the natural tension between these opposite personalities leads to a lot of fun friction, snark, and witty banter we all wish we could think of in the moment
- we all love a big ole' grump melting and turning into a teddy bear just for us

OBLIGATORY SCENES

THE BEGINNING:

You may choose to introduce your audience separately to the grump and sunshine characters, or you can choose one of these characters and throw him or her into a meet-cute with the other one.

Because this is an opposites attract story, there's almost always immediate friction between these two people no matter what situation you throw them into.

Your meet-cute may introduce a plot problem that will throw the main characters into repeated proximity throughout your story so they can get to know each other and eventually fall in love.

OR

The sunshine soul, having met the grump, assigns himself or herself a project to introduce the grump to everyone in town, to find friends for the grump, or to change the grump's...well, grumpiness. The sunshine soul is going to cheer up that grouch if it kills him or her.

Vice versa, the grump may assign himself or herself a project to protect the sunshine soul from someone who's taking advantage of him or her, to keep the sunshine soul safe from his or her own naïveté, or to keep the sunshine soul safe from some threat that the sunshine soul may or may not be aware of or may not fully appreciate.

No matter how you push these two people together, they have a rocky path forward at first as they drive each other crazy in the worst possible way. Their diametrically opposed world views clash constantly over the smallest of things.

One or both of these characters may grow exasperated with the other one and look for an exit strategy to get away from the other one before long. They both may seriously consider whether or not they've made a mistake getting to know the other one.

If there's an external plot problem throwing these two people together, the beginning usually ends with a mini-crisis in that problem that forces the grump and sunshine soul to work even more closely together, going forward.

If your story revolves primarily around the couple and their personal conflict, one of them tries to exit the relationship and the other one doubles down on "fixing" the one trying to exit.

THE MIDDLE:

Fully committed to their project—be it an external one or "fixing" the other one—the couple spends more and more time together.

They move from conflicts over superficial things to deeper conflicts of philosophy, world view, and views on humanity. Their pragmatism and idealism, pessimism and optimism, trust and distrust, come into more direct conflict as the problems around them grow more serious.

This trope is frequently paired with other, more plot-based tropes that put this couple on the run, in hiding, or dealing with some kind of threat. Typically the threat is to the sunshine character—after all, the grump is far too cautious and suspicious to wander into danger.

A bodyguard keeping a client safe is a classic grumpy-sunshine combination as is the naïve sunshine soul who has moved into a dangerous neighborhood with a grumpy protector for a next-door neighbor.

In these sorts of scenarios, the threat grows exponentially worse through the middle of the story. The sunshine soul's optimism and belief in a positive outcome are tested to the limit at the same time the grump's caution and preparation for and expectation of the worst are put to the test.

The middle often ends with some sort of very serious threat to the sunshine soul that grump may not be able to prevent or protect the sunshine soul from because of the sunshine soul's unwillingness to change or listen to the voice of caution.

Vice versa, the middle may end with some serious threat to the grump that he or she is unwilling to ask for help with and may be overcome by because of his/her failure to change.

BLACK MOMENT:

The opposite characters' failures to change or learn from each other cause the big. plot problem or big personal crisis between them to go very, very badly. They fail to fix the big plot problem, and furthermore, they fail to keep themselves or each other safe from harm.

This harm can be physical in a suspense story, or it can be emotional harm in a non-suspense story. Either way, the harm done is devastating. The sunshine character is emotionally crushed and loses his or her optimism, hope, and faith in humanity. The grump is crushed by the sunshine character's loss of joy and cheer.

Vice versa, the grump may be devastated by his or her failure to anticipate the worst and prepare for it. His or her pragmatism let him or her down and he/she didn't see the bad thing coming. This failure is devastating to the grump who may retreat completely into his/her emotional shell and physical reclusiveness. The sunshine character is devastated by his/her failure to help the grump be more open and instead having driven the grump even further away from any connection to others.

Not only have these two people failed to fix the big plot problem and not only have they broken up as a couple, but they've broken the other lover—or at least significantly harmed them. Each of them has taken what was best and strongest about the other person and damaged him or her.

All is well and truly lost.

THE END:

One or both of the lovers is miserable without the other one hanging around driving them crazy. They may irritate each other and banter constantly, but they really do love each other, and they finally realize they make each other better, more balanced people.

Without the other person in their lives to temper their most extreme impulses, they're not nearly as good a person nor are they prepared to deal with the world around them. Having learned that they're better together than apart, they now must find a way to fix the big plot problem tearing them apart, and moreover, they must make amends to each other and find their way back together.

One of the lovers approaches the other one, or possibly the big plot problem throws them together one last time (particularly if one of them is actively avoiding the other one). They work together to resolve the big external problem and may work out their differences while dealing with the big plot problem or may wait until after it's resolved to have a heart-to-heart conversation and confess their need and desire for each other.

They finally find the balance between their opposing approaches to life and find common ground where they work best together, balancing out each other's most extreme tendencies and finding happiness somewhere in the middle.

KEY SCENES

- the sunshine character steamrolls the grumpy character with his/her good cheer, upbeat personality, and complete obliviousness to the grump's attempts to get rid of him or her
- the grump goes full reclusive grouch on the sunshine character and shocks him or her
- the grump smiles or laughs for the first time
- the sunshine soul admits that he/she leaps before he/she looks and does get into trouble from time to time
- the grump's pessimism gets him/her into trouble and the sunshine soul rescues him/her
- the sunshine soul's optimism gets him/her into trouble and the grump rescues him/her
- the lovers work together for the first time and it goes better than either expected
- each of the lovers reverts to their old form and it goes terribly

THINGS TO THINK ABOUT WHEN WRITING THIS TROPE

Why is your grump a grump?
How will you show your audience his/her grumpiness initially?

Why is your sunshine soul the way he/she is?

How will you show your audience his/her cheerfulness initially?

How do your lovers meet each other?

How does their first meeting set the mood and tone for the rest of the story?

What big plot problem will the couple have to deal with over the course of the story?

How does this big plot problem require both of their social skills and temperaments to deal with it successfully?

How would each of them fail individually if they tried to handle the big plot problem by themselves? How will each of them try to do this over the course of the story?

What attracts them to each other in spite of their temperament differences?

What—besides the obvious—drives them crazy in a bad way about each other?

What will they each do to try to change each other? How does it go?

How does the grumpy character protect or defend the sunshine character or bring caution into his/her life? How does it go?

How does the sunshine character try to bring joy, companionship, and openness to the grumpy character's life? How does it go?

What forces or brings the lovers into repeated contact in your story so they can get to know each other and eventually fall in love?

What common core values, beliefs, ethics, or morals do the lovers share that they can build a healthy and lasting relationship on?

How do their differing personalities come into conflict in several tiny ways in your story?

How do their differing personalities come into conflict in several major ways in your story?

How does the big problem get worse over the course of the story? Much worse? Even worse than that?

How does each character, when under pressure revert to their original grumpy or sunshine form and get into big trouble or make the situation worse?

How does the grumpy character rescue the sunshine character from a difficult situation?

How does the sunshine character rescue the grumpy character from a difficult situation or make the situation worse?

How does the big plot problem become a crisis?

How does the big plot crisis trigger or exacerbate a personal, emotional crisis between the hero and heroine, and vice versa?

Why do the lovers fail to successfully solve the big plot crisis... which is to say, why do they fail to work together to solve it?

What lesson(s) do the lovers each learn from their failure to solve the big plot problem that allows them to succeed in the story climax?

What lesson(s) do the lovers learn that help them figure out how to have a healthy, long-term relationship together?

When do the lovers reconcile relative to solving the big plot problem?

How do the hero and heroine reconcile? Do they talk? Does someone apologize? Does one or both of them make a grand gesture?

TROPE TRAPS

The grump is SO cranky he/she is unlikable to your audience.

The sunshine soul is so obnoxiously perky or blindly optimistic that he/she irritates your audience.

The bickering between the two characters is so continuous or so mean that it puts off your audience.

There's nothing in your plot to keep drawing your main characters together and it seem implausible that they keep spending any time together at all.

The lovers share few or no core values in common and them finding true love is unbelievable to your audience.

The main characters try to change each other's actual personalities...at the end of the day it's extremely rare for any adult to change their core personality at all.

Each character is able to change behaviors too easily, without any mistakes or backsliding, and your audience doesn't buy it.

One or both characters is judgmental of the other one and deems him or her broken, wrong, or in need of fixing instead of accepting them as they are.

The characters fail to compromise. Ever.

One character is portrayed as a good and correct way to be as a person and the other is depicted as bad or wrong.

The lovers fail to work together and combine their strengths.

The lovers don't need to work together and combine their strengths to solve the big plot problem.

Neither character learns any lessons over the course of the story.

Neither character ever acknowledges or appreciates the strengths of the other character.

The lovers don't find solid enough common ground between them for the audience to believe they have any chance of being happy together forever.

GRUMPY-SUNSHINE TROPE IN ACTION
Movies:

- You've Got mail
- The Proposal
- Bridget Jones's Diary
- Breakfast at Tiffany's
- While You were Sleeping
- 10 Things I Hate About you
- Notting Hill
- When Harry Met Sally

Books:

- The Hating Game by Sally Thorne
- The Unhoneymooners by Christina Lauren
- Beach Read by Emily Henry
- The Wall of Winnipeg and Me by Mariana Zapata
- Act Your Age, Eve Brown by Talia Hibbert
- The Flatshare by Beth O'Leary
- You Deserve Each Other by Sarah Hogle
- The Simple Wild by K.A. Tucker
- The Love Hypothesis by Ali Hazelwood

16

HATE/SNARK TO LOVE

DEFINITION

This is arguably one of the most used of all romance tropes, and dare I say, the worst understood. This trope is almost always confused with the Enemies to Lovers trope (which I encourage you to take a look at to better understand the difference between it and this).

In short, enemies are two people working against each other with opposing goals. Only one of them can succeed, and the act of one succeeding causes the other to fail. It's a win-lose scenario. This has NOTHING to do with whether or not they like each other. Indeed, an Enemies to Lovers story is usually about two people who are desperately in love but forced to work against each other.

The Hate to Love or Snark to Love trope, however, is centered upon two people who initially dislike each other (possibly intensely) but who end up falling in love. The hook for this trope is a beginning where the future lovers irritate the crap out of each other, snipe at each other, and bicker constantly.

This couple may even feud with each other, argue, fight, sue each other, do rotten things to each other, retaliate and retaliate in kind. In short, they drive each other crazy.

Over the course of the story, however, as they gradually—and probably unwillingly—get to know each other, they realize there's more to the other person. They find things they have in common. They share fundamental morals, values, and beliefs that make them more compatible than they first realized.

The more things they learn about each other that they like, respect, and have in common, the more attracted they grow, until they eventually fall in love. By the end of this story, this couple has made up, set aside or resolved their differences, forgiven each other for past slights and insults, and they're ready to go forward into happily ever after.

However...

This trope has a couple of serious potential pitfalls you need to be aware of before you dive into a hilarious insult-fest. (And as a side note: humor is your best weapon for keeping a story of this type light and friendly and not falling into one of the following traps.)

First, if a boy pulls your hair or teases you, it DOES NOT mean he likes you. You have an ethical responsibility to your reader or viewer not to romanticize bad behavior and call it anything other than bad behavior.

Second, friction is friction. Sparks of dislike or hatred DO NOT automatically translate to hot sex. Real anger, dislike, and hatred lead to violence and rape—and victims of either are well aware of this. Sadly, many of your audience members will have experienced anger, dislike, or hatred in their lives leading to violence against them.

Third, angry sex only works if a basic level of respect has already been established and clearly communicated. Angry sex NEVER negates the necessity for consent. Indeed, it increases the importance of clearly established and communicated consent. Worth noting, anger of any kind when entering into a sexual encounter may be a severe trigger for any audience member who has been a victim of sexual assault.

Beware, beware, beware of portraying any violence in a story of this type. And be equally wary of portraying any situation that your audience believes might logically lead to violence between your main characters.

ADJACENT TROPES

- Enemies to Lovers
- Rivals/Work Enemies
- Everyone Else Can See It
- Opposites Attract
- Right Under Your Nose

WHY READERS/VIEWERS LOVE THIS TROPE

- we all wish we were as witty and quick with a comeback as the characters in this story
- this is usually a funny story, and we all can use a joyful, laughter inducing, uplifting love story now and then
- the back-and-forth between characters creates and builds huge romantic and/or sexual tension between them before they finally get together
- we love the idea of finding a way to make up with someone in our life with whom we clash or have had misunderstandings
- the contrast from beginning to end with this couple is especially dramatic and satisfying because of how far they've come
- we all would like to think seemingly hopeless relationships in our lives could come to a happy resolution like this couple's did

OBLIGATORY SCENES

THE BEGINNING:

The hero and heroine meet in what's technically a meet cute but might more accurately be called a meet feud. If it doesn't happen the moment they lay eyes on each other, very soon thereafter, these two people rub each other the wrong way.

While this can begin with a funny or "cute" misunderstanding, typically the hero and heroine's initial responses to each other include instant dislike and irritation.

It's not uncommon to begin the story with an initial moment of attraction to the future lover…until he or she opens his or her mouth and says something that purely sets the other character's teeth on edge. By establishing a spark of attraction, you mitigate the implausibility of two people who truly dislike each other eventually falling in love.

The external plot of your story typically has to include some element that forces the hero and heroine into proximity. This can be physical proximity as in one moves in next door to the other one at home or at work. Or it can be proximity based on a project they must do together, perhaps a work project or charity project. One of them may need a service the other one can provide, for example carpentry, house cleaning, or body guarding.

About as quickly as these two people meet, they commence bickering, arguing, or sniping at each other. This dislike or irritation builds quickly in the opening of your story, and these two people would logically walk away from each other and never have anything to do with each other if there weren't some reason they have to interact in your story.

The beginning often ends with a complication to this plot that forces the hero and heroine to stay together or to work together in spite of their intense desire to walk away from each other.

. . .

THE MIDDLE:

The middle of this story is devoted to three things:

1. The plot of the story, the thing that's forcing the hero and heroine to be together gets progressively worse or more complicated, forcing them to remain together whether they like it or not.
2. The snark, arguing, and bickering rise to a crescendo.
3. The hero and heroine get to know each other, discover things they actually like about each other, and fall in love.

The progression of the third story element can actually be fairly challenging to pull off depending on how intensely your hero and heroine dislike each other by the end of our story's first act.

One of the surest ways in real life for two people to form a strong bond quickly is to put them together in mutual danger.

Multiple psychological studies have paired two strangers together, simulated some kind of attack, crime nearby, or situation the test subjects will perceive as life threatening. At a rate 200% higher than the test subjects who are simply introduced and left alone in a room together, the first group ends up dating and romantically involved.

While threatening their safety may not work for your story, perhaps you can put your couple into a highly stressful situation together in the middle of your story that will nudge along the formation of a romantic relationship.

The middle typically ends with the external plot problem exploding into some kind of crisis that strains both the romantic relationship and the newly formed truce between the hero and heroine to the breaking point.

BLACK MOMENT:

As the plot problem goes wrong in every way it possibly can go wrong, one or both of your main characters backslides and returns to his or her snarky ways. By this point in the story the hero and heroine know each other fairly well, so a little snark from one to the other isn't a deal breaker in their relationship. When I say one or both backslides, I'm talking about a return all the way to the beginning of the story where one or both of them does something that well and truly ticks off the other character.

Whatever behavior or attitude drove them crazy in a bad way about each other at the beginning of the story comes roaring back, now, when everything's falling apart around them.

The fact that the hero and heroine can't find a way to work together peacefully and as a team is almost always the primary factor in their failure to resolve the plot problem in the black moment. It's their snark, independence, pulling against each other in the harness, and failure to compromise that causes them to be unable to solve the plot problem or to get the project across the finish line successfully.

The hero and heroine usually break up with each other at this point in the story and storm away from each other if it's possible in your story for them to do so.

THE END:

After the hero and heroine have gone their separate ways and had some time for their tempers or righteous fury/indignation to cool down, they typically start to miss each other. They remember all the things they loved about the other one, and they feel remorse for backsliding into their old, awful behavior patterns.

They learn the lesson that their worst behavior, their worst self is costing them the person they love and robbing them of their happiness. The hero and heroine resolve to change their ways for good and not backslide again.

They're usually brought together by the external plot problem one last time—the big fundraiser they've been organizing finally happens. The inn they've been renovating opens and is featured on the TV show that wants to interview them both. They have a final confrontation with the bad guy who's been chasing them.

The hero and heroine may get together and apologize to each other and make peace before this final event brings them together, but you generally should resolve the plot problem—which is less important than the romance—first and resolve the most important story thread of the romance last.

This couple may need to make grand gestures of apology and love to each other to break through the defensiveness and trust issues they may have with each other by this point in the story.

You may choose to have the hero and heroine forgive each other and resolve their differences during the final, climactic event of the external plot, of course. This works just fine for your audience.

Lessons learned, the hero and heroine finally work together seamlessly and cooperatively as a team, and by so doing they finally are able to resolve the plot problem successfully. It's worth noting that, should they have failed to come together as a team, they would surely have failed to succeed at resolving the plot problem this time, too.

This is a couple that you may need to give us a glimpse of after their happily ever after declarations of true love, proposals of marriage, or however else you choose to resolve their romance. Your audience may need to see this couple still getting along, not backsliding, and living in harmony, particularly if they've had a highly acrimonious relationship through the first portion of your story and in the black moment.

KEY SCENES

- the hero and heroine individually gripe to a friend, family member, or coworker about the other one
- the hero and heroine seriously consider walking away from the other one for good

- a friend, family member, or coworker advises the hero and heroine to ditch the other one for good
- unwillingly having to work on something together that they both believe in enough to set aside their differences temporarily
- the first truce when they're not having to solve a crisis... which is typically short-lived
- the first kiss
- the first argument after the first kiss
- the morning after argument (after their first big romantic encounter, whatever that looks like depending on the heat level of your story)

THINGS TO THINK ABOUT WHEN WRITING THIS TROPE

How will your hero and heroine be brought into proximity with each other in the first place, and how will you keep them in proximity with each other? Which is to say, what problem is going to bring these two people together?

Based on the thing that's going to force them together, what do the hero and heroine each do for a living? What skills does one or both of them have that brings them together?

Based on your answers to the above questions, what kind of person is your hero? What kind of person is your heroine?

What are the things about each other, the personality qualities or quirks, the habits, opinions, or actions they take that initially irritate the living heck out of each other?

Knowing all of that, what's the perfect way for these two people to meet that will most bug them and most highlight the things about each other that drive them crazy in a bad way?

Is this a funny event or scene or is it dominated by some other tone? Suspense? Danger? Friction? Reluctance? Duty? Responsibility?

What's the overall tone of your story going to be? Does your initial meeting between the hero and heroine reflect this...or will you transition the story to a different tone as the plot unfolds?

Is one of your main characters long-suffering and patient while the other takes all the pot shots and makes all the witty, snarky comments? Or are both of your main characters snarky, snappy with a comeback, and quick to give as good as they get?

What makes both your hero and heroine really likable to your audience?

Why don't your hero and heroine walk away from each other very quickly after they meet and realize how much they annoy each other? Why doesn't one or the other quit the project, turn down the job offer, find someone else to do the job, or start looking for somewhere else to live?

What about the other person do the hero and heroine find attractive? How will you show that in your story? When does it make sense to have this moment or realization happen?

Is it too superficial for your characters to only find each other physically attractive at first, or do these two people need to find something else attractive to build a real and lasting relationship on later?

How will you continue to force your characters into proximity with each other even after they really start to irritate each other?

What do friends, family, and coworkers think of this pair as a couple? Do they think they're perfect for each other? Counsel the hero and heroine to walk away from each other? Sit back, eat popcorn, and enjoy the fireworks between the hero and heroine?

What's something that happens fairly early in the story that forces the hero and heroine to set aside their bickering and differences for a little while to do something for a good cause, help someone else they both care for, or do something they both believe in strongly?

What sends them back to war with each other after this momentary lull in their mutual dislike?

What's the first really important moral, value, or belief they discover they have in common? How do they figure this out?

How do they each react to discovering they have something major in common?

What causes the hero and heroine, individually or together, to decide to try to give the other person a chance? What is that chance, by the way? A chance to prove the other person is competent at their job? A chance to prove they can be nice to each other for a little while as they do something together? Something else?

Do the hero and heroine ever decide to re-start their relationship, to give each other a do-over, or to wipe the slate clean and try again? If so, when, where, and how? How does it go? What causes this do-over to fail?

What are the steps along the way of the hero and heroine's romantic relationship forming and growing into love?

1. What progression of the romance makes most sense for this couple? Will they learn in small, incremental steps to get along, like each other, and fall in love? Will they fight right up till the moment they fall into bed together? Is whatever progression you choose **plausible** and **believable** to your audience?
2. How does the plot problem of your story unfold? How does it get worse? Much worse? Truly terrible? What are the steps along the way of this problem developing, and what are the steps the hero and heroine take to try to deal with it?

- With these two lists side by side, how does each development in the plot parallel a development in their relationship?

- How does each plot point provoke a development in their relationship, or vice versa, how does a development in their relationship provoke a development in the plot?

What additional likable qualities will you reveal about your snarky character(s) to the audience as the story progresses to keep the audience from getting tired of or starting to dislike them?

What qualities do the hero and heroine find lovable about each other?

After the first big, serious romantic encounter (the first sex scene if your story has that high a heat level or the equivalent scene if your story has a lower heat level), what happens to make them fight again?

How does this post-sex event, comment, realization, or internal moment of fear/doubt/panic send the conflict in the relationship to even greater heights than before?

How does the couple's inability to set aside their conflict and differences provoke the relationship's black moment and cause their failure to resolve the plot crisis that is the plot's black moment?

What behavior, reaction, or misbelief does the hero backslide into that causes one or both of the black moments (the relationship black moment and the plot black moment)?

What behavior, reaction, or misbelief does the heroine backslide into that causes one or both of the black moments (the relationship black moment and the plot black moment)?

What is the consequence of failing to resolve the plot problem in the black moment? What does it look like when it happens?

Do the hero and heroine break up after their relationship black moment? If so, what does that look like? How does this complicate the plot problem even more?

How do the hero and heroine feel after they've physically or emotionally broken up?

What event or realization provokes each of them to take a hard look at themselves and learn a lesson about themselves? What's that lesson?

How will you convince your audience that they've truly absorbed the lesson in a deep and intense enough way that they'll never backslide on it again?

Who needs to apologize to whom? For what? How will he or she make the apology? How does the other one react? Does the other partner accept the apology immediately or not? If not, at what point does he or she accept the apology?

Does one or both of them make a grand gesture of sacrifice or love to the other one? If so, what is it? How does the other one receive it?

How will the hero and heroine physically come back together so they can make whatever apologies or grand gestures you've decided to have them make?

How will the hero and heroine solve the big plot problem together?

What teamwork or cooperation do they exhibit this time around that allows them to succeed at resolving the big plot problem that they weren't able to do in the black moment or big crisis that caused the black moment?

When is the big plot problem resolved in relation to the big reconciliation between the hero and heroine? Before the reconciliation? At the same time?

What does happily ever after look like for this pair?

How will you convince your audience that this pair has truly learned their lessons and can sustain a happy, non-snarky, non-hateful relationship for the long term without any more emotional backsliding?

TROPE TRAPS

Your snarky character(s) isn't/aren't likable to your audience.

The bickering and attacks between your characters devolve into being mean.

The dislike between your hero and heroine is so intense or bitter that your audience doesn't buy this pair ever plausibly liking each other, let alone falling in love and ending up happily ever after.

The plot problem you built to force this pair together isn't strong enough to plausibly hold the pair together, given how much they dislike each other.

The hero and heroine have no motivation to stick around each other or their personal motivations for sticking around to solve the plot problem together aren't plausible.

Someone else could step in for one or both of the main characters to deal with the plot problem, yet neither the hero nor heroine asks to be replaced or leaves the situation.

The progression from snark or hate to love doesn't seem plausible to your audience.

The progression from snark or hate to love isn't believable to your audience.

The pace of the progression from snark or hate to love is too fast or too abrupt for your audience to believe.

Relying on the friction of snarky comments, bickering, or arguments to create sparks that will magically (and completely unbelievably) transform into sparks of attraction.

The plot problem and the progression of the romance between the hero and heroine don't affect each other in a meaningful way or proceed at different paces that are jarring to your audience.

The snark or hatefulness in the relationship is actually demeaning or toxic to one or both main characters.

The couple's friends, family, and coworkers respond inappropriately to the relationship (suggesting that hair-pulling is actually affection, encouraging the hero or heroine to forgive and forget things that are actually nasty or demeaning, or urging the hero or heroine to stay in what's actually a toxic relationship)

Romantic encounters between the hero and heroine are tinged with anger, disrespect, or a threat—no matter how small—of violence.

Failure to be very direct about consent in the couple's romantic encounters.

Triggering audience members with what might be construed by them as real anger, dislike, or hatred by one of the main characters toward the other one (that your audience members know from real life experience might lead to violence).

After the first love scene, failing to reestablish the tension and interpersonal conflict between the hero and heroine.

The plot black moment isn't caused, at least in part, by the hero and heroine failing to get along, work well together, or cooperate.

The final resolution of the plot problem isn't caused, at least in part, by the hero and heroine finally getting along, working well together, and cooperating.

The hero and heroine fail to learn a lesson about themselves, their behavior, their fears or insecurities, or how they express themselves, that will fundamentally and permanently change how they interact with the other main character.

Nobody apologizes for previous bad behavior or snark/hate toward the other one.

The character being apologized to shouldn't realistically accept the apology and should stay broken up with the other character in the eyes of your audience.

The character being apologized to should realistically accept the other character's heartfelt and sincere apology but fails to accept it or fails to accept it gracefully in the spirit that it is given and meant, thereby royally ticking off your audience.

Your audience doesn't believe for a second that these two people will stay changed and won't revert to bickering, arguing, or worse in the long run.

HATE/SNARK TO LOVE TROPE IN ACTION
Movies:

- Pride and Prejudice
- When Harry Met Sally

- 10 Things I Hate About You
- The Proposal
- You've Got Mail
- How To Lose A Guy in Ten Days
- The Hating Game

Books:

- You Deserve Each Other by Sarah Hogle
- Red, White & Royal Blue by Casey McQuiston
- The Spanish Love Deception by Elena Armas
- The Kiss Quotient by Helen Hoang
- The Unhoneymooners by Christina Lauren
- Beach Read by Emily Henry
- The Cruel Prince by Holly Black
- Act Your Age, Eve Brown by Talia Hibbert
- The Wall of Winnipeg and Me by Mariana Zapata

17

INNOCENT COHABITATION

DEFINITION

This trope is often called the Roommates to Romance trope. As cute as this title is, being roommates isn't the only method by which a hero and heroine might end up living together temporarily or permanently. Hence, I was forced to go with the imminently more boring title of Innocent Cohabitation.

At any rate, in this trope two people, who are not romantically involved, are forced to or choose to live together to begin your story. Feel free to get creative explaining why your hero and heroine find themselves cohabitating.

Once living together, they get to know each other, spend lots of time together, and at some point, friendship becomes boyfriend-girlfriend-ship, attraction becomes action, and liking each other grows into loving each other.

While this trope is often portrayed as a romantic comedy, it's by no means limited to that.

A bodyguard might move in with the person he or she is protecting from a dangerous stalker. A cult not far from where I live was in the news a while back for pairing up men and women and putting them in houses together with orders to fall in love and make babies.

What makes this trope different from a standard forced proximity trope is that these characters live together. They typically don't work together, which means they see each other at their most relaxed and natural time, being their "real" selves.

Indeed, this story has a lot of potential to have little to no conflict in it and no obstacles to the hero and heroine getting to know each other, falling in love, and continuing to live together until they feel like getting married.

Which is to say, this trope benefits greatly from some sort of external obstacle to love. For example, one of the roommates already has a boyfriend, girlfriend, or fiancé. This trope can also benefit greatly from some internal or personal obstacle to the hero and heroine falling in love. One of them may have commitment phobia, be celibate, or be painfully shy and awkward.

Personally, I would consider doing both since this trope doesn't bring a ton of conflict to the story on its own…unless one of the roommates is a total slob and the other one is an OCD neatnik, or something along those lines. In this case, the characters have flaws or incompatible traits that must be reconciled before they can fall in love and be happy together forever.

Other forced proximity stories rely solely on a shared work project, a shared threat, or some other situation where they must be together that comes with a certain tension, stress, or deadline pressure. Although this hero and heroine may share a situation like that, by living together too they get to see the off-duty moments—brushing teeth, cooking food and eating together, shopping, doing laundry—the small, necessary moments of everyday life that happen in between the moments of work, high pressure, or high danger.

It's in these moments that the hero and heroine's relationship has an extra chance to grow into true love and an eventual happily ever after.

ADJACENT TROPES

- Friends to Lovers
- Marriage of Convenience
- Guardian/Caretaker
- Pretend/Celibate Marriage
- Fake Fiancé/Boyfriend/Girlfriend
- Unconsummated Marriage

WHY READERS/VIEWERS LOVE THIS TROPE

- there's a strong forbidden fruit element to this story—the roommate is off limits, which makes him or her all the more enticing
- we love the idea of finally being seen—really seen—by someone we know, who then falls in love with us
- when living with someone, over time they see you being your most authentic self...and they fall in love with that version of you. They really love YOU
- many of us have friends with whom we secretly wonder what it would be like to end up in a romantic relationship
- we love the everyday intimacy, slow burn, and domestic proximity of this love story

OBLIGATORY SCENES

THE BEGINNING:

Your story might begin with the hero and heroine already living together in a steady-state friendship/roommate situation. Or you may start your story when the hero and heroine move in together. Your hero and heroine may know each other very well before they move in together or they might be total strangers.

If there's an unusual reason the hero and heroine are going to move in together, this reason may require some sort of inciting incident or other event to occur first that explains why the hero and heroine must now move in together. For example, there's an assassination or kidnapping attempt on the hero or heroine. After that, the other main character—a security expert—is hired to move in with him or her.

The living situation may be temporary or permanent.

Other people around the hero and heroine may have strong negative opinions about this living arrangement. Typically these people are from an older generation, or they have some moral objection to two people of the opposite sex living together (in a M/F relationship, at any rate).

Another variation on this story is boarding school or college roommates who've never met but are assigned to live together. In a dormitory situation, your main characters are more likely to be a same sex couple. But if they're sharing off-campus housing, any gender combination of roommates and romance goes.

The meet-cute of this story is often the roommates actually moving in together.

The beginning is taken up with awkward moments, working out bathroom and refrigerator sharing, and getting to know each other. It can be rocky at first, or it can be silly or hilarious.

There's always an adjustment period when two people who've never lived together before have to learn how to share space with each other all the time, even if they've been best friends forever. This period usually takes up the beginning of your story.

The beginning typically ends with the first serious challenge to the hero and heroine's living arrangement, usually caused by the external plot problem that poses an obstacle to them being together or caused by one of the main characters having some internal, personal obstacle to falling in love with the person they're living with.

OR

The beginning ends with the hero and heroine sharing a romantic or near romantic moment that makes both of them aware that there's more going on here than just a platonic cohabitation arrangement. The pair may exchange a look, a kiss, get drunk together and wake up in the same bed—use your imagination at how they become aware that there are romantic sparks building between them.

THE MIDDLE:

In the rom com version of this story, shenanigans ensue. In the suspense version, the danger ratchets up ferociously. No matter what flavor of story you're writing, the middle is usually where the casual friendship of the hero and heroine fully shifts into a romance.

We see more of the couple's day-to-day life together. Movie nights that weren't dates before become dates now. Cooking dinner and eating it together becomes a romantic tryst. Things that used to be mundane and uninteresting suddenly become romantic interludes as the romantic awareness and tension between them goes sky high.

The hero and/or heroine may resist the shifting of the relationship into something else. One or both of them may have a compelling reason for stopping the relationship from upgrading to the next level from friendship to romance. For example, one of them is protecting the other one and needs to pay attention to his/her job. Or, one of them is engaged to someone else.

Whatever external plot problem you've introduced to your story gets worse, and then much worse through the middle of your story.

As for the internal, personal obstacles the hero and heroine may have to love, those are challenged harder and harder as the hero and heroine start to shift their friendship into something more romantic.

Either the hero and heroine keep their budding romance secret, or the people around them will definitely react to this relationship shift.

The more in love they fall, the greater the complications become, and possibly the more complications pile on top of the lovers.

Whatever the things are acting as obstacles to the two of them falling in love, those obstacles come to a head at the end of the middle of the story.

BLACK MOMENT:

Whatever external obstacle has threatened the hero and heroine's budding romance finally succeeds at tearing them apart.

A boyfriend, girlfriend, or fiancé invokes the previous commitment the hero or heroine made to him or her and insists that either the hero or heroine move out. The stalker trying to kill one of the main characters makes a good faith effort to do the murder and nearly succeeds. The bodyguard main character reacts by resigning in guilt and shame while the other main character languishes in a hospital bed or safe house.

Whatever personal conflicts have been brewing between the hero and heroine explode into open conflict between them. They may have a huge fight. One of them may storm out of their shared living space. One of them may abandon the living arrangement temporarily or for good.

Not only may their living arrangement implode, but their romantic relationship also implodes. Not only have they lost the person they love, but they may have also lost their best friend or their place to live.

If there's some external problem they've been working on solving together, they fail to resolve it…in the most catastrophic way possible.

The stalker finds his or her target. The would-be killer nearly kills the hero or heroine. The kidnapper may nab his or her target person.

And, as bad as that external plot disaster is, the worst of it is the hero and heroine have each lost the person they love.

THE END:

This trope relies heavily on learning lessons to resolve the various plot problems you've thrown at this couple. They learn how much they miss each other once they're apart. They learn how much they loved living together when they're not living together anymore. They learn how safe, cared for, and not alone they felt when they were living together. They learn how much they valued the sense of shared partnership with the other person.

It's this lesson learned that usually drives the hero and heroine to come back together to find a way to resolve their internal and external problems so they can be together for the long term.

The hero and/or heroine may have to resolve the external problem to clear the way for the two of them to be together. A would-be kidnapper or killer must be caught. A blackmailer must be silenced. A fiancé, boyfriend, or girlfriend must be broken up with to clear the way for an open and honest relationship with the other main character.

Or of course, the hero and/or heroine may have to repair their broken relationship after repairing themselves.

The ending usually includes apologies, forgiveness, and gestures of love and acceptance.

The good news is this couple already knows how to live with each other very well. All they have to do is return to living together in a permanent situation, and happily ever after is already there for the taking. This is one couple your audience won't worry about surviving as a couple for the long term once they move in together.

. . .

KEY SCENES

- an argument over space or organization of their shared space
- one of them gets sick and cares for the other one
- one of them has a habit that drives the other one crazy, and this deal breaker habit must be fixed if they're to remain together
- an outside love interest (or friend/family member/coworker) accuses the hero and heroine of having something romantic going on between them
- one or both of the main characters is worried about losing their friendship if a romantic relationship between them doesn't work out
- the couple has a big fight...and they live in the same space so there's nowhere to retreat away from each other
- one of the lovers walks out on the other one
- the morning after their first big romantic encounter
- one or both of them backslide into behaviors that are destructive to themselves and the relationship

THINGS TO THINK ABOUT WHEN WRITING THIS TROPE

Do the hero and heroine know each other before your story begins? If so, for how long and how well?

How do the hero and heroine end up as roommates?

Do they choose to live together, do circumstances force them together, or something else?

Is the living situation permanent or temporary?

If temporary, is it long-term enough for them to relax and be themselves around each other, get to know each other, and fall in love?

Who objects to their living situation? Why? How loudly or publicly?

Does someone try to break them up? If so, who? Why? How?

What's the external plot problem they have to deal with over the course of your story?

Does the external plot problem endanger one or both of your main characters? If so, who and how?

What's the personal or internal problem each of your main characters has to overcome to successfully have a long-term romantic relationship with the other one?

How do the external problem and personal problem(s) threaten the couple's ability to have a long-term romance?

What drives them crazy in a bad way about the other one?

What habit does each of them have that annoys the other one?

What does a typical day or evening at their place look like? What do they do together? What do they do apart? Who does which chores? Who pays for what?

What are things they do together as friends that morph into dates or romantic time spent together as they start to fall in love?

Does one of them have a crush on the other one first?

When and how do they each realize they might be romantically interested in the other roommate? What do they do or say about it to each other?

When and how do they confess being interested in each other romantically?

Do they act upon that admission right away or try to resist their urges? Why?

What event, crisis, or realization drives them into each other's arms for the first time?

Do they feel guilty about their first romantic encounter or not? Why?

Do they keep their change in relationship status secret from anyone? Why or why not? And if so, whom?

How does their changed relationship status become public knowledge?

How does the external plot problem grow into a crisis? What's the crisis? How does the crisis threaten the couple's ability to stay together romantically?

How do their internal, personal conflicts, traumas, wounds, fears, or misbeliefs grow into crises that threaten to end their romantic relationship?

Is either of them worried about risking their friendship to attempt a romantic relationship? Why? What does the other one have to say about that?

What breaks them up to provoke the black moment or because of the black moment? How does the breakup happen? Why does it happen? Are the hero and heroine correctly identifying why it happened or not? What do they think happened?

What lesson do the lovers each learn about themselves in the wake of their breakup?

What have they lost beside their romance? Their friendship? Their housing? Their safety? Something else?

How can you make their breakup even more devastating?

How does the external plot crisis force the hero and heroine back together? How do they feel about that?

What do the hero and heroine do together to resolve the external plot crisis?

When and how do they resolve their relationship problems? Who apologizes to whom? Who forgives whom? Who makes a grand gesture of love?

What does happily ever after look like for this couple? Do they go back to their old place to live or someplace else?

TROPE TRAPS

The hero and/or heroine isn't likable.

The hero and heroine don't have anything in common other than their address and your audience doesn't buy them falling in love.

If they've already been living together for a while, failing to explain why they haven't noticed each other romantically before now.

One of them is already in a romantic relationship with someone else and fails to get out of that relationship ethically before diving into the new one with the roommate.

The hero and heroine live together in perfect harmony from day one and never butt heads over anything...which nobody will believe is plausible.

The hero and heroine fight over stupid things that aren't important.

The hero and heroine ignore or don't address the really important problems and conflicts between them and irritate your audience.

There's no significant conflict, external or internal, to challenge this couple deciding they're in love and building a romantic relationship and your story is boring.

The couple fights in an unhealthy way and resolves fights in an unhealthy way.

The resolution to their big breakup is nothing more than an honest, mature, adult conversation they could have had WAY earlier in the story.

The story lacks deep and meaningful emotional beats, focusing too much on the act of living together and on falling in love effortlessly and without obstacles.

The hero and heroine fail to learn anything important about themselves that makes them capable of sustaining a healthy, long-term romantic relationship.

The hero and heroine don't work together in the end to resolve the big plot problem.

Your audience doesn't believe they'll stay together forever based on the problem they've already had living together.

. . .

INNOCENT COHABITATION TROPE IN ACTION
Movies:

- Burlesque
- What If
- The Bodyguard
- No Strings Attached
- Passengers
- Outlander
- Just Friends
- The Flatshare
- Two Night Stand
- Sleeping With Other People
- The Mountain Between Us

Books:

- The Simple Wild by K.A. Tucker
- The Wedding Date by Jasmine Guillory
- The Kiss Quotient by Helen Hoang
- One Day in December by Josie Silver
- From Lukov with Love by Mariana Zapata
- Josh and Hazel's Guide to Not Dating by Christina Lauren
- The Bromance Book Club by Lyssa Kay Adams
- The Roommate by Rosie Danan
- People We Meet on Vacation by Emily Henry

18
LOVE AT FIRST SIGHT

DEFINITION

When people fall in love, they experience a whole host of wonderful sensations of intense attraction, connection, and euphoria. Indeed, the documented physical reactions to falling in love include instant physical attraction, decreased need for sleep or food, need to be with that person, increased heart rate, sensation of having known them forever, shortness of breath, going weak at the knees, and butterflies in the stomach.

Given that all of this feels pretty great, is it no wonder that people are thrilled when they see someone across a crowded room, lock gazes, and experience all these feelings all at once? And is it any wonder that almost all people believe that love at first sight is a totally real thing?

The reality, however, is that which people experience as love at first sight is more accurately described as instant attraction or powerful infatuation. It's definitely a real feeling and it's definitely overwhelming. But is it, in fact, love?

Psychologist, Robert Sternberg proposed in *Psychological Review*, 93(2), 119–135, A Triangular Theory of Love, a theory that all romantic relationships are fundamentally based on varying amounts of three key components: intimacy, passion, and commitment. The phenomenon of love at first sight falls into the passion portion of this triad.

Psychologists go on to say that, as powerful as the feeling of love at first sight is, it's NOT a predictor of long-term success of any relationship. Having checked off the passion portion of that triangle of love, the couple still must take the time and do the work to build intimacy and commitment. Only then, can they hope to achieve a long-term happily ever after.

Psychologists make three suggestions to couples who've experienced love at first sight with each other:

1. Don't rush the relationship
2. Identify common values
3. Set healthy boundaries and expectations

To expand on these a bit, psychologists are telling us to do the slower, harder work of getting to know each other and not to base the entire relationship on just those feelings of passion, which can be fleeting and don't last forever.

They're suggesting that two people have to make sure their core beliefs, morals, and values are in alignment before they dive into a long-term relationship. This is because relationships rarely survive a serious misalignment of values between the participants in the relationship.

Lastly, psychologists are suggesting that, just because you felt love at first sight with someone, be realistic and don't assume the two of you are fated to be together forever regardless of your differences, disagreements, or misalignments in expectations from this relationship. Be prepared to walk away from ANY relationship that is unhealthy or going to make you unhappy in the long-term...no matter how good it feels right now.

This, then, gives us our recipe for this trope.

Two people meet, and one or both of them experiences love at first sight. The lightning bolt of passionate attraction hits them out of the blue, and they're intensely attracted to the other person. The remainder of this story is the relationship building, development of intimacy, and building of commitment to each other (along with comparing core values, setting boundaries and expectations in the relationship, and dispassionately considering if this person will make you happy for many, many years—long after the intense passion you're feeling right now has faded).

All stories need conflict. Hence, you'll throw obstacles in this couple's path to building intimacy and commitment. The hero and heroine must overcome these obstacles as they attempt to build a solid and long-lasting triangle of love for themselves.

ADJACENT TROPES

- In Love with the Wrong Person
- Teen Crush
- Home for the Holidays/Vacation Fling
- Fated Mates/Soul Mates
- Engaged To/Marrying Someone Else
- Secret Crush/Secret Admirer

WHY READERS/VIEWERS LOVE THIS TROPE

- love at first sight is one of the most intense romantic experiences anyone can feel, and we all crave feeling like that (or if we've experienced it before, we crave it again)
- in a world that prizes instant gratification, very little is more instant than love at first sight or more gratifying than having someone fall in love with us at first sight

- this is the ideal romantic fantasy – he or she only had to see me to fall for me. How attractive and desirable would that make us feel
- the notion of love at first sight suggests we all get to skip the messy, difficult, sometimes painful work of building a solid, long-term relationship, and that's a fantasy that most people who've tried to build a relationship only to have it fall apart deep into the process can relate to
- as the intensity of our own passion for our partner fades, we enjoy the fantasy of experiencing that overwhelming intensity of feeling again

OBLIGATORY SCENES

THE BEGINNING:

This story has the most obvious beginning of all time. Two people see each other for the first time, lightning—or Cupid's arrow—strikes, and they instantly fall in love. This can happen in the most inappropriate of places, when the characters and your audience least expect it. It can happen in a humorous way or in a humorous situation. Or it can happen in the grimmest, darkest, most unexpected of circumstances.

It's worth noting that psychologists tie the passion of love at first sight to people's primitive desires to procreate and find the best possible mate to create the most survivable offspring with. Which is to say, if you're in a life-threatening, terrifying situation, you may not be thinking about mating and procreation, and your audience may not buy that this is the moment when you look across the bloody foxhole and spot your true love.

The rest of the beginning of your story may be taken up with the two people trying to find a way to get into physical proximity, to meet each other, or to get away from whatever else is going on around them to get to know each other.

It's not unusual in this story for the hero and heroine to spot each other, fall like a ton of bricks for each other, and regardless of the other people or obstacles around them, to steal away to a private place and have hot, passionate sex with each other. Even if this is *not* what the hero and heroine do, it's surely in both of their minds to find a way to do exactly this.

There may be a compelling reason why this couple can't indulge their explosion of mutual passion, and that becomes the first obstacle they must surmount in the beginning of their story.

The beginning of this story often ends with the couple finally making it into each other's arms (depending on the heat level of your story, this may be an explicit love scene or it may be something more restrained). As the couple emerges from this tryst, or possibly as the interruption that stops the tryst from being consummated, the first potentially relationship-ending obstacle presents itself and tears the hero and heroine apart.

THE MIDDLE:

The big external plot problem grows more complicated and more difficult to overcome. There might be a boyfriend/girlfriend/fiancé that one or both of the lovers must find a way to break up with. There may be a compelling reason why it would be terrible for the hero and heroine to be together forever—their families are at war, they come from wildly different cultures that would never approve of the match, they're enemy spies or combatants, or their relationship is illegal. Your world building may create some other external obstacle to this pair being together or getting married.

Also in the middle, personal differences in expectations, values, and boundaries emerge to cause problems for the couple.

They may have deeply different expectations of what they want from a marriage. She wants to settle down and have a bunch of kids;

he wants a partner to travel the world with and has no interest in children.

They may have deeply differing values—one is deeply religious and the other is not. One believes in marriage and one does not. They may disagree sharply about politics, which side in their family feud is correct, who started the war their two countries are engaging in. Or they may have fundamental core value differences. One values honesty above all else, the other does not. One values generosity greatly, the other values taking care of one's own above all others.

NOTE: Both people's values can be viewed as "good" by your audience. Neither of them has to have villainous values—although you certainly can, if you'd like. All that matters, if you're trying to create a major obstacle to their love, is that their values clash.

The hero and heroine may also have very different boundaries—they may have differing sexual fantasies, differing spending habits, differing ideas of monogamy, fidelity, substance use and abuse, or a host of other things couples might reasonably set boundaries for each other about.

Lastly, you can create an obstacle to love inside the heart or mind of the hero and/or the heroine. One or both of them may have some past trauma, failure, or wound that leaves them scarred in some way that poses an obstacle to them allowing themselves to love, something that makes them unaware of what healthy love looks like or that makes them afraid to let someone else love them.

In most cases, your story will benefit from you developing both an external obstacle to this couple being together and a personal or internal conflict for them to overcome.

As the middle of your story progresses, these obstacles get worse, and then much worse, building toward a crisis that explodes at the end of the middle of your story.

BLACK MOMENT:

For this couple, the black moment is when they break up or are torn apart—or when both things happen simultaneously. The big obstacles to being together that they've been struggling to overcome get the best of them.

In an external obstacle, whoever or whatever has been trying to break them apart catches up with them and physically tears them apart.

For a personal obstacle of values, boundaries, or expectations, one or both of the lovers backslides on his or her promise to do better or be different, breaks through a boundary the other lover has set, or reverts to his or her old ways of behaving or reacting.

By crossing this red line, the hero or heroine forces the other lover to walk away or break up with them completely. This does beg the question of did that person intentionally drive away the person they love? Did he or she self destructively sabotage the relationship, and if so, why?

THE END:

Having lost the person he or she loves, the hero and/or heroine is forced into a period of introspection and self-examination. What did he or she do wrong that blew up the relationship? What did they both do wrong to blow up the relationship?

Out of this period of devastation, loss, and mourning, the hero and heroine should both learn a profound lesson of some kind. Having learned this lesson, they can now move forward with apologizing, promising things will be different, and working together to solve the external plot problem together.

The trick is to convince your audience that the "I'll do better" is going to stick for the long term.

The way to do this is to portray it as a life-changing event to lose the person they're so passionately in love with and with whom they seemed to be building something strong and lasting. It has to shock and hurt your hero or heroine profoundly—profoundly enough to make a change at a deep, core level as a human being.

Most people in your audience know from hard experience that it takes something as huge as a life-changing event to trigger an actual, life-changing lesson. So, give the hero and heroine a life-changing event at the end of the story to make their epiphany, their big, life-changing lesson, feel real and lasting.

Having learned this huge lesson, the hero and heroine are now ready to apologize to each other, forgive each other, and work together to overcome any remaining obstacles to their being together forever.

They resolve the external plot problem, resolve the personal obstacles and internal obstacles to love, and they can finally be together, their triangle of love completed and built of solid intimacy, commitment, and yes, passion.

KEY SCENES

- the first moment of physical passion between them
- getting caught or nearly getting caught in a moment of stolen passion
- their first big fight, when differences in values, expectations, or boundaries rears its ugly head
- make-up sex (or whatever constitutes a passionate reconciliation based on the heat level of your story)
- friends, family, or coworkers tell the hero and/or heroine a relationship between them will never work or shouldn't happen
- the hero and heroine individually, and as a couple, doubt if they've got what it takes to stay together for the long term
- their reckless passion hurts someone else whom they love
- their relationship costs one or both of them something really important or valuable

- one or both of the lovers panics over some aspect of their relationship and quietly, or not so quietly, freaks out
- one or both of them nearly walks away or breaks up, but at the last moment decides against it or something intervenes to stop him or her from walking away/breaking up

THINGS TO THINK ABOUT WHEN WRITING THIS TROPE

Who are your hero and heroine? What are the traumas, wounds, fears, and misbeliefs one or both of them are going to bring to their future relationship? How did these things happen to each of them? Which is to say, you don't need to develop their entire life stories—just the traumas and life-changing events you plan to bring out as obstacles to their relationship later.

Later in the story how will you tell or show your audience how your hero and heroine became the person they are today and how they developed their traumas, wounds, fears, and misbeliefs that are going to be obstacles to the love story?

How do your hero and heroine first meet?

Which one of them—or both—experiences the love at first sight moment?

Whose point of view will we first see this moment in?

Will you shift to the point of view of the other character to replay the moment or show his/her reaction to the lightning strike moment?

Are the hero and heroine able to physically join each other immediately after they first see each other or not? If so, what do they do and where do they go? If not, who or what stands in their way? How will they physically get together for the first time?

What happens the first time the hero and heroine meet? Do they just talk? Trade contact information? Go somewhere private and make mad, passionate love?

How quickly do the hero and heroine commence seeing each other regularly? What obstacles stand in the way of them doing that? How do they overcome them?

What external plot problem or external obstacle is blocking the hero and heroine from jumping immediately into a romantic relationship?

What are the steps they'll have to go through to overcome this obstacle?

How does this external obstacle get worse and harder to overcome as the story progresses? How does it get much worse? How does it become nearly impossible to overcome?

What conflict in values, boundaries, or expectations between them will the hero and heroine have to confront? How does it first come up as a difference? How does it become a tangible problem? How does it get worse? Much worse? Threaten to break them up? How does it contribute to breaking them up?

How do the hero and heroine's individual traumas, wounds, fears, and misbeliefs first reveal themselves to each other? How do these become problems? How does this problem interfere with their relationship? How does it get much worse? Threaten to break them up? How does it contribute to breaking them up?

What lessons must the hero and heroine learn to be able to build a healthy relationship with each other for the long term?

Based on the lesson each of them must learn, what life changing event must happen to each of them to force them to learn that life-changing lesson? How will you build this life-changing event into your story?

Can the hero and heroine each learn their life-changing lesson from the same life-changing event? **NOTE**: This isn't necessary, but it's handy if you only have to construct one huge crisis for both of them to experience so they can each have their big aha moment/epiphany.

How are the life-changing events the hero and heroine have to experience to become ready for love tied to the external plot problem/crisis they need to resolve? Is there a way to tie these together? **NOTE**: It's okay if they don't...it's just handy not to have two personal crises and a plot crisis to cram into the back end of your story.

Who apologizes to whom? How? What do they say? How does the other lover respond to the apology? **NOTE**: If this is an apology the hero or heroine could have made earlier in the story, then it's not the right apology. This apology has to come as a result of their life-changing lesson learned.

Does one or both of them need to make some sort of grand sacrifice either to prove their love and commitment to the other one or to clear the way to be with the other one? If so, what is that? When and how does it happen? Does it happen before the big apology or after? Before the big plot crisis is resolved or after?

How does the lover who made a grand sacrifice let the other know about it? Do they do it in front of each other or tell each other about the sacrifice(s) after the fact? Or does someone else tell them about it?

How do the hero and heroine work together to resolve the external plot problem/crisis? Do they do this before, after, or at the same time as they resolve their personal issues?

How do the people around them react to them being together openly and headed for happily ever after?

What does happily ever after look like for this couple?

Do they need to go to a new place and make a fresh start or can they stay where they are now?

TROPE TRAPS

The hero and heroine make carnage of the lives of people around them in the name of their passion, and they come across as selfish, unlikable, and underserving of their love.

The hero and/or heroine is unlikable for some reason and the audience roots against them getting a happily ever after.

The hero and heroine are so wildly mismatched the audience doesn't buy that these two would experience love at first sight.

The place or timing of the love at first sight moment is wildly inappropriate or so stressful that the audience doesn't buy the lightning strike of love moment happening then or there.

There aren't enough obstacles for this couple to overcome to be together—they get their happily ever after payoff too easily.

The couple doesn't do the work of building a real and lasting relationship, and their whole love story centers on hot sex and lots of it.

The couple never gets to really know each other.

The lovers never show each other their true selves, warts and all.

The only obstacles to their love are external and the story feels shallow, the characters underdeveloped.

The character who has to learn a life-changing lesson does NOT experience an event traumatic or shocking enough in the story to convince your audience that he or she has changed at a core, deep, fundamental, and permanent level.

In the absence of a life-changing event, your audience doesn't buy that the hero and/or heroine will keep their promises to be different going forward.

Your audience doesn't buy for a minute that this couple has what it takes to stay together happily for the long term.

You fail to build one of the three legs of the triangle of love and your audience knows this relationship is fatally flawed.

You rely on passion to solve all of the couple's arguments.

The couple never sits down and has an honest, serious, open, adult conversation that could make it clear early on that they shouldn't be together for the long term or that would solve their personal and internal problems much earlier in the story.

The harm the lovers cause to the people around them is so great they don't deserve to be happy ever after with each other. (I give you one of my big problems with Romeo & Juliet.)

. . .

LOVE AT FIRST SIGHT TROPE IN ACTION
Movies:

- Romeo and Juliet
- Titanic
- Love Actually
- (500) Days of Summer
- West Side Story
- The Notebook
- Enchanted
- Slumdog Millionaire

Books:

- Twilight by Stephenie Meyer
- The Time Traveler's Wife by Audrey Niffenegger
- One Day in December by Josie Silver
- Love Story by Erich Segal
- Outlander by Diana Gabaldon
- The Statistical Probability of Love at First Sight by Jennifer E. Smith
- One Day by David Nicholls
- The Night Circus by Erin Morgenstern
- Eleanor & Park by Rainbow Rowell
- The Bridges of Madison County by Robert James Waller

19
MATCHMAKER GONE WRONG

DEFINITION

In this trope one character, a (professional or amateur) matchmaker tries to pair two people together. If the couple paired spends time together, falls in love, and ends up together happily ever after, that's great for them, but terrible for your story that's about the matchmaker finding love. Indeed, in that case, the matchmaker is a secondary character who facilitates a story element—the first meeting—but is nothing more.

If our matchmaker is going to be the focus of an entire story trope, the above story has to have a conflict, complications, and very different outcome.

In the Matchmaker trope, which I've called Matchmaker gone wrong for clarity's sake, a professional or amateur matchmaker pairs two people together in the belief that they're perfect for each other and will fall in love if they get to spend time together.

The matchmaker sets up an introduction, may coach one of the people in the pairing, and may engineer a series of dates. Indeed, the couple may dutifully go on those dates.

However, somewhere along the way, the person of the appropriate gender for your story in the matchmade pair falls not for the person they're being paired with but with the matchmaker himself or herself.

OR

Somewhere along the way, the matchmaker himself or herself falls for one of the people he or she is attempting to pair up with someone else.

Now we've got ourselves a complication from which the conflict and obstacles to true love can flow. We find ourselves in a love triangle where one of the people in the paired couple is falling for the matchmaker while the other person in the pairing falls for him or her. Or we may find a matchmaker struggling to remain professional, not fall in love unethically with a client, and consciously stay out of the paired couple's way while unconsciously attempting to sabotage the paired couple's relationship.

Regardless of who falls for whom, chaos and conflict ensue while the paired couple and matchmaker try to sort out who's in love with whom and who's going to end up with whom.

By the end of the story, the matchmaker and the (now former) client, end up in love and together for their own unexpected happily ever after.

As for the third person in this love triangle, he or she may be out in the cold. Or perhaps he or she gets their own true love along the way in this story. Or this jilted soul may even get their own story next.

ADJACENT TROPES

- Arranged Marriage
- Love Triangle
- In Love with the Wrong person
- Forbidden Love

- Right Under Your Nose
- Engaged to/Marrying Someone Else

WHY READERS/VIEWERS LOVE THIS TROPE

- we can relate strongly to someone who's great at managing the love lives of others but who can't seem to manage their own, which is how many of us feel
- while we all love the idea of someone being able to perfectly engineer love or engineer a perfect romantic relationship, we all relate strongly to the idea that love is messy and complicated and hard to navigate
- we relate to the struggle of maintaining professional boundaries with people we're attracted to
- we relate to the struggle between our logic and our emotions
- we, too, sometimes feel blind to our own needs and relate to a story about becoming aware of our own feelings and needs and taking care of ourselves for once

OBLIGATORY SCENES

THE BEGINNING:

Typically, this story is told from the point of view of the matchmaker in part or in whole. We meet this person and you may want to establish that he or she has no love life of his or her own or that he/she is terrible at navigating their own love life (or whatever trauma, wound, fear, or misbelief about love you want to stick your matchmaker with).

Very early on in the story, however, the matchmaker introduces one or both of the people he/she is going to attempt to pair up with someone else. This can be a professional encounter if your main character is formally a matchmaker, or it can be an amateur who has a friend he or she wants to help find love.

Also very early in the story, the matchmaker sets up the people to be paired together. You may choose to spend some time with the matchmaker coaching, role playing, or preparing the client or friend for the first date. If this is the case, this is inevitably the person who will fall in love with the matchmaker first or who the matchmaker falls in love with inadvertently.

The climax of the beginning is typically the first date between the paired couple. The matchmaker may or may not be present for it. He or she may witness the first date surreptitiously from afar or may be as close and intrusive as going on the date with the paired couple.

The beginning typically ends with the revelation that the matchmaker has feelings for one of the paired people or that one of the paired people has feelings for the matchmaker.

THE MIDDLE:

Whoever's having feelings realizes it's totally inappropriate and backs away from those feelings hard. He or she may or may not tell the person they're attracted to that they're having feelings for him or her.

We may see more of the matchmaker role-playing dates with the awkward client he/she is setting up with someone. The matchmaker may tag along as a third wheel on the paired couple's dates. The person the matchmaker is helping may contrive reasons to spend more time with the attractive matchmaker.

Meanwhile, the paired couple continues to see each other, and one or both of these people may develop feelings for the other one. You can set this up as a love triangle with any of the participants having feelings for one or more of the other triangle members.

As soon as the person falling for the matchmaker or for whom the matchmaker is falling reciprocates the other one's feelings, these two are going to enter into a secret relationship with each other. That relationship may consist of business meetings where they refuse to acknowledge their feelings for each other, even though the sparks are flying thick and fast between them. Or they may give in to their attraction and steal private romantic moments together.

Meanwhile, the appearance of pursuing the original pairing may be ongoing. It may even have progressed to declaring themselves a couple, appearing together in public, introductions to family and friends as a couple, or even an engagement.

This other relationship or other people's expectations of where this other relationship is going may be your primary eternal plot problem. Or you may choose to introduce an additional external plot problem that revolves around work, fame, politics, wealth transfer, or some other compelling reason for the paired couple to remain together and forge a permanent relationship.

Somewhere in the middle of the story—the midpoint reversal being an excellent candidate for this moment, the person having strong feelings for another character may confess they've fallen in love with the other person. This confession really amps up the tension and conflict in the story.

At the midpoint reversal, the matchmaker and love interest may reverse course and, instead of trying to find ways to sneak time together while the pairing continues, may turn their efforts to breaking up the pairing in a way that allows them to end up together without making enemies or harming anyone around them. For example, the matchmaker and/or the love interest may try to find someone else to pair up with the third wheel partner and lure them away from the current love triangle into a romance with someone else who's even more perfect for him or her than the love interest.

Meanwhile, personal or internal issues may be rearing their ugly heads and causing problems for the couple. The matchmaker may feel guilt for breaking up the paired couple. The love interest may feel shame for loving the wrong person. One or both of them may have other traumas, wounds, fears, or misbeliefs that makes it hard for them to allow themselves to be loved, to accept that the other person's love is real, or to see themselves as lovable.

Typically the matchmaker has some huge hang-up about love that explains why he or she is great at helping other people find love but absolutely sucks at finding love for himself/herself.

The love interest may also have some huge hang-up to explain why the matchmaker amateurly intervened to set up this friend or family member with someone else or why the love interest sought out the assistance of a professional matchmaker in the first place.

Both the matchmaker's and love interest's hang-ups are typically tropes in their own right within this story.

Overcoming these external, personal, and internal issues, however, is easier said than done. The various plot problems stopping the matchmaker and love interest from being together build toward a crisis or series of crises that the matchmaker and love interest can't control or prevent from exploding.

BLACK MOMENT:

If the relationship was secret until now, the lid is blown off of it and the relationship goes public. *Everyone* knows about it now.

All the obstacles to love blow up simultaneously or in some sort of daisy chain reaction where one crisis triggers the next and the next. Everything the matchmaker and love interest have been trying to prevent blows up and happens. The lovers are ripped apart physically, professionally, personally, and emotionally.

The matchmaker, who already knew he/she was cursed in love is reminded of that fact. The love interest who sought out a matchmaker or went along with a friend's matchmaking is reminded why he or she isn't worthy of or able to love.

The other person who was originally paired with the love interest is betrayed, disillusioned and devastated, enraged, or both.

The matchmaker and love interest are torn apart, and the people around them whom they were trying to protect are as hurt or more hurt than the lovers anticipated and feared.

All is well and truly lost.

THE END:

All the members of the love triangle have some things to sort out. In their loss of relationship and love, the matchmaker and love interest grieve and discover how devastated they are by the loss of the other person. Indeed, they're devastated enough that they're willing to face anyone, any problem to have each other back.

In their grief and loss, any lessons they need to learn are provoked and happen. Taking this new knowledge forward, the lovers find a way to meet up in private and make their apologies and/or grand gestures of true love to each other. They work together to resolve all the remaining problems between them and being together forever. In the act of working side-by-side as a team to fix the problem(s) their inappropriate love has caused, they find the proof they need to believe that the other one truly loves them.

Once the final obstacles are removed from their path, they're able to come together as a couple at long last, free of problems, conflicts, and obstacles and move forward into their own happily ever after together.

KEY SCENES

- the first look or realization by one or both of the future lovers that they are having very inappropriate romantic feelings for the other person
- the first, forbidden romantic moment
- the matchmaker and love interest decide they mustn't go forward with any kind of relationship with each other

- someone else catches them together, catches a romantic look, or suspects the matchmaker and love interest are fooling around and accuses or confronts one or both of them
- the paired partner of the love interest is blissfully oblivious of the budding romance behind his/her back
- the paired partner begins to suspect something is going on behind his/her back
- the matchmaker and love interest consummate their relationship or something of that degree of involvement depending on the heat level of your story
- the matchmaker and love interest confess to the spurned partner that they're having an affair or serious relationship
- the matchmaker and love interest are discovered or go public or both

THINGS TO THINK ABOUT WHEN WRITING THIS TROPE

Who is the matchmaker? Is he or she a friend of one of the paired partners? Is he/she the person who's going to set them up with each other?

Does the matchmaker know both of the paired partners before they're put together as a couple or not? If so, how? If not, how does the matchmaker know one of them?

Is the matchmaker a professional or an amateur matchmaker?

Why is the matchmaker single? What's his or her hang-up or curse when it comes to finding love for himself or herself?

Why is the matchmaker good at solving other people's love problems but not his or her own?

If the matchmaker is a professional, which person in the paired couple goes looking for a professional matchmaker? How does the matchmaker know the person with whom he or she pairs up the client?

What makes the matchmaker think the paired couple is perfect for each other?

What non-love aspects of the paired couple's lives, families, social positions, or something else makes the pairing a good match?

What's the main reason both of the people in the pairing are desperate to find someone and get married? That is, what do they want?

What's the unconscious need each of the partners in the pairing are looking to fulfill by going along with a matchmaker's help?

How does the future pair meet? Does the matchmaker set up the date or does one of them?

How does the pair's first meeting go? What's their first impression of each other? Does this remain consistent through the story or does it change? If it changes, how does their impression of the other person change and what causes that shift in perception?

What does the matchmaker think of their first date?

Who's first attracted to whom in your story? Is one of the partners attracted to the matchmaker, or is the matchmaker attracted to one of them?

Why is it inappropriate for the matchmaker and one of the paired partners to get involved romantically?

What's the big external plot obstacle to the matchmaker and the love interest being together besides the ethics problem or it being unprofessional?

What's the big personal obstacle to the matchmaker and the love interest being together?

What's the big internal obstacle for the matchmaker and for the love interest being together?

How will all these obstacles get worse over the course of the story?

How will the love interest try to get out of the relationship with the paired partner so he/she can be with the matchmaker? Does it work? Why or why not?

How does the matchmaker try to fix the situation? Does he/she vow to stay away from the love interest or try to find another partner for the paired partner? Does it work? Why or why not?

Who first suspects something's going on between the matchmaker and love interest? Do they confront one or both of the lovers? Does this person promise to keep the secret? Aid and abet the couple? Threaten to reveal all if they don't break it off? Blackmail one or both of them? Something else?

What kinds of meetings or encounters do the matchmaker and love interest keep having that gives them lots of time together to get to know each other and fall in love?

How do the lovers sneak away for private moments or dates together? Where do they go? What do they tell other people they're doing?

How do the obstacles to love get much worse? How do they become insurmountable?

How secret does the lovers' relationship remain? For how long? When and how is their secret blown wide open?

What precipitates the big crisis that blows up the whole relationship between the matchmaker and love interest?

Why does the matchmaker recognize this mess? Has he or she been in it before? Has he or she been burned by the same decisions, same problems, same fears, insecurities, wounds, traumas, or misbeliefs before?

Who learns what lessons?

Who owes whom apologies?

Who forgives—and doesn't forgive—whom?

What are the consequences of the matchmaker and love interest's secret relationship becoming public?

Will those consequences blow over or are there real and lasting consequences they'll have to live with? If so, what are they?

What do the matchmaker and love interest have to do to make the situation right? Do they have to do it together, or does only one of them have to fix things?

Who makes a grand sacrifice or grand gesture of love to the other one? What is it? How is it received?

How do the matchmaker and love interest make things right with the other people they've harmed?

How do they make things right with each other?

How will their relationship be different going forward now that they've both learned a hard lesson?

What does happily ever after look like for them?

TROPE TRAPS

The matchmaker looks like a terrible friend or terrible professional for moving in on one of the people he/she is trying to set up with someone else.

The paired partner who falls for the matchmaker seems flaky or creepy for falling for the matchmaker instead of the person he or she is being set up with.

The other paired partner (the friend of the amateur matchmaker and a client of the professional one) seems naïve or stupid for not realizing sooner that there's something going on between the matchmaker/friend and the person he or she has been set up to date.

The love interest is a jerk for not breaking things off with the paired partner as soon as he or she realized he or she was having feelings for the matchmaker.

The love triangle seems wildly imbalanced—either the matchmaker is way hotter and more attractive overall than the partner he or she is stealing the love interest from. Or that partner is way hotter and more attractive overall than the matchmaker, and the love interest would never plausibly go for the matchmaker over the paired partner.

The drama between the three people involved in the love triangle is way overblown based on the lack of real and serious stakes built into the story. Break up already and date the person you like!

The external plot problem that makes it bad for the matchmaker and love interest to date is nonexistent or so lame none of your audience buys it or sees it as a serious problem.

The personal problem—the matchmaker and partner whose match is being stolen from them are good friends, for example—is lame or so huge a problem the matchmaker would never go there in real life.

The love interest is perceived as a complete schmuck for ditching the person he or she has been set up with to fool around with the matchmaker.

The matchmaker and love interest don't appropriately or sufficiently angst over the ethical dilemma of dating each other or not.

Instead of being honest up front and coming clean with everyone, the matchmaker and love interest sneak around behind a lot of people's backs, lying to them and hurting them all—or being highly unlikable and unheroic to your audience.

Relying solely on a single obstacle to the lovers being together and not bothering to flesh out several plausible obstacles to their being together.

The audience prefers the ditched partner over the matchmaker and is mad the love interest chooses the matchmaker over the other partner.

Appropriate apologies or amends aren't made by the lovers once they've gone public with their romance.

The promised consequences of their affair never land on their heads and turn out to be an empty threat that was a lot of bluster and concern for nothing.

The matchmaker and love interest are so selfish that your audience doesn't like them as a couple and hopes they're unhappy ever after.

. . .

MATCHMAKER GONE WRONG TROPE IN ACTION
Movies:

- Hitch
- Emma
- My Best Friend's Wedding
- The Wedding Planner
- The Matchmaker
- Made of Honor
- Hello I Love You
- Whatever It Takes
- Drive Me Crazy
- Some Kind of Wonderful

Books:

- Match Me If You Can by Susan Elizabeth Phillips
- The Matchmaker's Replacement by Rachel Van Dyken
- The Accidental Match by Tina Gabrielle
- Something Borrowed by Emily Giffin
- The Viscount Who Loved Me by Julia Quinn
- Before We Were Strangers by Renée Carlino
- The Matchmaker's List by Sonya Lalli
- A Bollywood Affair by Sonali Dev
- The Arrangement by Mary Balogh
- Josh and Hazel's Guide to Not Dating by Christina Lauren
- The Best Man by Kristan Higgins
- The Happy Ever After Playlist by Abby Jimenez

20
MAY-DECEMBER

DEFINITION

A May-December romance is one in which there's a large age gap between the hero and heroine. It's up to you what constitutes a "large" age gap and whether it's the hero or heroine who's much older than the other.

A large age gap, while a potentially interesting character element, doesn't make for an entire trope all by itself. The age gap between the hero and heroine has to pose or cause a serious obstacle to the two of them being together as a couple to rise to the level of a trope.

The age gap may pose a problem to the couple themselves. One or both of them may be uncomfortable with the age difference. Or they may encounter differing beliefs, morals, or values because of their age difference that cause issues in their relationship.

However, a large age gap between two romantically involved people typically doesn't bother them anywhere near as much as it bothers the people around them. This is a relationship that has potential to come under severe external pressure from people who think it's wrong or a terrible idea.

Family, friends and coworkers may question the motives of the hero or heroine. Is one of them trying futilely to recapture a lost youth? Is one of them gold-digging by getting involved with a much wealthier person of a very different age? Is the younger one seeking a parent figure? A frequent complaint is that the younger lover is the same age as the older lover's children, and a romantic relationship with someone their child's age is squicky or weird.

There may also be issues of the younger partner wanting to have children and the older partner having already finished raising a family and not wanting to start over.

The couple's financial places in life can be very different as well. While the older partner is typically wealthier than the younger one, the older partner may be more focused on preparing for retirement while the younger one may be interested in working and building wealth or, conversely, experiencing life and spending money freely.

The May and December lovers often counter all these arguments against their relationship by pointing out that, if someone makes them happy, who cares what the age difference is?

It's up to you how you want to handle the arguments for and against the hero and heroine ending up together in the long run. They will certainly have to arrive at answers they're personally comfortable with.

They may or may not feel a need to make the people around them comfortable with the relationship before they make it permanent. That said, be sure to introduce at least some obstacles to the relationship that the couple must resolve before they can be happy together forever.

ADJACENT TROPES

- Opposites Attract
- Forbidden Love
- Rags to Riches

- Billionaire
- No One Thinks It Will Work
- Guardian/Caretaker
- Boss-Employee

WHY READERS/VIEWERS LOVE THIS TROPE

- there's a strong aspect of forbidden love to this couple and we may find it romantic, titillating, or taboo to imagine getting involved with someone scandalous
- there's potentially a power dynamic differential between an older, more experienced person and someone much younger and less experienced that your audience finds sexy
- this couple is subversive and challenges stereotypes and norms that many of us may find limiting, constricting, or annoying and enjoying seeing busted
- this story fulfills the fantasy of being with someone who can teach you what you don't know about sex, romance, or love
- this story fulfills the fantasy of being with someone younger and more energetic (in bed and out of it) who can make us feel younger and bring excitement into our lives

OBLIGATORY SCENES

THE BEGINNING:

The hero and heroine, of widely differing ages, meet. Because people tend to spend time with others of similar experience, social status, or career, this usually means people tend to hang out with people of similar age as well. Hence, your hero and heroine of widely differing age may not normally cross each other's paths, and hence, a meet cute is common for this couple.

Keep in mind that while it's called a meet cute, there may be nothing cute about it at all. This couple may meet under dangerous, unusual, or downright strange circumstances. This meeting sets the tone for the rest of the story. While many people think of a May-December romance as comic, there's no reason at all this can't be any kind of romance story. Although the couple is likely to use humor from time to time when they encounter generational or age differences, that doesn't automatically relegate this story to solely romantic comedy by any means.

At any rate, the hero and heroine are attracted enough to each other to pursue a relationship right away (even if their initial intent is simply a short-term fling).

OR

Circumstances in your story or the plot of your story bring the hero and heroine into repeated proximity so they have time to get to know each other more slowly and gradually develop a romantic interest in each other.

The beginning typically ends with the couple realizing (often with dismay) that they actually have romantic feelings for each other...and these are a big problem. If their attraction exploded immediately when they met, then instead of the couple realizing they have feelings for each other, someone close to them may realize the hero and heroine have romantic feelings for each other and may turn it into a big problem for them.

The beginning also may end with the first big complication to the external plot of the story. This may happen simultaneously to the couple realizing they have feelings for each other or someone else realizing they have feelings for each other.

Either way, what seemed fairly simple at first has just become a whole lot more complicated and problematic.

THE MIDDLE:

The couple's own reservations come into play along with the objections of people around them to their budding romance. The hero and heroine may initially resist their feelings and try to avoid any situations that might become romantic.

But, as their feelings for each other continue to grow and intensify, the couple may go secret with their relationship and hide it, particularly from the people around them who object to it.

The plot of your story may continue to throw the hero and heroine together in comic or suspenseful situations, or both. As the reasons why they should not be together mount, their growing feelings for each other counteract those reasons…for now.

External pressure may build to a nearly unbearable level for them not to be together. Meanwhile, their own conflicts may be growing. Differences in outlook, generational culture, and expectations may be causing friction.

Any internal traumas, wounds, fears, and misbeliefs either of them has are also bubbling up to cause them stress individually and as a couple. Regardless of their age difference, they're both humans first and foremost and come with their own emotional baggage.

As if all of that's not enough to stretch a new romantic relationship to its limits, the plot problem builds toward a crisis and finally explodes to end the middle of the story.

BLACK MOMENT:

Both the plot and the lovers' relationship implode. One may provoke the other, or they may simply happen in quick succession.

One or both of the lovers walks away from or backs out of the relationship.

The naysayers around them have won. The external disapproval, internal doubts, and seemingly insurmountable problems around and between them tear the hero and heroine apart.

On top of all that, the plot problem that they were both trying to resolve has gone as badly as it can possibly go. They've failed in every way it's possible to fail.

THE END:

This is typically a couple who didn't want to break up. They genuinely care for each other but everything and everyone around them are just too much to deal with. Then, their own doubts, fears, and insecurities have finished off the work of breaking them up. But it was never about not loving each other.

Once separated from each other, their feelings for each other become even clearer to them both. They now have some hard choices to make. Will they ignore what others think of their relationship and do what makes them happy? Will they set aside their own hang ups so they can be together? Is there some life lesson one or both of them must learn before they're ready to reach for this relationship they know could make them happy forever? What must they do—individually or together—to once and for all resolve the external plot problem, and are they ready and willing to do it?

Once the hero and heroine have answered these questions, they're ready to come back together, resolve their differences, fix the plot problem, make apologies or grand gestures of love to each other, and get on with the business of being a couple, no matter what anyone else thinks.

When they've finally come back together as a couple after having to fight through all the obstacles in their path, they're never going to let go of each other again. They can go forward into their happily ever after, and your audience can be confident this couple will never break up again.

KEY SCENES

- the hero and heroine find out each other's ages
- friends, family, and coworkers find out their ages and react
- they encounter some generational difference that's a stark reminder of their age gap
- their first romantic encounter, which they each approach differently and have to resolve
- their first big argument, which they also approach differently
- people around them tell them this relationship will never work
- a moment when the younger partner is wiser than the older one
- a moment when the older partner is more of a risk taker than the younger one
- a moment where they laugh together about their age difference
- a conversation where they honestly express their doubts about overcoming their age difference

THINGS TO THINK ABOUT WHEN WRITING THIS TROPE

How old are your hero and heroine?

In what ways are they similar to each other? In what ways, other than their ages, are they different?

Has either of them been married before? Does one or both have children, and if so what ages?

What do they each do for a living?

What attracts the hero and heroine to each other?

What fascinates the hero and heroine about each other?

How do they meet? How does this meeting set the tone for the rest of the story?

What's their first impression of each other? How is this correct? How is it incorrect?

How will you bring them into proximity over and over so their romance can develop and unfold? **NOTE**: Usually, this is some sort of plot device—a charity auction they're planning, they're at the same resort, one works at a place the other frequents.

Will they resist their initial attraction to each other? Why or why not? If so, how?

What do the people around them initially think of the hero and heroine spending time together? Is it obvious to others that they're attracted to each other or not?

When and how do the hero and heroine find out each other's ages? How do they react to that?

When and how do other people find out the hero and heroine's ages? How do they react to that?

Who thinks them being a couple is a terrible idea? Why? How does this person express it? Who else has big opinions on the subject? How do they express it?

How does the plot problem, which may or may not be the same thing that forces them into proximity, make the hero and heroine ending up together have terrible consequences? Can you make these potential consequences worse? Much worse?

What are some age-based differences the hero and heroine run into? Do these emerge in a funny way? A problematic way? A tragic way? An infuriating way?

What's the couple's first big argument about? What provokes it? How do they make up after this fight?

How does their first romantic encounter go? What's the tone of it? What does it say about how they feel about each other?

Will the hero and heroine be secretive about their relationship from the very start? Do they go secret later, after people object to the idea of them as a couple? Are they public about their relationship the whole time? Why do they make this choice? How do they feel about it?

What traumas, wounds, fears, insecurities, and/or misbeliefs do the hero and heroine each bring to this relationship? How will these rear their ugly heads and cause a problem in their relationship?

How do the various obstacles to their relationship—external, personal between them, and internal—combine to cause stress on the romance? Can you make this stress worse? Much worse? Terrible? Enough to tear them apart?

Does the big plot crisis provoke the big relationship crisis or vice versa? If so, how? If not, what does provoke both of these crises?

Why ostensibly do the hero and heroine break up? What reason do they give to other people? What reason do they give to each other? What reason do they tell themselves? What's the real reason (which one or both of them may not be aware of)?

What realization, lesson, or epiphany does the hero have about himself and their relationship after the couple has broken up?

What realization, lesson, or epiphany does the heroine have about herself and their relationship after the couple has broken up?

What do the hero and heroine have to learn and change about themselves or their beliefs to become able to overcome the obstacles to their being together? How will they realize or learn this? What do they do about it after they learn it?

How will the hero and heroine come back into physical proximity with each other so they can work out their remaining issues? Does the big plot climax force them together or something else?

Do the hero and heroine, individually or together, have to confront anyone else and/or overcome that person's objections to their being together before they can actually be together? If so, who?

What will the hero and heroine say? Do the hero and heroine care what that person ultimately thinks?

Rinse, lather, and repeat the above series of questions for everyone who objects to their romance.

What do the hero and heroine have to do to resolve the big plot problem(s)? Can you make that harder? Much harder? Almost impossible? Only possible if they work together?

What does happily ever after look like for this couple?

TROPE TRAPS

The age difference between your hero and heroine is so large that it's implausible to your audience.

Failing to include differences that would logically exist between the hero and heroine given the ages you chose for them.

Neither the hero nor heroine ever questions their age difference or doubts that a relationship is a good idea.

The people around the hero and heroine spout stereotypical objections to their age difference that are offensive to your audience.

The hero and heroine don't have enough in common for a relationship between them to seem plausible.

Your audience believes the younger partner is, in fact, a greedy gold digger and doesn't genuinely care for the older partner. Which is to say, failing to show genuine affection and feelings between them.

The external plot problem pushing them together is lame.

The external plot problem tearing them apart is lame or wildly implausible.

The hero and heroine care too much about what the people around them think and tick off your audience.

Relying solely on their age difference to cause problems in the couple's relationship.

Failing to develop the hero and heroine into fully realized people with hopes and fears, dreams and doubts.

Never addressing their potentially very different expectations from a long-term relationship (kids, money, jobs, travel, hobbies).

Never honestly addressing the age difference and what it means for the long term.

The hero and heroine are too willing to let other people break them up and don't fight hard enough for the person they love.

The hero and/or heroine don't learn any big lesson after they break up that explains how they can get back together and make their relationship work this time.

A simple, honest, adult conversation between the hero and heroine would have solved their big problem(s) much earlier in the story, but they acted immature or selfish and never just acted like adults and talked things out.

MAY-DECEMBER TROPE IN ACTION
Movies:

- Harold and Maude
- Lost in Translation
- The Graduate
- Sabrina
- As Good As It Gets
- An Education
- Something's Gotta Give
- Venus

Books:

- The Reader by Bernhard Schlink
- Birthday Girl by Penelope Douglas
- On the Island by Tracey Garvis Graves

- Memoirs of a Geisha by Arthur Golden
- Unsticky by Sarra Manning
- Elemental by Amanda Curtin
- This Man by Jodi Ellen Malpas
- The Pilot's Wife by Anita Shreve
- Jane Eyre by Charlotte Brontë
- The Idea of You by Robinne Lee
- Gabriel's Inferno by Sylvain Reynard

MISTAKEN IDENTITY

DEFINITION

In point of technical fact, a mistaken identity happens when one person mistakes someone for someone they're not. These two people become attracted or fall in love before the mistake is corrected and complications ensue.

While this classic version of mistaken identity is certainly included in this trope, this category of trope also includes situations where someone (innocently or not so innocently) pretends to be someone they're not. While pretending to be someone else, the main character meets the love interest and ends up getting stuck in the pretense or else risking losing the love interest or risking getting in trouble for their pretense.

In either version of this trope, the main character is mistaken for someone else and doesn't correct that mistaken impression immediately. By not doing so when he or she first meets the love interest who mistook them for someone else, the main character has created a problem for himself or herself.

The problem may be external. For example, he or she has gotten a job under the guise of being someone else or has been asked out on a date in the guise of being someone else.

Or the problem resulting from the mistake in identity may be more personal. For example, the main character would be caught in an embarrassing lie or the love interest would walk away from them if he/she realized the main character lied to them.

This first (small) mistake on the part of the main character, not correcting the mistaken identity the love interest takes him or her for, compounds into more and more complicated problems that make it harder for the main character to tell the truth and correct the mistaken identity.

Twins Switching Places is a separate trope because the twins typically do it intentionally, and it's very easy for anyone to mistake one for the other. They may switch back and forth between each other's lives whereas in this trope, once the main character is mistaken for someone else, he or she cannot readily undo that mistake.

While this is often thought of as a comic trope, it's entirely possible for this to be serious or suspenseful. The tone of the story will be set by the potential consequences of the main character revealing the truth. For example, if a criminal who's posing as someone else reveals his or her true identity, he or she could be hauled off to jail for a long time. In a less extreme example, if someone got a job under false pretenses, he or she could expect to be fired immediately upon revealing his or her true identity.

All other consequences aside, the main character has good reason to expect the love interest will dump him or her upon learning of the deception. This is the most important and real danger of all, regardless of how funny the complications may be that lead up to this serious threat of heartbreak.

ADJACENT TROPES

- Twins Switch Places/Lookalikes
- Clumsy/Thoughtless/Bumbling Hero/Heroine

- Dangerous Secret
- Forgiveness

WHY READERS/VIEWERS LOVE THIS TROPE

- we all love to know something that others don't, and in this case, we know the secret but the love interest doesn't
- the main character, by assuming another identity, lives out our fantasy of getting to live a different, sexier, more glamorous life for a little while
- the constant threat of discovery lends excitement and tension to this story that we all find thrilling and engaging
- we all can relate to the appeal of leaving behind our own boring, mundane existence and getting to be someone else
- most people have told a little white lie in their lives and can relate to the main character's impulse to do so…and can cringe sympathetically as that one lie spins completely out of control

OBLIGATORY SCENES

THE BEGINNING:
The hero and heroine meet or cross paths. This may be when the main character allows the love interest to mistake him or her for someone else and doesn't correct that mistake or the main character introduces himself/herself as someone else—perhaps because it's expedient and he or she never expects to see the love interest again or

perhaps because the main character has a good reason for concealing his or her true identity.

Of course, the main character and love interest do cross paths again very soon. In that second meeting, the love interest mistakes the main character for someone else a second time. The main character wants something that happens because of the mistaken identity, and for a second time, the main character doesn't correct the case of mistaken identity with the love interest.

Now the main character is committed to the mistaken identity.

Every single time the main character lets the love interest mistake his or her identity, it gets harder and harder to correct the mistake.

If there's a compelling reason for the main character to maintain the mistaken identity, this reason is introduced in the beginning of the story.

It's okay for the big plot problem to be caused by the main character's willful maintaining of a mistaken identity. It's also common for the big plot problem to happen independent of the main character and to trap the main character in a mistaken identity that he or she has accidentally or intentionally assumed (even if the plan was to pretend to be someone else for a very short time or for a single interaction).

Whatever the big plot problem is, it's typically introduced in the beginning of the story as well.

The beginning usually ends with the main character hitting the moment of no return for correcting his or her mistaken identity with the love interest. Something happens that the main character can't resist…but it requires him or her to stay in the mistaken identity. By buckling in his or her desire or resolve to correct the mistake, the rest of the story will move forward with the mistaken identity firmly in place.

OR

The person the main character has replaced shows up…for the

job interview the main character did in this person's place, shows up to do the work he or she was hired for, to be the mail order bride the love interest expected, or to do something else altogether.

The main character must act fast to get rid of this person before the person whose identity the main character has assumed reveals the truth and gets the main character in trouble.

THE MIDDLE:

The complications of living under a fictitious, mistaken, or stolen identity stack up as this story moves forward. The main character may continue to live part-time under his or her real identity and part-time under the false or mistaken identity. If this is the case, the juggling act becomes more and more challenging for the main character.

If the main character abandons his or her real identity to live fully in the assumed identity, the difficulties mount while trying to be someone else in a believable way. Not slipping up and getting some detail of that alternate life wrong becomes more and more challenging. Particularly if someone suspects something is off about the main character, someone may intentionally try to trip up the main character in his or her ruse.

Meanwhile, in either case, the love interest is falling in love with the main character in their guise as someone they're not. This puts even more pressure on the main character to maintain the façade of being someone they're not.

For his or her part, the main character is also falling in love with the love interest...all while living a lie. The worst part is, if the main character confesses his or her lie, they risk losing the person they've fallen in love with.

The main character may come close to confessing everything in the middle of the story, as the external problem and romantic pressure mount. But every time the main character gets close to telling the truth, something or someone always intervenes, or the main character's own fear of losing the love interest prevents him or her from confessing the truth.

Someone who knows the truth may pressure the main character, demanding that he or she reveal the truth to the love interest, or vice versa, someone may prevent the main character from confessing all.

The plot problem grows toward a crisis at the same time the main character's guilt and shame grow toward a crisis. The stakes couldn't be any higher—there's no way the main character can tell the truth, but the consequences of doing so are unthinkable to him or her. He or she is completely trapped in the mess he or she has made for himself/herself.

To end the middle of the story, that mess inevitably blows up in the main character's face. Despite his or her best efforts to find a way to reveal his or her true identity without destroying his or her life and without devastating the love interest, the main character has been unable to find a way to do so.

The big plot problem may provoke the revelation of the main character's true identity. Or the revelation of the main character's true identity may provoke the big plot problem blowing up into a crisis and going all wrong.

The person whom the main character has been mistaken for all along may show up again (if he/she showed up in the beginning of the story) or for the first time at the end of the middle to reveal the truth. You may choose not to use this device, of course, and never have the person whom the main character has been mistaken for show up.

BLACK MOMENT:

Regardless of which crisis provoked the other one, the combination of the big plot problem and the revelation of the main character's true identity devastates the love interest who has been lied to this whole time. The couple's entire relationship is based on a lie.

The love interest may break off the relationship after discovering the lie, or the main character may beat the love interest to it out of guilt, shame, and self-recrimination. Either way, the couple's relationship implodes.

The main character's deception has cost him or her everything. While he or she may vow to the love interest that the initial lie about identity is the only one they've ever told, it's likely the love interest isn't interested in excuses or explanations. Trust is a fragile thing that, once broken, is very difficult to restore.

Whatever thing the main character wanted way back in the beginning of the story that he/she got by allowing the love interest to mistake his/her identity is now lost.

The devastation is complete, and there doesn't appear to be any way back to trust and love between the hero and heroine.

THE END:

This trope has a lesson learned specifically built into it. The main character learns a very hard and painful lesson about taking the easy or expedient path and failing to tell the truth scrupulously. By delaying correcting the mistaken identity even a little, a chain of events was started that has cost the main character the person he or she most love and hoped to spend their life with.

This trope also has a built-in, and pretty close to mandatory, apology. The main character, who allowed the love interest to mistake him or her for someone else for so long, owes the love interest a huge and sincere apology.

If the main character has deceived anyone else over the course of the story, he or she owes them an apology along with the love interest. Your main character may choose to apologize to everyone else before he or she works up the courage to apologize to the love interest.

For his or her part, the love interest has to find it in his or her heart to understand why the main character allowed the case of mistaken identity to happen in the first place and then to forgive him or her for doing it. Ideally, the main character has proven that he/she has so many other wonderful qualities and is such an honorable person with a strong sense of integrity that the love interest can find his or her way through to forgiving the main character and trusting him or her again.

In the midst of all these lessons learned and apologies, the hero and heroine must resolve the big plot problem. Coming together to solve the big plot problem may give the main character the opportunity to apologize that he or she has been looking for.

Also, the lessons learned and new honesty of communication between them may allow the hero and heroine to succeed at resolving the big plot problem this time around (after failing to resolve it in the crisis leading to the black moment).

With all their problems resolved, the hero and heroine can finally be together once more. They may choose to start over, redoing their relationship honestly this time. Or they may choose to move forward from where they ended the story and continue on with their relationship much as it was before with only the main character's name/identity having changed.

KEY SCENES

- the main character decides to tell the love interest the truth but something stops him or her—an interruption, an event, fear, or something else—and this scene should recur multiple times
- the love interest sees some evidence that suggests the main character might be lying about his or her identity, but dismisses it as paranoia, overactive imagination, or a ridiculous lack of trust
- someone who knows the truth tells the main character to 'fess up, but the main character doesn't listen
- the awful consequences of confessing to having lied are demonstrated to the main character in some parallel

event, for example, the love interest reacts terribly to someone lying to him or her
- the main character has an attack of guilt after the couple's first big romantic encounter
- the main character tries to tell the love interest the truth, but the love interest changes the subject, misinterprets what the main character is trying to say, distracts the main character, or in some other way doesn't let the main character confess
- the love interest sits with the fact that the main character allowed him or her to believe a lie and act on it...for a long time
- the love interest mentally tries to put himself or herself in the main character's position to understand why the main character did what he or she did

THINGS TO THINK ABOUT WHEN WRITING THIS TROPE

Who are the main character and love interest? What about them is going to intensely attract them to each other? Do they see these things in the moment they meet?

How do they meet?

Who does the main character claim to be and why? Is this relatable to your audience? How can you make it even more relatable?

When does the case of mistaken identity happen? Does the love interest make an assumption about who the main character is and the main character doesn't correct it?

Does the main character portray himself or herself as the other identity of his or her own volition and decision to do so? If so, why and how?

What does the main character stand to gain by playing along with the mistake in his or her identity? Can you make this bigger and more enticing? Much bigger and much more enticing?

What does the main character stand to lose by correcting the mistaken assumption about who he or she is? Can you make this bigger and worse? Much bigger and much worse?

Are the things the main character stands to gain and lose going to be highly relatable to your audience? If not, how can you make them that way?

When is the second time the love interest mistakes the main character's identity, and why is it *really* important to the main character in that moment not to correct the love interest?

At what point in your story is the main character committed to the lie?

When does your main character start having serious doubts about keeping up the mistaken identity?

What's a moment in which the main character almost gets caught or revealed to be pretending to be someone he or she is not? How does the main character get through it?

What are a bigger moment and a much bigger moment in which the main character almost gets caught or revealed to be pretending to be someone he or she is not? How does he or she wiggle out of the trap, dilemma, or awkward situation?

What core values, morals, and ethics do the lovers have in common? Are these big enough to overcome the fact that the main character is lying to the love interest?

How is the main character honest with the love interest in some other situation where it might be awkward or difficult to do so?

How will you demonstrate the main character's core honesty to your audience and the love interest before the big reveal of the mistaken identity?

Who knows the truth about the main character's identity? What do they think about his or her deception of the love interest? Does this person help the main character or try to convince him or her to tell the truth?

How does the main character stop this person who knows the truth from revealing it themselves?

What's the big plot problem in your story?

How will the big plot problem go very badly if the main character reveals he/she isn't who everyone thinks he or she is? Can you make this a disaster? A catastrophe?

How does the main character's guilt, shame, and stress manifest itself over the course of the story?

How is the truth finally revealed? Is it revealed privately or publicly? To whom? Who tells the love interest the truth? Is it the main character or someone else?

How does the love interest react?

Does the revelation of the truth provoke the big plot crisis or vice versa?

What lessons do the main character and love interest learn in the aftermath of their breakup? Does something or someone provoke these lessons? If so, what or who?

How does the main character make amends to the love interest?

What are the consequences of the truth being revealed? Can you make these worse?

How will the main character and love interest get into the same place to talk? Does one avoid the other? If so, who and how? Does someone help engineer this encounter?

How will the main character and love interest resolve the big plot problem in the end? What new information, new resources, or new relationship situation between them allows them to fix the big problem?

Who besides the love interest does the main character need to apologize to for the deception? Does this happen before or after the main character apologizes to the love interest?

Does the love interest have anything to apologize for? If so, what is it?

Has the main character suffered and paid for his or her mistake enough by the end of the story that your audience believes he or she will never do anything like that again, and that the love interest can trust him or her?

TROPE TRAPS

Your main character doesn't have a good enough reason for maintaining the mistaken identity, and your audience dislikes him or her for not correcting the mistake immediately.

The love interest does nothing to help make telling the truth to him or her hard in the first two encounters, setting up the main character to be a bad person in the audience's eyes.

The main character has multiple great opportunities to tell the truth early on and no good reason for not using one of them.

Nobody who knows the truth tells the main character that he or she is headed for a disaster.

The main character doesn't exhibit enough guilt, shame, and stress to be believable.

The love interest is so judgmental and sets such high standards of perfection that the main character could never meet them even if he/she wasn't lying.

The love interest is so rigid and unforgiving that the audience hates him or her and doesn't care if the main character continues to lie to him or her.

The love interest seems dimwitted for not figuring out that case of mistaken identity on his or her own.

There are so many hints and clues that the main character isn't who he/she says they are that everyone else continuing to believe the ruse is totally implausible to your audience.

The main character isn't clever enough in dealing with situations that might expose the truth for the audience to believe that he or she pulls off the ruse.

The promised consequences of the mistaken identity being revealed are never delivered.

Failing to convince the audience that the lovers truly, deeply love each other before the truth is revealed.

The revelation of the truth has no effect on the big plot problem of the story.

The love interest is more of a jackass when the truth is revealed than seems plausible for him or her. A big reaction is fine...just keep it in character for that person.

The love interest is too fast to forgive the main character.

The love interest is too slow to forgive the main character.

The main character doesn't pay a high enough price for the deception to convince your audience that 1) he/she has learned their lesson, 2) he/she deserves to be forgiven, or 3) the love interest has good reason to trust him/her going forward.

The main character doesn't apologize to any of the other people he/she has deceived.

The love interest has never made a mistake themselves and is so rotten to the main character after the revelation that the audience doesn't want the couple to reconcile.

The main character's apology isn't heartfelt enough to be believable.

Your audience believes the main character will lie again and mess with the love interest again someday, and this couple is doomed to fail.

MISTAKEN IDENTITY TROPE IN ACTION
Movies:

- While You Were Sleeping
- The Truth About Cats and Dogs
- Mrs. Doubtfire
- The Princess Switch
- Just Go With It
- To Catch A Thief

Books:

- A Kingdom of Dreams by Judith McNaught
- Suddenly You by Lisa Kleypas
- You've Got Mail by Cathie Linz
- The Bride by Julie Garwood
- The Wedding Trap by Tracy Anne Warren
- The Masqueraders by Georgette Heyer
- The Notorious Rake by Mary Balogh

22

NANNY/TEACHER-SINGLE PARENT

DEFINITION

In this trope, a child or children are the catalyst for the hero and heroine meeting and falling in love. One of the lovers is a single parent raising one or more children. More importantly, this parent needs help. He or she is in over his/her head, or too busy working to parent properly, may be new to being a single parent, or may be new to being a parent at all.

Enter the calm, collected, child-experienced teacher or nanny to help out this beleaguered single parent. This person takes control of whatever mess the single parent has made of parenting and provides stability, order, and control over the child or children.

Of course, the single parent is intensely grateful for the help. But beyond that, he or she takes a romantic interest in the person helping out him or her with the child(ren).

The teacher or nanny, for his or her part, loves kids, and especially loves this kid or kiddos. **NOTE**: Any time I make a comment like that, I'm delighted to see a writer turn the assumption on its head and make it work in a story. How fun would it be to write a story where the teacher can't stand the child's awful behavior and it takes the parent to show him or her the lovable side of that child?

Mind you, it's going to be very hard to make a character appealing to your audience if they actively hate any child. After all, children are, to a great extent, the products of their circumstances and not to be blamed for having been taught bad behaviors or never having been taught good behaviors. Also, it's way too likely that a child who behaves badly is acting out on something bad in their lives that they, as children, aren't responsible for.

At any rate, the teacher and single parent typically come together on multiple occasions to help the child fix some sort of problem, do some sort of project, or achieve some goal. It's these meetings and proximity that allow them to get to know each other and eventually to start dating and fall in love.

For the nanny, he or she moves into the single parent's home and life part-time or full-time, and proximity is plentiful for these two to get to know each other.

In both cases, there's an ethical issue of whether or not it's appropriate to be dating a student's parent or to be dating one's employer. Also, the child or children may have strong opinions on the subject. Depending on the child's age, he or she may be embarrassed if it gets out that his or her parent is dating the teacher. Conversely, a child may be all for a beloved teacher or nanny making mommy or daddy happy again, and this child may actively throw the adults together or try to get them to spend more time together.

Because this is largely a plot of feelings and ethics as opposed to actions, it's the norm to include some sort of external plot problem to this story—for example, the school board may plan to cut funding for a program the teacher is passionate about and the single parent is on the school board, a lawyer who can argue against the school board, or someone wealthy enough to fund the program through a grant to the school.

Complications ensue when the teacher/nanny and single parent start to fall in love, and the couple must navigate their own conflicts and issues, the child's feelings, and whatever external obstacles you throw in the way of their happily ever after.

But in the end, the couple finds their way through to true love and the formation of a whole new family.

ADJACENT TROPES

- Single Parent
- Instant Family
- Widowed Hero/Heroine
- Boss-Employee
- Rebound Romance
- Raising Child Together

WHY READERS/VIEWERS LOVE THIS TROPE

- anyone who's ever had a child left in their care for any period of time has felt overwhelmed or in over their heads at some point and relates strongly to the idea of someone knowledgeable and wise about kids rescuing them from the nightmare
- anyone who loves my beloved child can't be all bad
- the powerful fantasy of filling the hole in one's family that has occurred by death, divorce, or some other loss and making it whole once more
- being rescued from the daily, exhausting grind of parenthood, even if just for a little while
- we can't all have blood families, but we can all have our own found family or intentional family
- teachers and nannies are perceived as especially nurturing and caring people who are heroic for rescuing children from bad situations…and sometimes rescuing their parents from bad situations.

OBLIGATORY SCENES

THE BEGINNING:
The meeting between these two people almost always revolves around the child in the story. Something about the child, something he or she is doing or has done, or some goal the child has typically brings this couple into closer contact with each other, or perhaps the parent has finally accepted that he/she needs help and hires a nanny.

Now and then, this trope includes a nanny who shows up uninvited and unasked to sort out the family's chaotic situation.

Perhaps a family member, friend, or coworker has sent the nanny. Perhaps a grief counselor, pastor, or school official asks a professional to visit the beleaguered single parent and lend a hand. In a few classic stories, the nanny magically shows up where he or she is needed most.

Sometimes this story's opening scene establishes the single parent's need for help. Her or she may forget something important, miss an important event or meeting, or simply be completely overwhelmed trying to juggle parenthood, job, and whatever other responsibilities he or she has.

Only after this scene of complete, chaotic, meltdown does the nanny or teacher enter the scene to help out.

The single parent may initially turn down help...or this overwhelmed parent may exuberantly accept help. Indeed, one of the first major plot complications of this story is often the single parent turning over all parenting duties to the teacher or nanny who has stepped in to help.

Often, the beginning of this story ends with the teacher or nanny refusing to completely replace the single parent and demanding that the single parent step up to do something important for or with their child.

This event typically goes terribly, and it's clear the single parent still needs a lot of help and support to figure out how to do the parenting thing, or to do it well, or to balance the demands of his/her job with parenting.

THE MIDDLE:

If any trope was more set up for true shenanigans to ensue, I'm not sure what it might be. The child or children run amok through this story in the most creative, silly, imaginative, or destructive ways you can cook up.

They drive mom or dad to distraction, and only gradually does the teacher or nanny gain control of them and teach them to behave like orderly, well-behaved children and not the heathens they start the story as.

In addition to kiddie shenanigans, your single parent may have no clue how to properly parent a child, and this also may be a source of chaos, humor, and calamity. The teacher or nanny not only has to wrangle the wild child, but also has to wrangle the completely hopeless, helpless, clueless parent.

In the middle of all this chaos, whatever big plot problem you've built to drive the action of your story grows more complicated and more demanding of the single parent, the teacher/nanny, or both of them.

Somewhere in the midst of it all, your hero and heroine must also notice each other romantically and carve out bits of time to be alone together so their romance can unfold.

For the live-in nanny, these moments may be after the kids are finally put to bed and the adults finally get some quiet time together. For the teacher and parent, one of them asking the other out on a date may be necessary to get time away from the child(ren). Or the teacher and single parent may have some project they're working on in the evenings that drives them together on a regular basis.

This story is always complicated by who's looking after the

child(ren). Beware of abandoning young children by themselves in your story or in any other way neglecting them or putting them in an unsafe situation. Your audience won't stand for that, even if you treat them to a smoking hot love scene while the baby's home alone.

Whatever personal issues your single parent and teacher/nanny are working through become more pronounced and more of a problem as your story progresses.

The single parent may feel guilty for falling in love again after tragically losing a spouse. The teacher/nanny may struggle with commitment issues or ethical issues. They may disagree on parenting styles.

Meanwhile, the external problem grows toward a crisis. The school board is about to cut funding for the program that is helping the single parent's child and which the teacher is in charge of. The single parent's ex becomes a bigger and bigger problem as the teacher/nanny moves into a more parental role with the ex's child, and the ex is threatening to sue for custody.

If the lovers have been keeping their relationship secret, the end of the middle is when something or someone threatens to make it public.

The middle ends with the external plot problem blowing up into a crisis and with the romantic relationship between the teacher/nanny and single parent imploding.

BLACK MOMENT:

Everything that can go wrong does. The external plot problem and internal relationship problem tear apart the lovers and they break up. The child(ren) may be caught in the middle of the mess as well, only adding to the overall stress, guilt, and sense of loss.

The single parent's failure to learn how to be a competent parent or to juggle the demands of parenting and work may cause the external plot problem to blow up. The single parent, when faced with a choice between work and child, may choose child over work, precipitating a disaster at work and potentially costing the parent his or her job.

Likewise, the teacher/nanny may choose the welfare of the child over their own position and may do something that will end up getting him or her in trouble or fired.

The little family that was starting to form falls apart. Everyone's despondent, and everyone feels terrible. Everything good that has happened is erased and everyone's back to square one...or worse off than before.

THE END:

One of the family members—the single parent, the teacher/nanny, or the child(ren)—does something to begin to reverse the disaster. The lovers get together and apologize for messing up each other's lives and for upsetting or disappointing the child(ren).

By realizing how miserably unhappy they are apart, and by realizing how much the teacher/nanny has helped the parent and child learn to function together as a family unit, it becomes clear that they all belong together as a family, no matter what obstacles stand in their way. They love one another and miss one another, and nothing is more important than family.

A new approach to fixing the big plot problem is found by one or all of them. By working together the lovers (and possibly the child/children) fix the big external plot problem. If your plot problem doesn't involve the children and is an adult-oriented problem, then the child(ren) probably won't have much to do with its solution.

By reprioritizing their lives, by working together, by sticking together, and by trusting the power of their love for one another, the single parent, teacher/nanny, and child(ren) have come together to form a new, strong, resilient family who can go into the future together, safe in the knowledge that together they can get through anything.

KEY SCENES

- a scene of utter chaos between the single parent and child that the teacher/nanny walks in on
- the single parent has a minor or major emotional breakdown at being completely overwhelmed
- the teacher/nanny refuses an offer of a date or other potentially romantic encounter
- the teacher/nanny admits to being overwhelmed sometimes
- the child(ren) surprise the adults by doing something nice or thoughtful
- the teacher/nanny and parent argue about some aspect of raising the child(ren)
- the first big romantic encounter without the child(ren) around
- the child(ren) interrupt a big romantic encounter
- the teacher/nanny has a frank conversation with the parent about getting his or her act together
- the single parent chooses work over kids and upsets both the teacher/nanny and the child
- the child is embarrassed by the teacher/nanny's and parent's romantic relationship
- the single parent has to choose between the child and the teacher/nanny
- the teacher/nanny has to choose between the child and the single parent

THINGS TO THINK ABOUT WHEN WRITING THIS TROPE

How did your single parent become single? How did he or she become a custodial parent?

Is having solo custody of the child new or has this been going on for a while?

How old is the child or children? How does the child or children feel about only having one parent?

Is the other parent alive? Does he or she have visitation rights or take the child(ren) for weekends, holidays, evenings, or some other arrangement?

What about being a single parent is overwhelming the single parent now?

How do the teacher/nanny and single parent meet?

Has somebody asked the teacher or nanny to help out the single parent? If so, who?

What problem with the child brings the teacher/nanny and single parent together?

What's the ethical problem between the teacher/nanny and single parent that gets in the way of them dating? How do they each feel about it? What are the consequences to each of them if they date each other anyway?

Do the teacher/nanny and single parent keep their relationship secret? Do they need to? If so, why? Or do they simply choose to? If so, why? If no to both questions, why not?

How aware is the child (ren) about the budding romance? How does/do the child/children feel about it?

Does the child(ren) keep the secret of the budding romance between mom or dad and the teacher/nanny? If so, why?

Who else knows about this budding romance? How do they feel about it? What advice do they give the teacher/nanny or the single parent?

How quickly does the teacher/nanny tame the chaos at the single parent and child's home? What does the teacher/nanny have to do to get control of the chaos?

Why is the single parent not able to successfully juggle work, kids, home, and whatever else he or she is juggling?

What kind of help does the single parent ultimately need? Organization? Understanding children? Learning how to parent? Something else?

How are the single parent and teacher/nanny pulled into repeated and frequent proximity to each other so they can get to know each other?

How do the single parent and teacher/nanny arrange to spend time together alone without the child(ren) present?

How does or do the child/children interrupt the adults trying to spend time alone together? Is this intentional or accidental? Does the child know what's going on or not?

If the other parent is alive, how does he or she feel about this new person in the single parent's and their child(ren)'s lives?

If the other parent is not alive, how would he or she feel about the single parent falling in love again and about having the teacher/nanny replace him or her?

What internal traumas, wounds, fears, or misbeliefs are each of the adults laboring under that cause problems for their relationship?

Does the teacher/nanny want a family and kids of his or her own, or does he/she want nothing to do with his/her own family after dealing with other people's all the time?

How do the teacher/nanny and single parent disagree on how to raise the child(ren)? Can you make this disagreement bigger?

How does each of the adults face a dilemma of having to choose work or family but not both? Why and how do they each choose work over family? What problems does making this choice cause in their relationship?

What keeps each of the adults from committing to a long-term relationship with each other?

How does or do the child/children feel about a long-term romantic relationship between their parent and the teacher/nanny? How does this affect the adults' relationship?

Does a crisis in the big plot problem provoke the couple to break up or vice versa? How?

What old behavior does the single parent revert to that provokes the black moment or is a result of the black moment?

What lessons, realizations, or epiphanies do each of the adults have after they've broken up? What are they now capable of doing as a result of their realization? How are they now capable of committing to a long-term relationship and a new family in a way they weren't before?

How does their decision to prioritize family over everything and everyone else change both adults' situations at the end of your story?

How are the kids better off after the adults prioritize family over anything else?

What does becoming a family look like for this new family? How will you give your audience a glimpse of the "after" family that the characters have formed?

TROPE TRAPS

The single parent is initially such a jerk about being a parent that your audience hates him or her.

The single parent is so incompetent at even basic parenting that your audience doesn't buy it at all or thinks this character is too stupid to be allowed to raise his or her own children.

The kids are WAY too mature or worldly for their age.

The kids are WAY too immature or naïve for their age.

The teacher/nanny doesn't have any good reason or right to help out the single parent in an official capacity, but that's how you explain his or her involvement with the parent and child(ren).

The teacher/nanny and parent magically get big blocks of time together where no child interferes or asks for anything...and your audience, particularly the parents, find it wildly improbable.

The child(ren) is/are such insane, wild brats the audiences spends the whole story wanting to smack them.

The reason the single parent is single or just got custody of their child isn't properly explained or the explanation is lame and cliché.

Failing to explain why there's nobody else helping out this poor, beleaguered single parent. Where are the grandparents, other family, friends, neighbors, social workers, or other helpful people who would reasonably help a newly single parent figure out the whole parenting thing?

The single parent is too wrapped up in his or her work and is unlikable to your audience for not giving more time and attention to his/her child(ren).

Failing to explain why this single parent can't muddle through parenting any better than they are.

Your single parent is unlikable for not doing a better job of parenting or at least trying harder.

The teacher/nanny is superhumanly organized, on top of work-life balance, and all children magically do whatever this person wants them to without a single whine or word of backtalk...and your audience finds him or her totally unbelievable.

The teacher/nanny fails to set limits for the child(ren) and is too cool to be believable or to actually control the children.

Never addressing the ethical issues of dating a parent of a student or of dating an employer.

Failing to portray any growing pains of two adults and at least one child learning to live together, learn one another's routines, or adjust to the different ways they do simple things.

The teacher/nanny completely takes over raising the child(ren) and the single parent abdicates way too much of the parenting responsibility, coming off as a bad parent and rotten human being for not engaging more with his or her child(ren).

The child(ren) never, ever get in the way of the romantic moments the adults are trying to have...and no parent buys that for a second.

The adults act sophomoric or immature in their romantic interactions but act mature and wise in the parental interactions with the child(ren) and don't come off as consistent or plausible characters.

Nobody ever asks the child(ren) what they think of a romantic relationship between the parent and the teacher/nanny.

Conversely, the child(ren) have too much say in what happens between the single parent and teacher/nanny.

Failing to create any consequences for getting caught if the romance between the single parent and the teacher/nanny must be kept secret for some reason in your story.

The parent never does prioritize family over something else important to him or her.

The teacher/nanny never grows out of the role of babysitter for the child(ren).

The single parent and teacher/nanny never become equal partners in raising the child(ren) and in building or maintaining the family.

The child(ren) never learn how to be helpful, thoughtful, or respectful members of a family, or remain spoiled and self-centered with everything the adults do having to be centered around them.

NANNY/TEACHER-SINGLE PARENT TROPE IN ACTION

Movies:

- The Sound of Music
- Mrs. Doubtfire
- Daddy Day Care
- The Nanny Diaries
- Jersey Girl
- Raising Helen
- The Pacifier
- One Fine Day

Books:

- The Undomestic Goddess by Sophie Kinsella
- Daddy's Girls by Danielle Steel
- The Nanny Arrangement by Rachel Harris
- The Nerd's Lesson in Love by Trish Jensen
- A Nanny for the Rogue by Lily George
- Teach Me by Olivia Dade
- The Nanny Trap by Cat Schield
- Starting Over on Blackberry Lane by Sheila Roberts
- The Brightest Star by Fern Michaels

23
ONLINE LOVE/PEN PAL

DEFINITION

Ahh, the power of the written word to woo and win over your true love...that's what this trope is all about, at least on its surface. The conceit of written communication as the means by which two people meet and fall in love is a classic that's been around forever and will remain as long as two-way, remote communication of some kind continues to exist.

In this trope, two people communicate by some remote format (see how I'm leaving room there for technology to evolve and your stories to include anything from note by carrier pigeon to something ultra-cool yet to be invented?).

They may or may not be truthful with each other, although traditionally, people tend to reveal their innermost, private thoughts and selves on the written page in ways that they do not in person or with people they don't know very well.

Our lovers, after writing poetically and profoundly to each other and forming a deep, personal connection, finally meet in person—and that's when the trouble begins. That's when the masks, social roles, and dishonest, inauthentic behaviors and personas people show the world at large come into play.

The poet at heart has to act like a cool kid at school. The tortured soul has to show a brave front to coworkers or the rest of the world. The young parent who loves his or her child but yearns to travel, see the world, do more—be more—must pretend to be delighted with life never leaving home.

This trope is a deep exploration of the facades we show others and how very hard it is for most of us to reveal our most vulnerable, honest selves to others. Of course, this trope can be cloaked in humor, shenanigans, or fraught suspense. But at its core, this story is about two people struggling to be honest with each other and with the rest of the world at the same time.

Sometimes, one or both of the lovers in this trope is (are) portrayed as a kind of Jekyll and Hyde character—loving, tender, and kind in private, but an insensitive, emotionally closed off jerk in public. It's also common to see one of the lovers able to be authentic and honest about who they are in public while the other one struggles to match his or her open and vulnerable approach to life.

The story revolves around the scared or wounded character learning to be the same warm, wonderful person he or she is in writing (or other private communication format) with everybody, all the time. It's a journey from dishonest to honest, inauthentic to authentic, afraid to show warmth, affection, and love in public to courageous about doing so.

ADJACENT TROPES

- Beauty and the Beast
- Cold/Serious/Uptight Hero/Heroine
- Socially Awkward Hero/Heroine
- Friends to Lovers
- Long Distance Romance

WHY READERS/VIEWERS LOVE THIS TROPE

- we all crave honest communication and deep connection with someone else, even if it's in some remote format
- by not knowing everything about our pen pal or online friend, we're free to idealize them and fill in the blanks however we'd like, creating the perfect friend or lover in our minds
- somebody knows the real me and sees the real me...and still is willing to write to or communicate with me
- this could happen to any of us. It's an accessible way to really get to know another person that doesn't revolve on some big, high concept event happening to us
- we all crave more intimacy than we get
- the ability to be authentically ourselves...and still be loved

OBLIGATORY SCENES

THE BEGINNING:

The hero and heroine engage in some sort of remote communication with each other. For ease, I'll discuss it as writing letters, but it can be any form of back-and-forth exchange that doesn't involve the main characters being in physical contact with each other.

Indeed, you may spend the entire first act of your story with the hero and heroine having never met. We may see vignettes of their individual lives and your audience may get to know them separately as they write back and forth to each other.

It's a common device for the hero and heroine's lives to cross in the beginning of the story without them knowing who the other character is —they're actually neighbors or work in the same place but have never met in person and don't recognize each other. Writers use this device to get the main characters on screen or on the page together quickly while still maintaining the distance between them required by the pen pals trope.

This physical distance, this separation if you will, is when the main characters reveal in writing their authentic selves. They share their private thoughts, feelings, fears, hopes, and dreams with each other in a way that would be very difficult to do in person with someone they've never met.

In short, the hero and heroine fall in love in the beginning of your story with an idealized, imagined version of the other person.

Typically, the beginning ends with the hero and heroine finally meeting in person for the first time.

Typically, some sort of external plot event or plot problem is what brings the hero and heroine together. They're assigned to work together on a project. They contrive to attend the same party and agree to meet there. One of them arranges to take a vacation and visit the other one.

THE MIDDLE:

The first meeting between the hero and heroine doesn't have to go disastrously badly for this story to become extremely complicated very quickly. All that has to happen is the hero and heroine discover something unexpected about the other one that startles or alarms them.

It would be easy and logical for these two people, disappointed that the reality of the other one doesn't meet their imagined expectations of the perfect lover, to walk away from each other after one meeting; hence, it's important to build some reason into your plot that they cannot just walk away from each other immediately after they meet.

This plot problem forces the pair to stay in physical proximity long enough for them to start finding new things about each other to love or to start revealing the person from their letters to each other in person.

Because both of them have fallen in love with an unreal construct of who they think the other person is, they're both bound to be disappointed in some way and surprised in other ways. In the act of meeting, the hero and heroine both realize that, while they may know some aspects of the other one very well indeed, there are large aspects of each other they know nothing about.

The perfect simpatico of their written communication breaks down when they meet in person and have to deal with moving their relationship into the real world. They both question if they would have even become friends, let alone fallen in love, had they not already exchanged their letters with each other.

They question whether or not anything in their letters to each other was real at all, or just a fiction they both made up. They struggle to reconcile their imagined version of their lover with the real one.

Misunderstandings, disagreements, and incorrect expectations abound as the hero and heroine get to know the public persona each of them show the world.

And yet, throughout this story, there may still be letters exchanged Alternately, the couple experiences moments together where they show each other the person from their letters, the one they each fell in love with in the first place.

Through the middle of the story, the hero and heroine fall in love again, this time with the real person and not the idealized one they each imagined.

The middle typically ends, however, with one or both of the lovers backsliding to their public personas and denying or rejecting their private, personal feelings, hopes, or dreams that they previously shared in written form with each other.

The plot problem may provoke this emotional retreat, or their emotional retreat may provoke a crisis in the plot problem. Either way, a crisis ensues that encompasses both the external plot events of your story and the internal, emotional love story.

BLACK MOMENT:

Both of your main characters have, for some reason, retreated from trying to be their open, authentic, vulnerable selves in a public situation. They can do it in writing, but they can't bring themselves to do it in person. The other lover's request for honesty has been denied.

This gigantic betrayal of their written relationship, their real and honest relationship, is devastating to both of them. Each of them has succumbed to fear and has run away from doing the one thing their lover has asked of them—showing the world the person that the lover sees in their letters.

Not only is their real-world relationship betrayed and destroyed, but now their written, private relationship has also been betrayed. All is well and truly lost between the hero and heroine.

It may be almost an aside in the minds of your hero and heroine that the plot problem has also gone to hell. But don't forget to do this in your story as it's an effective way to pile on the loss and failure and acts as an outward representation of the internal failure of the hero and heroine's relationship.

THE END:

The hero and heroine are devastated by the loss of what they each believed was their one true love, the one person who really knew them and loved them just as they really are. In the aftermath of this tremendous loss, each of the lovers is forced to engage in some serious introspection. It's in this time of self-examination and asking themselves what went wrong that each of them learns an important lesson about themselves.

They may change their priorities and walk away from some external goal they thought was more important than love. They may cease caring what other people think of them. They may overcome their greatest fear, which keeps them from being totally honest with each other. The lesson they each need to learn is up to you, and you have a broad range of choices at this point in your story.

Once the hero and heroine have had their respective epiphanies, they finally have arrived at a place where they can be their authentic selves, not only with each other but in front of the world. Having arrived at this moment, they now can come back together and make up with each other.

Furthermore, they can now resolve the external plot problem(s) together, united as a team. With the plot problem(s) out of the way, the couple can, at long last, be together. They can step out into the world together, both of them showing the world the person they each fell in love with. The written romance has now become their public, real-world love story.

KEY SCENES

- the hero and heroine each receive a letter and read it
- they dread and anticipate meeting each other
- they reread old letters and wonder what happened to that person
- they quote to each other in person something the other one wrote in a letter (this may be an argument or may be a romantic scene)
- he/she accuses the other one of lying in the letters
- a moment when they show the other one in person a vulnerable part of themselves that they've only revealed in letters in the past
- they write each other one more letter to share their honest feelings after they've met each other or after they've broken up
- they write letters they don't send to each other

. . .

THINGS TO THINK ABOUT WHEN WRITING THIS TROPE

How do the hero and heroine start writing to each other? What's the device or who introduces them?

When in your story do you want the hero and heroine to meet?

Will you include the text of the letters themselves in your story or not? If so, do the voices in the letters sound different and unique—as if two different people wrote them and not you, the writer, penned both?

Will you use flashbacks or backstory to reveal any of what was written in the letters, or will you tell your story entirely in current time?

What do the hero and heroine each reveal about themselves in their letters that they would never tell each other in person if they'd just met?

Is their letter exchange secret? If so, why? If so, from whom?

Why do these two start writing personal, private, or intimate things about themselves to the other one?

What are each of the main characters secret fears, traumas, wounds, hopes, and dreams that they'll share in the letters?

In the letters, what about the other one makes each of the main characters fall in love with the other?

What do they each imagine the other one to be like before they ever meet?

How will the hero and heroine meet in person?

What's different about the hero and heroine in person that neither of them expected? Can you make that bigger? Even bigger?

What's better than they each expected about the other one? What's worse?

What external plot event or plot problem is going to keep them from walking away from each other and never seeing each other again after they first meet?

How does their meeting in person complicate one or both of their lives?

What part of themselves, revealed in the letters, do they not show to other people? How do they hide this about themselves?

What does each of the main characters think of the other one's public persona? What do they say to each other about these facades they both show the world?

How will the hero and heroine spend private time together where they can let down their public facades and be themselves?

Once in person, is one or both of them reluctant to talk about something in their letters? If so, what is that thing? Why don't they want to talk about it? How does the other lover feel about this reluctance?

What are some private and personal things they learn about each other in person that weren't included in the letters?

What's a moment of connection and intimacy between them that draws them closer?

What's a moment of disconnect and friction between them that pushes them apart?

What do their friends, family, and coworkers think of their relationship...both the written one and the one after the pair meets in person?

What do they love about each other in person that goes beyond what they love(d) about each other in writing?

How does the external plot problem provoke a crisis in their relationship or vice versa?

What old behavior pattern does one or both of the lovers revert to that breaks them up? Why does he, she, or both of them backslide like this?

What's the deal breaker for each of them in their relationship? How does the other partner do this thing?

What do each of the main characters need to learn about themselves to be able to have a healthy, long-term relationship with the other one?

What do each of the main characters need to learn about each other to be able to have a healthy, long-term relationship with each other?

How will the main characters learn both of these lessons? Does something or someone provoke that lesson, or do they have this epiphany spontaneously?

After their epiphanies, how do the lovers get into physical proximity, or communicate in writing, so they can work out their problems?

How do the lovers resolve the external plot problem?

Does solving the external plot problem push the lovers back together, or do the lovers have to get together first to be able to solve the plot problem?

Who apologizes to whom and for what?

Does one of them make a grand gesture of sacrifice or of love to the other one? If so, what?

What does happily ever after look like for this pair?

TROPE TRAPS

The letters are so extravagantly romantic so quickly that your audience doesn't buy them as expressing authentic feelings.

The hero and heroine, prior to meeting, are such strangers that they wouldn't plausibly share the things about themselves that they do. Some things are simply too personal ever to share with a stranger.

Failing to explain why both characters engage in their pen pal exchanges using the method of communication that they do.

One or both of the main characters isn't likable.

One or both of the main characters comes across as excessively needy—it's one thing to share honest feelings. It's another to burden a stranger with terrible secrets.

It's implausible that these characters wouldn't meet in person much sooner than they do.

It's implausible that the main characters wouldn't figure out who the other one is if they already know each other. Which is to say, they give away so much about themselves in the letters that the other one would surely recognize the other one.

Their first meeting goes so badly they would never plausibly stick around to get to know each other better.

The other lover is exactly the way they each imagined and there's no internal conflict in the story between the idealized and real versions of each of them.

One writer is WAY more forthcoming about his or her feelings, thoughts, fears, wounds, traumas, and the relationship is wildly unbalanced.

The real-world versions of the lovers don't have enough in common for your audience to believe that they would ever end up together.

The reality of the other person is so different from their fantasies of each other that the audience thinks each of them is unrealistic or doesn't deserve the other one.

None of the idealized versions of each other that the main characters each imagined are true...and your audience doesn't believe this pair would ever fall in love.

The lovers don't have enough day-to-day things in common for your audience to believe that this pair will stay together and be happy for the long-term.

The people around the couple never accept the relationship, leading your audience to ask what they know that the audience doesn't about this pair.

Neither lover learns a lesson that makes him or her ready to accept the real person over their fantasy of the other person.

The lovers are never as honest with each other in person as they were in writing.

Failing to convince your audience that this couple is better off together than apart (as pen pals or not).

. . .

ONLINE LOVE/PEN PAL TROPE IN ACTION
Movies:

- You've Got Mail
- The Shop Around the Corner
- The Lake House
- Sleepless in Seattle
- Must Love Dogs
- A Cinderella Story
- The Perfect Man

Books:

- Attachments by Rainbow Rowell
- The Flatshare by Beth O'Leary
- Tweet Cute by Emma Lord
- To All the Boys I've Loved Before by Jenny Han
- The Guernsey Literary and Potato Peel Pie Society by Mary Ann Shaffer and Annie Barrows
- Dear Aaron by Mariana Zapata
- Alex, Approximately by Jenn Bennett
- This Is What Happy Looks Like by Jennifer E. Smith

24

OPPOSITES ATTRACT

DEFINITION

This is one of the foundational tropes of all romance stories and many, many other popular romance tropes are some version of this classic, archetypal love story. This trope is exactly what it sounds like. Two people who are opposites meet, drive each other crazy in their opposite-ness, eventually fall in love, and live happily ever after.

But here's the reality. People who are actually opposites in some deep, fundamental way are probably doomed not to be happy with each other. Ever. People with conflicting morals, values, and core beliefs aren't likely to even like each other, let alone fall in love with each other and stay happily in love forever.

Picture the following:

- a profoundly religious or spiritual person with someone who scoffs at the mere idea of faith
- a pathological liar with someone who values honesty above all else in life
- two people from completely opposite ends of the political spectrum who passionately believe their view of the

world is the only right one. (And I'm not just talking a liberal and a conservative from the same political system. I'm talking a committed fascist and a committed communist, a committed socialist and a committed anarchist.)
- A serial, violent criminal and a cop or prosecutor.

None of these couples are likely to meet, get to know each other, fall passionately in love, and stick around for a life-long relationship with each other. They're going to argue, despise the other one's beliefs, and identify each other with ideas and/or behaviors they cannot or do not wish to tolerate, and have no desire to be around each other constantly.

There's an old saw in the romance writing world about the love interests: if one is a firefighter, make the other an arsonist.

I'm in agreement with this saying to the extent that conflict is the heart and soul of any good romance. But I disagree completely with the saying if you ask your audience to believe that two people with completely different morals, ethics, and core values can successfully find a way to live with each other's conflicting fundamental beliefs.

A firefighter and an actual arsonist could only plausibly end up together if the arsonist had a damned good reason for burning down one building, made sure nobody would get hurt in the fire, and had no impulse *ever* to light anything else on fire. In this scenario, setting a fire would not constitute having an ethical and moral compass that thought burning down buildings is fun, destroying thousands or millions of dollars' worth of other people's property—potentially everything in the world that person owns and loves—is cool. It's never heroic to endanger the lives of innocents, including the elderly, disabled, children, pets, firefighters, first responders, good Samaritans, and anyone else who could be harmed or killed in a fire.

Of course, the arsonist could have seen the light, reformed his or her ways and now be someone who helps with arson investigations. In this case, though, the lovers' core values, ethics, and morals have come into alignment. A firefighter and this ex-arsonist could plausibly be happy together for the long term.

To be clear:

- Two people can certainly have personality traits that conflict as in the Grumpy-Sunshine or Beauty and the Beast versions of this trope.
- They can have other traits that conflict as in the May-December, Across the Tracks, or Goody Two Shoes versions of this trope.
- They can have upbringings, opinions, and beliefs that conflict as in the Cross-Cultural or Burned By Love versions of this trope.

But the hero and heroine of any romance must have similar enough views of what constitutes good and evil, right and wrong, to like and respect each other sufficiently to sustain a long-term relationship.

Most people hold a few beliefs that are absolutely sacred and inviolable to them and cannot tolerate a life partner who continuously violates or denigrates these beliefs. Your audience can believe that a character might change something that's important to him or her. But they won't buy a character being willing to change their **core** beliefs, the morals, ethics, and values that define who they are.

It is worth noting, however, that in reality, very few people actually make any significant changes to their belief systems with suffering a significant, life changing event.

Also worth noting, people can make short-term behavior changes and sustain them for around six months fairly easily. But after that, it becomes harder and harder to sustain a change that sticks if it's not rooted in a really deep, personal, powerful commitment to change.

- Conflict is fine.
- Being opposites in superficial enough ways that one or both partners is willing to revise a trait, belief, or behavior to be with the other one is fine.
- Having traits that cause friction, chaos, or humor is fine.
- Disagreeing about beliefs that the main characters are willing to compromise over or live with is fine.

But don't ask your audience to accept that a serial arsonist, one who delights in causing death and destruction and who will never see anything wrong with torching the whole world for his or her personal entertainment, is ever going to be the true love of a firefighter committed to saving and protecting his or her fellow man from harm, one who is willing to give his or her life to do so.

ADJACENT TROPES

Rather than list dozens of obvious 'opposites' tropes, here are a few less obvious examples:

- Bad Boy/Girl Reformed
- Feuding Families
- No One Thinks It Will Work
- Rags to Riches
- Not Good Enough for Him/Her

WHY READERS/VIEWERS LOVE THIS TROPE

- the unexpected connection of two people who, on the surface, seem completely opposite or who come from very different backgrounds, surprisingly having very similar core values

- the dynamic tension of a heightened conflict between the hero and heroine is exciting and entertaining
- there are lots of quips, jabs, and snappy comebacks between the hero and heroine that we all wish we could come up with on the spot like the main characters do
- we would love to have someone love us enough to change something about themselves that's important to them
- comparing and contrasting two very different characters in a story allows us to reevaluate our own beliefs and ideas about some topic or conflict
- we love the idea of people with opposing views or ideas being able to balance each other out and find compromise

OBLIGATORY SCENES

THE BEGINNING:

The hero and heroine meet. Typically, this story begins with a meet cute, or more accurately, a meet-instant-friction. It can be funny or suspenseful but be careful to establish at least a tiny spark of attraction between these people who instantly disagree and rub each other the wrong way.

Having met and irritated the crap out of each other, you'll need to give this couple a reason to see each other again, multiple times, so they have a chance to get past their instant dislike and get to know each other.

OR

The hero and heroine may already know each other when your story starts and already heartily dislike each other. In this scenario, the story begins with some incident that forces the couple into physical proximity and promises to keep them together or coming back together frequently through the story, regardless of how much they dislike each other.

The beginning typically ends with these two people doing something to absolutely infuriate the other one, sending their distant and possibly casual dislike to a whole new level of infuriation.

THE MIDDLE:

Into this active dislike and friction, the plot unfolds, forcing these two people into ever more frequent contact with each other. This trope is often paired with another one that explains their requirement to be with each other a lot. One could be a bodyguard and the other his or her protectee. Their children could become best friends. They could be assigned to work on a project at the office together.

Feel free to be creative with why and how you shove these two opposite souls together. Indeed, I encourage you to be creative. This popular trope is rife with clichéd grumpy-sunshine neighbors, coworkers with opposite approaches to problem solving, and bored billionaires introducing their spunky secretaries to how the ultra-wealthy live.

Also feel free to play with what's opposite between your main characters. There are all kinds of things two people might disagree about sharply but which your audience might really enjoy watching —knitting versus crochet, rival sports teams, the best sci-fi movie franchise—you get the idea.

Also, in the middle of your story, you may want to develop secondary "opposites" between your main characters that spring from the main "opposite" between them.

Likewise, you'll need to explore and develop the things the main characters have in common and the things that attract them to each other. After all, the idea is for this pair to fall in love eventually.

However, as the couple is growing a romance and falling in love, an unresolved conflict between them builds toward a crisis. It can be an opposite trait, behavior, or belief associated with the external plot problem, or it can be an opposite trait, behavior, or belief associated with their personal relationship or with their internal fears, insecurities, traumas, or wounds.

Whatever conflicts you place between the main characters, they build to a crisis that explodes at the end of the middle of your story.

BLACK MOMENT:

One or both of the main characters, who was/were doing so well with compromise or change, reverts to his or her old ways for some reason.

Perhaps the external plot crisis provokes this backsliding. Perhaps their own fears and insecurities cause them to revert to old behavior patterns. Perhaps the other lover triggers the snapback to old patterns of thought and action.

This return to the behavior that drove the hero or heroine crazy in the first place causes him or her to break up with the love interest... or they both are triggered to break up with each other. This way one of them isn't cast as the villain in your story while the other one, the partner who remained willing to compromise and work on the relationship doesn't look like a victim or appear taken advantage of... unless of course, he or she was and that has to get worked out by the end of your story.

Torn apart by their differences, the hero and heroine are devastated. They'd come so far and were really optimistic that they had overcome the worst of their differences...but obviously not.

THE END:

This deep pain and terrible loss is finally sufficient enough to cause each of the main characters to make a real and lasting change in his or her behavior, beliefs, habits, or ideas. Having finally overcome the thing that has been a deal breaker up till now, the hero and heroine can finally resolve their differences and come together as a couple.

This lesson learned or change made may happen as a result of having to face and fix the external plot problem or the act of learning the lesson/making the change may finally allow the main characters to resolve the external plot problem. Either way, the couple is finally able to forgive each other, resolve their personal differences, and move past the ways in which they've been opposite until now so they can be together forever.

Your couple may compromise on the way in which they're opposite and change to be more alike. They may remain opposite but learn to value that opposing quality, behavior, or belief in the other one. They may learn to love the other person enough to deal with that opposite trait just the way it is and accept that occasional friction between them isn't going to destroy their relationship.

However you resolve the lovers' opposite-ness, they've found a solution that works for them and will hold up for the long-term, and one that your audience believes will hold up forever.

KEY SCENES

- the hero and heroine are supremely frustrated by something the other one does
- knowing that it drives the other one crazy, the hero and heroine do something intentional to irritate the crap out of other one
- each of them laugh at something the other one does that usually makes them crazy
- the hero and heroine find something about the other one that they like or admire

- the couple bickers or argues about their oppositeness and resorts to a romantic interlude to conclude...but not solve...the argument
- another conflict arises from the initial opposite-ness-based conflict
- a friend, family member, or colleague tells the hero or heroine it will never work between the hero and heroine
- the couple's opposite qualities work well together to solve a minor problem
- the couple's opposite qualities work well together in the romance department
- when faced with the major plot problem, the couple's opposite qualities work against each other and cause them to fail to solve a (or the) major problem

THINGS TO THINK ABOUT WHEN WRITING THIS TROPE

Who are your hero and heroine and in what way are they opposite?

What are the core morals, ethics, and values the hero and heroine have in common?

How to the hero and heroine meet? How does it highlight their opposite qualities?

Do they already know each other when your story starts or have they never met before? If the hero and heroine already know each other, how do they know each other?

What drives them crazy about each other the instant they meet?

What causes a tiny spark of attraction between the hero and heroine when they meet? What do they notice about each other that keeps them from simply despising the other one?

What plot problem is going to force the hero and heroine to come into repeated proximity with each other over the course of the story?

What about that problem will ultimately force them to interact with each other repeatedly?

Can you make that plot problem more complicated? Bigger? Require the hero and heroine to interact a lot more?

How do their opposite qualities mesh to work well on the plot problem together?

How do their opposite qualities clash to work against each other on the plot problem and cause delays, setbacks, and failures?

How does the plot problem parallel their relationship problem(s)?

What is something related to or adjacent to the original thing that they're opposite about that they can also be opposite about? Is there another opposite quality they can have?

What brings the couple together for their first romantic moment?

What do they each think about the possibility of a romance with this irritating, annoying, frustrating person?

How does their opposite-ness work well together romantically?

What do the people around this couple think of their budding romance? Do they think there's no way it will work, or do they see the benefit of the couple's strengths and weaknesses complimenting each other?

Does anyone around the hero and heroine try to sabotage the relationship? If so, who, how, and why?

What changes do the hero and heroine each make over the course of the story?

What causes each of them to backslide into their old habits or way of being? What does that look like? Do they do it intentionally or unconsciously? How does the other one react?

How does the couple's failure to resolve their differences cause the major failure to resolve the big plot problem? What are the consequences of this failure? Can you make the consequences worse? Much worse?

What finally causes the differences between the hero and heroine to blow up into a relationship crisis that tears them apart?

Do the big plot crisis and big relationship crisis mirror each other? Does one cause the other, and if so, how?

What is the one big thing about the hero and heroine that they each just can't get past and that they cannot live with forever?

Who ultimately changes and how? What revelation or event happens to the person doing the changing that's powerful enough to motivate him/her to not only make the change but stick with it forever?

How will you demonstrate the hero/heroine's commitment to the new behavior? How is it tested? Can you make that test worse? Much worse?

How will the hero and heroine ultimately resolve the big plot problem? Does this happen before, at the same time, or after they resolve their "opposite" relationship issues? Does solving the plot problem help them resolve their relationship or vice versa?

Who apologizes to whom? How, when, and why?

Who forgives whom? How, when, and why?

Will the couple compromise or does one of them capitulate entirely to a new way of being?

What does happily ever after look like for this couple?

TROPE TRAPS

The hero and heroine hate each other so thoroughly when they meet that the audience doesn't believe they'll plausibly ever like each other, let alone love each other.

The hero or heroine is so unlikable initially that your audience hates him or her and never warms up to him or her.

One or both of the main characters doesn't become likable until so late in your story that much of your audience has quit reading/watching.

The hero and heroine have nothing at all in common from the beginning to make any romance between them seem plausible.

Failing to explain why or how one or both main characters have adopted an extreme attitude or behavior about whatever it is that makes them uniquely different than most "average" people.

Failing to establish the core values, beliefs, morals, and ethics the hero and heroine have in common and how they learned or adopted those.

Failing to set up situations in your story in which the main characters get to see the other one's core values exposed and acted upon in a positive way.

The attraction between the hero and heroine seems forced or contrived in the midst of their bickering.

Arguing—genuine disagreement—is portrayed as sexy (it's not).

Relying on attraction or sex to get past their unresolved conflicts.

Bickering that crosses over from funny to mean,

One character is forced to do all the changing, growing, and evolving while the other character remains exactly as they were from the opening.

The plot problem has nothing to do with and is completely unaffected by the couple's relationship issues, and vice versa.

Your couple has one and only one minor area of disagreement, conflict, or oppositeness, and everything else between them is perfect yet this thing is (implausibly, unbelievably, or insanely picky) a deal breaker for the couple.

The area of oppositeness between the hero and heroine involves a core value, ethical belief or moral code that most people would never change or compromise on.

Nobody ever backslides as they try to change their behavior patterns.

Failing to test the changes the characters make so they can be together in front of the audience in a way that will let the other main character (and your audience) believe these characters have actually committed to changing forever.

There are no negative consequences to the plot problem when the lovers fail to resolve their differences and/or break up.

Introducing a friend, neighbor, or coworker who's so much better suited to be the love interest that your audience roots for him or her to get the main character instead of your other main character.

Failing to convince your audience your main characters are more alike than they are different and that they're actually well-suited for each other even if they don't appear that way at first or on the surface.

The event or revelation that causes one or both of the main characters to change behavior isn't significant enough to provoke a plausibly permanent change in behavior.

The opposite-ness between the hero and heroine never causes serious problems or outright failure in dealing with the big plot problem.

Nobody ever apologizes for behaving badly, if one or both of the main characters did behave badly.

Failing to show your audience this couple embarking on or fully living their happily ever after...happily and peacefully.

OPPOSITES ATTRACT TROPE IN ACTION
Movies:

- Pretty Woman
- The Proposal
- Grease
- The Breakfast Club
- 10 Things I Hate About You
- Notting Hill
- Harold and Maude

Books:

- Pride and Prejudice by Jane Austen
- The Hating Game by Sally Thorne

- Me Before You by Jojo Moyes
- The Rosie Project by Graeme Simsion
- Act Like It by Lucy Parker
- Red, White & Royal Blue by Casey McQuiston
- The Wedding Date by Jasmine Guillory
- Beach Read by Emily Henry
- Ayesha at Last by Uzma Jalaluddin
- The Bromance Book Club by Lyssa Kay Adams

25
RAISING CHILD TOGETHER

DEFINITION

In this trope, two adults—neither of whom are a parent of the child—are tasked with or end up through chance or circumstance raising a child together. Over the course of the story, the adults end up falling in love, and by the end, they've formed a new family.

If one of the adults were the parent, he or she would be the clear decision maker and primary caregiver. But in this trope, the key is the two adults must work together to raise the child.

In reality, the child in this trope is a MacGuffin, which is to say the child is mainly the excuse for these two adults being forced together to live, work, parent a child in close proximity, fight, laugh, get to know each other, and eventually fall in love. But, because this MacGuffin is a living, breathing person with opinions, wants, and needs of his or her own, the child can be quite a lively MacGuffin who throws complications and monkey wrenches into the story that an inanimate MacGuffin cannot.

Two adults might have been named the godparents of a child who's later orphaned. They could have been named co-guardians in a will. One of them may find a child and the other may be an employee of the first adult and be recruited to help deal with the child until family members or authorities can come for the child. Feel free to be creative in how you force your future lovers together to deal with this small, messy, human MacGuffin.

There can, of course, be more than one child, and the child(ren) can be any age in your story. It goes without saying that children of different ages each pose their own special parenting challenges that will form much of the plot and parenting conflict in your story.

This trope almost always includes humor as an element both because children are delightful and funny but also because humor is often the best tool for dealing with the stresses of parenting.

The external plot of the story may revolve around finding the identity of a child and locating living family members to claim the child. The plot may revolve around working through the government child protection/foster care/adoption system. It might revolve around one or both adult caregivers trying to break a will or get out of being responsible for the child. There may be a threat to the child that provides suspense and the external plot.

The love story revolves around the adult caregivers getting to know each other if they don't already, figuring out how to parent a child and co-parent together, and falling in love.

The internal plot of the story likely revolves around the reasons why these two adults aren't already married to other people and raising children of their own already. It may revolve around their personal hang-ups about family and parenthood or about why these adults have, to date, chosen something else in their life over family and children.

At its core, this is a story about creating a family.

ADJACENT TROPES

- Baby On the Doorstep
- Instant Family
- Nanny/Teacher and Single Parent

- Single parent
- Is the Baby Mine

WHY READERS/VIEWERS LOVE THIS TROPE

- having to raise a child forces characters to mature and develop into true adults and become their best selves... something we all want for our co-parent(s) of our children
- for those who don't have a family but want one, the fantasy of not only a child but a partner in raising the child landing in your lap out of nowhere is a powerful one
- we love watching a healthy, loving family unit form out of nothing and wish for the same type of family in our own lives
- the funny, scary, frustrating, challenging situations the main characters find themselves in are deeply relatable and familiar to anyone who's ever raised a child
- becoming a parent reveals your deepest hopes, dreams, and fears and forces you to deal with them, and we get to do this vicariously through the parents in this story
- the dynamics of a family coming with built in conflict and stresses that we're all intimately familiar with and can sympathize with the main characters having to navigate...hopefully successfully, and hopefully teaching us how to do it better

OBLIGATORY SCENES

. . .

THE BEGINNING:

We may get a brief glimpse of the two adult's normal, childless lives before the inciting incident. Typically, the adults are busy, happy, fully engaged in their own lives, or at a minimum, they're very busy and deeply engaged in a life that no way, no how a child would fit into.

Then the inciting incident happens. It may be:

- The audience seeing the child's actual parent(s)/guardian(s) dying, particularly if this is a suspenseful story where some sort of danger is going to follow the child.
- The reading of a will naming the adults who have been chosen to raise the surviving child.
- Notification in person, by phone, or by mail/email to the two adults that they have been assigned custody of a child.
- A lawyer or government official showing up at their door with a child in tow.
- One or both of the adults finding the child and taking him or her in while they search for the missing parents.

Typically, one or both adults want NOTHING to do with having responsibility for raising a child. But the will is ironclad or the situation is such that there's no other alternative for now. Until the situation is straightened out or dealt with in some way, these two adults are stuck with this child.

The two adult guardians may or may not know each other. Their first moment of personal connection may be commiserating over how on earth they got stuck in this predicament.

The beginning may end with the adults taking delivery of the child if there's an elaborate set-up of how this custody arrangement has come about. Or the beginning may end with the first parenting disaster where the child's presence completely blows up some event, relationship, job, encounter, or physical space in the adults' lives.

THE MIDDLE:

In this story it's literally accurate to say that shenanigans ensue. Children as characters are nothing if not sources of shenanigans!

The journey of learning how to raise a child isn't easy in the best of circumstances with the most committed and eager of parents. But having to go from knowing nothing about raising a child and having no immediate plans to do so, to being thrust right into the middle of it is a difficult and challenging transition for anyone.

Then, to have to go through this really difficult challenge with a stranger, or an old friend but not one whom you've ever considered parenting with, makes the adjustment to being an overnight parent even more stressful.

As the two adults try to figure out how to be parents, who's responsible for what, how to divide and conquer the parenting responsibilities, and trying to mesh their separate and largely unformed parenting styles, they get to know each other. They'll undoubtedly have disagreements and outright fights, but they'll also share laughter, tender moments, and sweet encounters with and about the child.

As the adults fall in love with the child, they also fall in love with each other. This tends to be a slow-burn romance given the many time constraints and distractions inherent in raising a child as a new parent. It's not uncommon to be very near the end of the middle before the adults figure out they have feelings for each other.

These stories tend not to be ultra sexy simply because exhaustion and lack of free time tend to dampen the ability for the adults to spend lots of time having raunchy or wild sex. That said, if you can make a steamy or hot story work in the midst of two people becoming parents, more power to you!

Through the middle of the story, the external plot problem simmers early while parenting shenanigans take center stage but then starts to make itself more and more felt as the story progresses. As the adults get the hang of being parents and domestic crises tend to diminish, that's when the external problem rises to the fore.

Likewise, the more exhausted the adults get as the story progresses, the more their personal hang-ups and conflicts with each other will tend to surface. The presence of a child and the unexpected role of parent may cause havoc on one or both of the adults' pre-child lives, and these problems also build to a crisis as the middle of the story concludes.

Last but not least in this conflict-rich trope, the personal, relationship-based conflicts brewing between these two adults who've been thrust together to more or less live as spouses build toward a crisis by the end of the middle of the story.

BLACK MOMENT:

All the conflicts you've chosen to build into your story explode. One may cause a cascade of other crises, or they may all be interlinked. However you've chosen to construct the various tensions in the plot, everything—literally everything—falls apart. The adults may lose jobs, other romantic relationships, friends, their entire life prior to becoming a parent.

The romantic relationship between the two parents implodes. This may arise from their own personal hang-ups roaring forth to destroy the relationship. They may have some conflict of values, beliefs or ethics that they can't resolve. They may have an intractable disagreement having to do with their differing parenting styles or decisions. Or, they may have some conflict between them that has nothing whatsoever to do with the child but that they fail to resolve. Regardless of what does it, the lovers break up...and break up the budding family while they're at it.

Something goes terribly wrong as a result of a major parenting mistake. The child is hurt, sick, hospitalized, lost, run away, or in some kind of grave danger. The adults blame themselves for it or may blame each other. They realize, too late, how much they love the child and how desperately they want to be good parents and keep the child safe, happy, and healthy.

The external plot turns into a full-blown catastrophe and goes absolutely as wrong as it can. For example, the adults did something at the beginning of the story to attempt to relinquish custody of or responsibility for the child. They filed a motion with a court, made an official request of someone else to take the child, or the like.

By late in the story, however, the adults have changed their minds. They want to keep custody of the child and remain a family. But their earlier attempt to get rid of the child is finally granted and provokes the black moment, when the parents lose custody of the child and the child may actually be taken away from them. Not only are they devastated, but the child is also devastated. The adults have potentially promised the child they'll never leave the child, never abandon the child, or the child will never be alone...but now that has happened.

All is lost and the family unit is obliterated.

THE END:

The adults have to repair their own relationship AND they have to repair the destroyed family. But doing both of these things takes maturity, selflessness, and potentially is very hard. Which is to say, the adults have to learn lessons, have epiphanies, change for the better and grow up before they can fix all the terrible things that happened in the black moment and put their family back together again.

The order that all the problems get fixed in and the conflicts get resolved in can vary greatly in this trope. Sometimes the child is saved first and then the couple fixes their relationship problems. Sometimes the couple must reconcile before they can convince a court or official that they're fit to be parents and get the child back. Sometimes the lessons and epiphanies happen first, sometimes they happen somewhere in the middle of trying to repair the disaster.

That said, the ending usually includes most or all of the following elements in whatever order makes sense for your story:

- Lessons and epiphanies.
- Reconciling the adults as a couple.
- Recovering custody of the child, saving the child, or making the child safe.
- Restoring the family legally.
- Restoring the family in private at a personal level.
- Making apologies.
- New promises never to break up the family again.

It's important in this trope to give your audience a glimpse of the family unit fully restored, happy, safe, and living together. Readers and viewers get very worried about children and will insist on seeing with their own two eyes that the child is safe and happy.

So, this story ends with the family established as a forever family, the adjustments to parenthood complete in the adults' lives, the adults are a happy couple, and they all live together in a safe, happy home.

KEY SCENES

- the first time the adults meet each other
- the first time the adults and child meet
- the presence of a child causes chaos or completely blows up each adult's life in some way
- the parenting goes terribly and one or both of them reach out to other friends, family, coworkers, or parents for help and advice

- whoever's been helping the new parents get the hang of it refuses to bail the adults out of some parenting crisis, saying the only way to figure it out is to deal with it themselves
- the hero and heroine commiserate in their exhaustion
- a romantic moment is interrupted by the child
- the hero and heroine disagree strongly about some parenting decision
- the hero and heroine each lose something really important to them because of having to raise this child
- the new parents get cocky and think they've got this parenting thing licked when the child does something unpredictable that nearly gets the child hurt, possibly seriously
- the first love scene or romantic encounter between the parents…and it complicates one or both of their "real, pre-child lives" or causes some huge complication to their current situation

THINGS TO THINK ABOUT WHEN WRITING THIS TROPE

Who's the child and who are the adults to the child? Do the two adults know the child's parents? Do they know each other?

Why are these two adults named to raise the child? Are they simply in the right place at the right time to save the child and take it in? Is one or both of them very rich and well able to give a child a good life? Is one or both of them a close friend of the child's parent(s)?

What happens to the child's parent(s) to trigger this custody arrangement?

Is the custody of the child permanent or temporary? Why? If temporary, for how long?

What are each of the new parents' lives like before the child comes along? How would having a child totally wreck their lives?

Why don't each of these adults have a family or child of their own already?

How old is the child? Is it more than one child?

How does the child feel about this custody arrangement? How does he/she express these feelings? How does it affect his/her behavior?

Based on the child's age, what are some age-appropriate parenting challenges for kids of that age and developmental level? What are some challenges of raising a slightly younger child in case this child regresses in behavior somewhat in response to the stresses of this new situation?

How do the two adult guardians each find out they've been given responsibility for raising this child? Is it a surprise to them or not? How are they each notified? How do they react to the news? Is there other news, like the death of a close friend, that they also react to?

How is the child delivered to these people?

Where will the two adults and the child live? Whose home? Is it outfitted for kids or not? If not...how not child-proofed, not child friendly is it?

How are the two adults different and living different, clashing lives?

What do the two adults have in common beneath the very different surfaces of their lives?

What drives them crazy in a bad way about each other?

What drives them crazy in a good way about each other?

Which of the adults does what initially when it comes to caring for the child? Does one of them do most of the parenting, or do they split it equally?

Does either adult have any experience raising a child of this age? If so, what experience and when?

How is this child very different from any other children they've had experience with, such that even the experienced parent feels out of his or her depth and unsure?

How do the adults' lives get completely destroyed by the abrupt introduction of a child into them?

What are some adorable, funny, or groan-worthy things the child does or says that will tickle your audience and make the audience like the child?

How do the two adults first notice feeling attraction for the other one? Do they say anything about it or do anything about it…or do they ignore it initially?

How do they both first feel mutual sparks at the same time with each other? Where? When? What happens in response?

What people around the couple help them with the child? At what point do these people stop helping and force the new parents to figure it out for themselves?

What's the external plot problem in your story?

Do the new parents initially try to get out of being parents? Do they do anything that comes back to bite them late in the story like file a court motion to get out of being custodial parents?

Is there any danger to the child? Is this an external danger…like someone's trying to kidnap the child and collect a fat ransom? Or is it an internal danger…like the child has an illness that needs care?

How will the child be protected from danger if there is any and by whom?

How do the new parents make parenting decisions together for the child? What's a decision they disagree about but must find a compromise solution for?

What sort of routine does the family settle into as it finds a rhythm together?

What personal hang-ups or emotional baggage do each of the adults have about being a parent?

What conflict(s), completely separate from the child, do the two new parents have with each other? How will these become bigger and bigger and cause more and more conflict and problems as the story progresses?

What event triggers the series of black moment crises, failures, and breakups?

What happens to the child as everything falls apart? Where does he or she land? Is the child safe or not? If not, who's doing what frantically to make the child safe once more?

Does either parent briefly return to his or her pre-child life and try to resume it? If so, how does that go? What does he or she think of that life having now experienced having a child and family of his or her own?

What lessons do each of the adults learn after they've lost everything? What causes them to have the epiphany or finally see the lesson?

Who apologizes to whom? Is the child owed an apology?

How will the external plot problem be resolved? Who has to do what to fix it? Do the adults have to get back together as a couple before the eternal plot problem can be solved? If so, why?

How will the adults work out their romantic relationship separate from the child?

How will the adults put the family back together? Do they need to make promises to the child and then follow through on those promises in some way before the family is restored (or fully restored)?

What does happily ever after look like for this family? Where will they live? Who's doing what for work, daily life, leisure, family time?

TROPE TRAPS

Someone else would logically end up with custody of this child and not the two adults who ended up with him or her.

A relative or government agency would step forward to take custody of the child or do it much sooner than actually happens in the story.

No sane parent would have left these two people in charge of their child and no good reason is given for why it happened like this.

The abrupt custody of a child doesn't cause chaos in one or both adults' lives. Just how boring are they that instant parenthood doesn't cause any problems?

The two adults are wildly mismatched with each other and have disconnects in their core values, morals, ethics, and beliefs that would a) cause any long-term relationship between them to be very likely to fail, and b) make for lousy parenting with lots of strife and mixed messages to the child.

No romantic chemistry is established between the two parents.

Too much romantic chemistry to be plausible in the midst of being new parents is established between the two parents.

Failing to develop a fully realized love story between the adults in and around their learning to be parents and learning to be a family unit.

Relying on the child to always be the interruption that stops the adults from having romantic moments or love scenes, depending on the heat of your story.

The parents seem to decide to be a couple because it's convenient and not because they genuinely have feelings for each other.

The child acts and speaks WAY older and wiser than his or her age would suggest.

We don't see the adults growing up and maturing over the course of the story as they transition into being parents.

The parents magically get time to themselves for romantic interludes without explaining who's keeping an eye on the child.

The new parents never make mistakes or do anything dumb, selfish, or thoughtless.

The new parents argue in front of the child enough or seriously enough to scare the child.

The child adapts too quickly to the new situation or not quickly enough to be plausible to your audience.

The external plot problem and internal or romantic conflicts have no impact on or relationship to one another and the story feels disjointed.

People who should apologize to others don't.

Forgetting to give the child an apology if one is owed.

Never asking the child what he or she wants if the child is of an age to speak.

Doing the pieces of resolving the story in an order that doesn't make sense.

Failing to show the family happy and together and the child safe, healthy, and happy by the end of your story.

RAISING CHILD TOGETHER TROPE IN ACTION
Movies:

- Raising Helen
- Life As We Know It
- Instant Family
- About A Boy
- Three Men and A Baby
- Two Is a Family
- Martian Child

Books:

- Maybe This Time by Jennifer Crusie
- The Substitute by Denise Grover Swank
- A Family for the Billionaire by Dani Wade
- The Bridesmaid's Baby Bump by Kandy Shepherd
- Surprise Baby, Second Chance by Therese Beharrie
- Suddenly a Father by Michelle Major

- Falling for the Foster Mom by Kathy Douglass
- His Baby Dilemma by Catherine Lanigan

26
RIGHT UNDER YOUR NOSE

DEFINITION

In this story, the main character is blissfully unaware of the future love interest who is already in close physical proximity to him or her. The love interest may or may not be aware of the main character, either. Which is to say, both of the main characters may begin this story having regular contact with each other but being completely oblivious to each other's existence.

Whereas in the Oblivious to Love trope the main character notices the love interest but never considers the love interest's romantic potential, in this trope the main character never even notices the love interest at all. The love interest is literally or figuratively right under the main character's nose but goes unnoticed until this story begins.

This trope almost always begins with a meet-cute, keeping in mind that the phrase merely refers to a clever, interesting, or entertaining way that the hero and heroine first meet and become part of each other's lives. This story necessarily begins with that moment.

Now, the main character and love interest don't have to fall in love or even be romantically interested immediately. They merely have to see the person who's been under their nose all along.

But having once seen the love interest, now the main character is extremely aware of him or her.

Typically something changes in the meet-cute that forces the hero and heroine to continue interacting as the story progresses.

Often this trope relies on an external plot problem of some kind to throw the hero and heroine together repeatedly or continuously so their romance can develop and grow.

This trope is often combined with another plot-based trope that shapes the external plot problem. (My various Tropoholic's Guides to Thrillers, Mystery, Sci-Fi, Fantasy, Westerns, and Melodrama, for example, contain largely plot-based tropes.)

At any rate, this trope may also be combined with another character or relationship-based trope that acts as an obstacle to love and explains why the hero and heroine don't immediately fall in love after having finally noticed each other.

ADJACENT TROPES

- Oblivious to Love/Belated Epiphany
- Girl/Boy Next Door
- Best Friend's Sister/Ex
- In Love With the Wrong Person
- Unrequited Love
- Boss-Employee
- Ugly Duckling
- Makeover

WHY READERS/VIEWERS LOVE THIS TROPE

- going from unseen to seen is a powerful moment of

recognition and acknowledgement of lovability for any person
- the fantasy that our own everyday interactions with others might abruptly shift and turn into something magical and romantic
- these characters have a shared history, even if they're not aware of it, that feels more intimate and stable than meeting a complete stranger and trying to form a relationship
- your audience realizes the potential for romance before the hero and heroine do, which readers and viewers find engaging and are eager to see play out

OBLIGATORY SCENES

THE BEGINNING:

You may choose to start the story by establishing how the lives of the hero and heroine intersect and how they actually cross paths, see each other, or even interact with each other regularly...but without ever having really noticed each other. In this case, the meet-cute isn't the first scene of your story. Rather, it's more likely to be the second or third scene.

You may also choose to establish that one of your future lovers is, in fact, vividly aware of the other one before the meet-cute. He or she may have a crush on the oblivious main character or may even be in love with him or her.

Something happens to force the main character to notice the right under his or her nose love interest. Typically this meeting not only makes the hero and heroine aware of each other, but it also sets up a situation in which they're going to have to actively interact with each other again going forward.

You may choose to establish why the main character(s) is oblivious to someone whom he or she already has contact with, is acquainted with, or sees regularly.

If the meet-cute doesn't set up the external plot problem that's going to force the hero and heroine to interact with each other going forward, that's also set up in the beginning (typically immediately after the meet-cute).

Lastly, the beginning usually establishes the reason why the main character is oblivious to, objects to, or fears a romantic relationship. Vice versa, the beginning sets up whatever issues the love interest has with love…or with loving this particular person who has ignored his or her existence for some amount of time.

The beginning often ends with the moment that the hero and heroine first experience a mutual romantic spark.

THE MIDDLE:

It's not uncommon for the main character or love interest to think it's a terrible idea to develop romantic feelings for the other person and to recoil from that first romantic spark or to resist it…sometimes forcefully.

Often, an issue for the love interest to overcome before he or she can fall in love with the main character is finding out why the main character totally ignored or didn't notice him or her. Indeed, the main character may owe the love interest an apology or amends for his or her oversight or outright ignoring of the love interest in the past. If you're using some sort of transformation trope for the love interest, that transformation may have already taken place by the time the main character finally notices him or her. Or the transformation may begin and then the love interest gets noticed.

Personally, I'm not a big fan of stories where a character has to change physical appearance to become lovable and neither is the general public these days. You can certainly write this type of story, but be careful about sending out a message of anyone having to look a specific or certain way to be "lovable".

That said, a story of personal transformation can be one of gaining confidence, overcoming crippling shyness, or in some other way changing one's life or attitude in a way that makes the love interest more noticeable to the main character. If you're using this trope, it is typically completed sometime in the middle of the story so that the love interest is ready, able, and willing to explore a fully romantic relationship with the main character before the end of the story.

The external events and/or plot problem in your story throw the hero and heroine together, whether they like it or not. And now that they're aware of each other, they're vividly aware of each other and can't unsee each other.

The romance typically develops in a pretty straightforward way. They don't want to be in love, they have obstacles to falling in love, they fight the romance while being forced to work together to overcome or solve an external problem, and bit by bit, they get to know each other. The more they get to know each other, the more they find to love about each other. The more time they spend together, the more romantic sparks they experience, and the harder they find it to resist each other.

They eventually give in to their feelings and have a romantic interlude or express their romantic feelings for each other.

This event causes a whole new set of complications. Either it greatly complicates their relationship, one of both of their relationships with someone else, or it complicates solving the plot problem. It may also set off a series of internal, personal crises as the hero and/or heroine have to deal with their personal hang-ups, wounds, traumas, fears, or emotional baggage regarding being in love in general.

The problems, conflicts, and growing romance of the middle of the story all build toward a crisis that explodes to end the middle of the story.

. . .

BLACK MOMENT:

This is when everything falls apart. The external plot problem explodes into a crisis and the hero and heroine fail to resolve it. Things go as badly as they can possibly go. At the same time, the hero and heroine's relationship implodes and falls apart.

The main character may revert to his or her old behavior of ignoring the existence of the love interest. Or, in the moment of crisis, the main character may completely fail to reach out to the love interest for help and support in a way that makes the love interest feel completely unseen once more.

Whatever internal or personal issues the hero and heroine have been having with the idea of love or of loving in a healthy, positive way come crashing back. Any personal insecurities, wounds, fears, or emotional baggage do their worst and break up the lovers or mess with their heads until they break up.

There seems to be no way out of this internal and external crisis. There's no visible path forward, no solutions, and no hope.

THE END:

The ending typically begins with the hero and heroine taking a hard look at themselves and having some sort of epiphany or learning some lesson about what they did or didn't do that caused their relationship to fail.

The hero and/or heroine gets new information, new help, or finds a new way of thinking about the external plot problem that makes a possible resolution seem possible—if not easy, at least possible.

The hero and heroine may need to work together to solve the plot problem, which is an excellent opportunity for them to be forced back into physical proximity with each other once more. Being together is also an opportunity for the main character to demonstrate that he or she sees the love interest and notices him or her.

The act of resolving the external plot problem may be the same moment the hero and heroine resolve their personal relationship problems. Or they may need to resolve their relationship and then solve the big plot problem, or vice versa. Traditionally, the relationship is the most important element of a romance novel, and in that case, it would be resolved last.

If you're writing a story where the romantic relationship is a secondary plot and the external plot problem is your primary story line, you may choose to resolve the romantic relationship first and then solve the big, external plot problem.

It's not uncommon in this trope for the main character to make some sort of grand gesture of apology, love, and "I see you" to the love interest. It tends to be public, dramatic, and possibly over the top. You might take inspiration from the meet-cute in designing this grand gesture. If the meet-cute and grand gesture mirror each other or in some way relate to each other, it creates elegant bookends at each end of your story.

Armed with new information and new personal strength and resolve, the hero and heroine resolve the big plot problem, clearing the last obstacles from their path to true love and happily ever after.

Lessons learned, apologies made and accepted, grand gestures of love and appreciation delivered, the couple reconciles, this time in a healthy, happy relationship free of the wounds, fears, traumas, and issues that made it problematic in the past.

They move forward together into their future together, and your audience leaves your story deeply satisfied and convinced that these two people are headed for their well-deserved storybook ending.

KEY SCENES

- the love interest is ignored by the main character and reacts to it (with annoyance, hurt, frustration, or some other strong emotion)
- the love interest ignores or doesn't notice the main character at some point after they're engaged in a

relationship and it bothers the main character...and may be a learning moment
- the main character acknowledges or recognizes the love interest in some public way in front of other people for the first time
- the love interest tells the main character that he or she ignored or didn't notice him or her and how it made the love interest feel whenever he/she did that
- the hero and heroine resist the budding romance they sense starting to develop between them
- someone sabotages their relationship or tells one of them this relationship will never work
- after the first big romantic encounter (depending on the heat level of your story this might be a love scene, a kiss, or even a simple touch) a big complication happens
- the potential consequences of that big complication if the hero and heroine don't break up are made clear (and this may happen before the first big romantic encounter)
- the external plot problem causes complications/conflict in their relationship and vice versa
- the main character ignores the love interest or fails to turn to the love interest for support in a small way, foreshadowing the black moment when the main character does it in a big way

THINGS TO THINK ABOUT WHEN WRITING THIS TROPE

Who are the hero and heroine and how do their lives intersect before this story begins?

Do they actually know each other before the story begins? If so, how? How well do they know each other? How much do they know about each other?

Why does the main character have zero romantic interest in the love interest when or just before the story begins?

How does the love interest feel about the main character just before the story begins and before the main character notices him or her for the first time?

How does the main character finally notice the love interest for the first time?

How does this first meeting set the tone and mood for the rest of the story?

Does the first meeting set up the external plot problem? If so, what's that problem? If not, how will you introduce the big, external plot problem of your story?

What's the tone, mood, and danger level of the big plot problem in your story?

Does the love interest undertake some sort of self-transformation project before or during your story? If so, what is it?

What's the potential risk of offending some audience members with the type of transformation you've chosen, and how will you handle it in a way that doesn't get you negative blowback?

Does the love interest undertake some project or scheme to attract the notice of the main character or not? If so, what is it and why?

How do the hero and heroine feel about each other immediately after the meet-cute?

What about your story is going to force the hero and heroine into each other's physical proximity repeatedly and force them to interact for long enough to get to know each other and fall in love?

What attracts these two people strongly to each other?

What do they like about each other?

What do they dislike about each other?

Why hasn't the main character noticed the love interest before now? Why does he/she notice the love interest in a big way *now*? What's changed from before till now to make the main character abruptly so aware of the love interest?

What personal wounds, fears, trauma, or misbeliefs do the hero and heroine each bring to this romantic relationship? How will they be forced to face these things by the other person or by events over the course of the story?

Which of their friends, families, or coworkers supports this relationship? Why and how?

Which of their friends, families, or coworkers sabotages this relationship? Why and how?

How does the external plot problem pose growing problems for the couple's relationship?

How does the couple's growing relationship cause growing problems for the external plot problem?

What complication or bad thing will happen if this couple goes ahead and falls in love and gets together as a couple? Can you make it worse? Much worse?

Do they have an "almost" encounter before the first big one that gets interrupted or that one of them stops for some reason? If so, what happens and how is the "almost" encounter halted?

When and how do the hero and heroine have their first big romantic encounter?

What's the worst thing that could happen if the hero and heroine fail to resolve the big, external plot problem? Can you make that worse? Much worse? Even more awful?

When does the main character revert to his or her old pattern of ignoring or not seeing the love interest? How does the love interest react? Can you make that reaction bigger? Worse? More dramatic? More problematic?

Does the big crisis in the plot problem provoke the hero and heroine to break up or vice versa? If they don't cause each other, which one happens first? Why?

What personal issue causes the hero and heroine to break up?

How do the main character and love interest individually feel after they've broken up? Do they feel self-blame? Anger? Shame? Guilt? Something else?

In the painful aftermath of their breakup, what lesson(s) do the hero and heroine learn about themselves and about their relationship? Do they need to make changes in themselves or their behaviors going forward? How will you show the audience each character making these changes?

What new information, new help, or new perspective do the hero and/or heroine get that makes it seem possible to resolve the big external plot problem now, when it didn't seem possible before or when the hero and heroine utterly failed to resolve it before?

How will the hero and heroine resolve the big plot problem?

In what order will you resolve the big external plot problem and the hero and heroine's relationship?

Who apologizes to whom?

Does the main character make a grand gesture of some kind to the love interest? If so, what is it? How is it received?

How will you show your audience the hero and heroine's commitment to being their best selves for the long term?

What does happily ever after look like for this couple and how will you give a glimpse of that to your audience?

TROPE TRAPS

The main character is so unlikable, arrogant, or oblivious at the beginning that your audience never warms up to him or her.

The love interest is so shy, mousy, self-effacing, or insecure at the beginning that your audience never warms up to him or her.

The main character comes across as extremely rude for failing to notice this other human being existing right under his or her nose.

The meet-cute is so implausible or contrived that the audience isn't willing to suspend its disbelief to go along with it.

The main character's sudden and intense interest in the love interest after the meet-cute doesn't come across as reasonable, plausible, or realistic.

Failing to explain why, if the main character is so attracted to the love interest now, why wasn't he or she yesterday?

Relying solely on a physical transformation or makeover of the love interest to explain why the main character now notices the love interest and making the main character come across as shallow, materialistic, or only able to see the love interest's surface and not the real person.

Failing to give the love interest his or her own character arc and having him or her act only as a MacGuffin that the main character does or doesn't notice.

Failing to set up any real conflicts between the hero and heroine once they've met that threaten the survivability of their relationship.

The main character had a great reason for not getting into a relationship before noticing the love interest but you fail to explain or resolve that reason in your story.

Failing to explain why the main character is completely oblivious to anyone, let alone the love interest.

Failing to create any negative complications to the hero and heroine getting together as a couple and your story lacking any tension as a result.

The big external plot problem has no impact on the hero and heroine's relationship and vice versa.

The reason the hero and heroine fail to solve the big plot problem going into the black moment is lame, stupid, or contrived, and your audience doesn't buy it.

There's an obvious solution to the big plot problem that your characters completely fail to see but every audience member sees clearly, hence your hero and heroine come off as too stupid to live.

The reason the hero and heroine break up seems lame, dumb, or implausible to your audience.

The hero and heroine don't have any major epiphanies or learn any lessons before they get back together and are the same people who broke up before when they reconcile...leading your audience to believe they won't end up staying together for the long term.

The big external plot problem fixes itself and the hero and heroine don't actively have to do anything to resolve it and clear the way for themselves to be together.

No apologies are made for mistakes or bad behavior.

By the end of the story, your audience doesn't think the main character has suffered enough or changed enough to deserve the love interest.

Your audience thinks the love interest shouldn't take back the hero and is weak, self-destructive, or lacks enough self-esteem to deserve a happy relationship with a loving, attentive, respectful partner.

RIGHT UNDER YOUR NOSE TROPE IN ACTION
Movies:

- When Harry Met Sally
- Clueless
- 13 Going on 30
- Made of Honor
- Some Kind of Wonderful
- My Best Friend's Wedding
- 10 Things I Hate About You
- Just Friends
- Love, Rosie
- What If

Books:

- Emma by Jane Austen
- The Friend Zone by Abby Jimenez

- Josh and Hazel's Guide to Not Dating by Christina Lauren
- The Hating Game by Sally Thorne
- Attachments by Rainbow Rowell
- The Boy Next Door by Meg Cabot
- On Dublin Street by Samantha Young
- Friendship for Grown-Ups by Sophie Ranald

27
ROAD TRIP/ADVENTURE

DEFINITION

In this story, two people take a trip of some kind or travel together to some destination and fall in love along the way. There are endless reasons why two people might choose to travel together over days or weeks—and you'll need at least a few days of travel for your hero and heroine to get to know each other and plausibly fall in love.

The hero and heroine may or may not know each other when your story begins. Two strangers stranded at an airport might rent a car to get to the same destination. Or two best friends might take one last vacation together before one of them moves far away to a new home, job, or place.

What makes this trope interesting is that both characters are removed from their usual environments and their day-to-day lives for the duration of the trip. Their journey represents a complete departure from their ordinary worlds and thrusts both of them into new places, new situations, and the unknown...together.

It's likely this sense of the unknown and facing together any challenges that come their way is what pushes your hero and heroine together.

Also, this is a concentrated opportunity for your hero and heroine to get to know each other in a way that most people never experience. How often have you met someone and immediately spent days on end, from waking to sleep, being together with nothing better to do than talk and get to know each other?

The act of traveling removes the vast majority of life's distractions from this relationship. There are no kids to feed, no jobs to go to, no daily home chores to attend to. It's just you, the other person, and a strange new world going by.

A journey offers opportunities for challenges that one or both of your main characters may never have faced before. The pair will have to rely on their wits, their knowledge, their creativity, and their teamwork to overcome the obstacles you throw in their path to reaching their final destination.

There's a powerful sense of exploration and discovery built into this travel trope that mirrors the sense of exploration and discovery the hero and heroine do of each other. It's common for the journey itself to act as a metaphor for the unfolding romance growing between the travelers.

The tension in this trope arises from the ever-present and looming question of what will happen to the hero and heroine when they arrive at their final destinations and resume their ordinary lives? Will their relationship survive beyond the journey, or will it end along with the trip itself? It's this question that will keep your audience engaged in the story all the way through to the end.

At its core, this is a forced proximity trope, except in a place unfamiliar to either main character and to which they may never return.

ADJACENT TROPES

- Fresh Start
- Fish Out of Water/Cowboy In the City
- On the Run/Chase
- Quest/Search for the MacGuffin

- Runaway Bride/Groom
- Running Away
- Forced Proximity

WHY READERS/VIEWERS LOVE THIS TROPE

- traveling creates a sense of escape from real life and we all love the idea of getting away from absolutely everything and everyone in our lives for a little while
- we love the idea of going new places and seeing beautiful places…and how much better would that be if we could experience this with someone we love or while finding romance ourselves
- we love the idea of slowing down for once and taking the time to really get to know someone and have someone really get to know us
- feeling truly, deeply, intimately seen and loved by someone who knows more about us than anyone and still finds us lovable
- not having to go through something daunting, unfamiliar, or scary alone, but rather with someone who's there to support us and help us whenever we stumble or feel afraid

OBLIGATORY SCENES

THE BEGINNING:
The hero and heroine start a road trip or journey together. This may be set up by some sort of meet-cute. It may be spontaneous and

happen with little to no warning. Or the hero and heroine may have planned this trip for a long time, down to the last detail. How you set up this journey that your hero and heroine take, it will set the tone and mood for the rest of the story.

The journey begins. This may be easy or getting the journey started may be a huge project and the first major obstacle your hero and heroine must overcome together. They may have to find the last rental car in town. They may have to obtain a vehicle in which to make the journey. They may have to navigate a foreign language, unknown place, or strange culture to get the journey started at all.

Once they're on the road, the hero and heroine may need to overcome initial discomfort, strangeness between them, or some other obstacle to even talking and getting to know each other. The journey itself may dictate that they interact, however. For example, only one may speak the local language and be able to read road signs, but the other is the only one who can drive the vehicle they're in.

The hero and heroine start talking and getting to know each other. This trope threatens to become an entire story of talking heads, so it's important to consider the types of obstacles and action sequences you'll intersperse with what might otherwise become long, boring periods of traveling and talking.

The beginning usually ends with the first big problem in the journey. They run out of fuel. They get lost. Something is stolen from them. They have an argument. Sky's the limit on the first big problem you choose to throw at your travelers. The only requirement is that it should threaten to derail the entire journey and end it before it has hardly begun.

THE MIDDLE:

The same problem that threatens to derail the physical journey may be a metaphor for the first big relationship problem the travelers face.

In the middle, the hero and heroine will go back and forth

between getting along and getting to know each other better with running into things they dislike about each other, disagreeing on how to handle the various problems that come their way on the journey, and potentially the pesky attraction that start to form between them.

Sleeping arrangements could become an embarrassing (and sexy) problem. Sharing a bathroom, catching each other in compromising states of undress, close physical contact, or other shenanigans can plague their allegedly platonic trip together and cause the first romantic tension to form between them.

This talk-heavy couple may actually discuss the situation as they resume/continue traveling and reach some sort of accord about what the ground rules between them will be for their journey. Of course, your job as the writer is to force them to break every one of these ground rules along the way, breaking down the emotional, cultural, social, or other barriers between them.

The more the couple gets to know each other, the more they're attracted to each other. Because there's nothing to keep them apart and no one else to break up their budding romance, you the writer are likely to have to create some sort of complication or negative consequence that would occur should these two fall madly in love and decide to be together forever over the course of their journey together.

The middle is punctuated by setbacks, detours, side trips, and any conceivable problem you can cook up for the hero and heroine to be faced with along the way in their journey. Not only will they have multiple physical obstacles to completing the trip, but their relationship itself will have all of these same metaphorical obstacles.

The closer the hero and heroine grow and the more in love they fall, the more the end of the trip and whatever's waiting for each of them when they resume their real lives looms as a threat to their romance. They could have spouses or family obligations waiting for them. Their destinations may be in different places. They may have homes, jobs, family, friends, or other obligations to tend or places to be that will irrevocably separate them when their journey ends.

The hero and heroine may try to prolong the journey to hold off the inevitable, but the middle of the story ends with the big, external plot problem becoming a crisis or possibly with the end of the journey. Regardless of how it ends, the middle's ending is usually marked by the couple breaking up and going their own ways physically and/or metaphorically. Their magical journey is over.

BLACK MOMENT:

The hero and heroine part ways and return to their own lives but feel bereft and lost. Their real lives are no longer what they would choose for themselves if they had a choice. They long for a return to the escape from this reality they found with the other person.

If the journey's purpose was to help solve a big external plot problem, it has failed utterly. The journey was for naught, and all their suffering, hard work, and effort to complete the journey has come to nothing. Furthermore, they've lost the person they've come to love, and they feel that loss far more keenly than they expected to.

Indeed, neither the hero nor heroine wants to continue on in life without the other one. Except, they've said their goodbyes and walked away from each other with no intent to get back together. They've both lost their chance at love with each other.

THE END:

After trying to resume their "real" lives and being absolutely miserable, both the hero and heroine learn what and who it is that makes them truly happy. They each have to make major changes and potentially major sacrifices to walk away from their old lives and seek out each other.

The hero and heroine may have to solve the big plot problem before they can be together and they may work on their own or together to do so.

The hero and heroine may each have to make another physical or metaphorical journey—this time alone—to return to the other one and to find each other. But, once united, they both declare their love and desire to be together forever.

Finally, having overcome separation of a physical, emotional, and metaphorical nature, they vow never to be apart again. They've found each other again and know it for the miracle it is, and this time they're not going to turn their backs on their love.

They go forth into their new life together on a journey to and through happily ever after.

KEY SCENES

- leaving on the trip
- they get lost
- the first awkward sleeping situation
- the complication if they get romantically involved is laid out and possibly the negative effects demonstrated
- catastrophe strikes and they may have to abandon the trip altogether
- the awkwardness in the aftermath of a romantic encounter that was accidental or a mistake and having to sit together in close quarters and travel
- having to travel together during or after a major argument between them
- arriving at their destination and having to say goodbye
- one contacts the other (surreptitiously) after they've gone their own ways
- the realization that they hate their ordinary life and want the magical life from the journey back

THINGS TO THINK ABOUT WHEN WRITING THIS TROPE

Who are the hero and heroine?

Where do they want to go—individually or together? Why?

How are they going to take this trip? What conveyance will they use?

Do the hero and heroine know each other before this trip or not? If so, how? How close are they? How well do they know each other (or not)? Why do they decided to take this trip together?

If the hero and heroine have never met, why do they decide to take this trip together? Are they forced to do it? Do they have no choice? How do they feel about making this trip with this stranger?

What "real" life does each major character leave behind when they start the journey?

What real life awaits each major character at the end of their journey?

How talkative or not talkative are the hero and heroine? How will you get them talking to each other freely as the journey proceeds?

How long is the journey they're making? Is it going to run into major difficulties that extend it?

Map out the major secrets about themselves that each character will reveal to the other one over the course of the journey? What order makes sense for this person to tell these secrets and intimate, personal things about himself or herself?

What actions are going to happen in your story that keep it from being merely two people staring at a ribbon of highway talking to each other for the entire story?

Is there an external plot problem that will spice up this trip and give the hero and heroine non-road trip problems to overcome? How tense, suspenseful, or dangerous is the external plot problem? Can you make it bigger? Much bigger?

How can you force the hero and heroine off their intended route and force them to go in some whole new direction to get to their ultimate destination? How does this change mirror some aspect of their relationship and correspond to some large shift in it?

How does the entire journey acts as a symbol or metaphor for the hero and heroine's relationship as it forms, unfolds, and grows during the journey?

What do these characters disagree about adamantly?

What do the hero and heroine dislike about each other?

What do the hero and heroine admire about each other?

What common core values, morals, ethics, and/or beliefs do they share? How will they figure this out? Can you make the hero and heroine appear different enough on the surface that it surprises your audience members to find out these two people are actually a lot alike at a core level?

When does a setback in the journey provoke a setback in the hero and heroine's relationship?

When does a setback in the hero and heroine's relationship provoke a setback in the journey?

How does the romantic relationship unfold over the course of your story?

When is the first romantic spark between the hero and heroine? How do they each react to it?

Do the hero and heroine lay out any ground rules for behavior toward each other during the trip? How do they break every rule by the end of the journey? How do they feel about that?

At what point do the hero and heroine each or both stop eagerly anticipating arriving at their final destination and start dreading arriving at it? Why? Do they express this to each other or not? Why?

At what point in your story do you want to have the hero and heroine arrive at their final destination? The very end? Just before the black moment? Is their actual arrival the black moment? The middle of the story, acting as a midpoint reversal?

Is this the only or primary plot of your story? If so, how will you end the journey with a big bang?

Is this a secondary plot for your story? If so, when in the overarching story does it make sense for the journey to end?

Are the hero and heroine's efforts to get back together after they've parted ways more or less interesting than the journey itself? How will you devote the majority of your time in the story to the most interesting part of this love story?

How does the big external plot problem go as badly as it can possibly go? What or who causes this? Can you make it all go worse? Much worse?

What lessons about themselves and about each other do the hero and heroine learn over the course of their journey together?

How do these lessons allow them to make the changes necessary to have a healthy and happy long-term relationship together?

What new information, help, or insights do the hero and heroine get that finally help them resolve the big external plot problem?

How do the hero and heroine each feel when they say goodbye to each other at the end of their journey?

What do they each do after the journey ends and they part ways? How unhappy are they? Can you make them more unhappy? A lot more miserable?

What event brings the hero and heroine back together after they've parted ways forever or at least for a long time? Is it the big plot problem that draws them back together or something/someone else?

Do the hero and heroine have to get back together to deal with the big plot problem?

How does the reunion go? What outstanding personal, relationship issues remain between them in need of resolving when they finally get back together again?

How will the hero and heroine resolve their personal issues? Does someone apologize? Do they share their lessons learned with each other? Is it mostly a joyful reunion? Does someone make a grand gesture of love?

What things about their separate lives have to change for them to be together forever? How will they do these things? When in the story, which is to say, when do they start moving around their "real" life to be with the other person? How will you show these things to your audience? When does the other main character find out about these changes and accommodations?

What does happily ever after look like for this couple?

TROPE TRAPS

The hero and heroine could get where they're going by other means that makes more sense for each of them.

The trip they undertake is so difficult, ambitious or dangerous that it makes no sense for these two to embark on it without additional traveling companions (or more than they have).

The hero and heroine have so little in common that your audience doesn't buy the two of them ever falling in love.

The hero and heroine have clashing core values, morals, ethics, or beliefs that make a long-term, happy healthy relationship extremely unlikely.

The hero and heroine are romantically attracted too fast to be plausible or too slow to be plausible.

The story ends up being way too much talking heads and not very much ever happens in the story to break up the monotony.

The characters over share or under share about themselves over the course of the story and the audience knows too much or too little about them.

The number of personal secrets, revelations, or information shared is wildly unequal between the two main characters.

The characters are willing to reveal things about themselves that nobody would ever plausibly reveal, not even to a total stranger.

We never see the "real" lives of the two travelers when they're not on this journey, or they don't have "real" lives.

The hero and heroine's real lives never intrude into the magical separation from the real world that this journey constitutes.

The physical trip itself in no way mirrors the hero and heroine's journey to love and vice versa.

The hero and heroine never dread the end of the trip and saying goodbye to each other.

There are no setbacks, detours, or disasters along the way in this journey, and there's never any doubt that the journey will reach its planned conclusion.

The hero and heroine are never awkward together, never disagree, and never fight. Neither ever threatens to walk away from the journey.

After they've parted ways, there are no obstacles from their real lives to the hero and heroine getting back together as soon as they realize they hate being apart.

No one learns any lessons along the way about themselves, about their relationship, or about love or life.

The characters are unchanged at the end of their journey together.

Their happily ever after is extremely mundane, boring, regular, and contains none of the elements of magical separation and romantic love that they experienced on their journey of falling in love.

ROAD TRIP/ADVENTURE TROPE IN ACTION
Movies:

- Before Sunrise
- When Harry Met Sally
- Roman Holiday
- Midnight in Paris
- The Darjeeling Limited
- The Holiday
- Leap Year
- One Day

Books:

- People We Meet on Vacation by Emily Henry
- The Road Trip by Beth O'Leary
- Amy & Roger's Epic Detour by Morgan Matson
- One Italian Summer by Rebecca Serle
- The Tourist Attraction by Sarah Morgenthaler
- The Simple Wild by K.A. Tucker
- The Wanderlust Crew by Abbie Greaves
- Two Steps Forward by Graeme Simsion and Anne Buist
- Shipped by Angie Hockman
- The Friend Zone by Abby Jimenez

28
SECRET CRUSH/SECRET ADMIRER

DEFINITION

The main character in this trope has a secret crush on the love interest (who I'll also call the object of the crush, with the understanding that no person is ever an actual object), and at some point, the main character may anonymously let the love interest know someone is interested in him or her, at which point, the main character shifts into being a secret admirer.

The hero and heroine in this trope already know each other or are at least in close proximity to each other on a regular enough basis for one to have developed a crush on the other.

In today's technological age, it's certainly possible to have a crush on someone from afar and to act as a secret admirer online. But in this case, you'll need to be very careful that the admiring doesn't cross over into stalking and that the object of admiration doesn't file a restraining order. Also, the more remote the crush and admiration, the more difficult time you'll have plotting a story in which the person with the crush and the object of the crush can actually get together and have a fully realized love story.

It's possible to get to know people online, but it's more difficult to fall completely and fully in love with someone you've never met in person and to be sure you've found the person you want to spend the rest of your life with. Mind you, a fully online love connection is possible...just difficult. For the purposes of this trope entry, I'm going to assume that you're going to place the crusher and crushee into physical proximity when your story begins.

The object of the crush is typically a physically attractive person with other admirable qualities that are frequently on public display and which explain why the person with the crush develops it in the first place.

However, the main character is usually too shy to tell the object of his or her crush that he/she is interested in them. Or there may be a compelling reason why the crusher feels he or she cannot tell the crushee about the crush. They may come from extremely different cultural or financial backgrounds. One may be the boss of the other and it wouldn't be appropriate. One may be a cop doing surveillance on the family of a mobster and who develops a crush on the mobster's daughter. You get the idea.

At any rate, the movement of this story is created by the main character working up the nerve or overcoming the obstacles to telling the person he/she admires that the main character likes him or her.

Once this gigantic obstacle is overcome, a whole new set of obstacles present themselves and now must be overcome by the couple as they get to know each other. The main character finally gets to know the love interest for real and replaces his or her imagined wonderful qualities with his or her real ones. Meanwhile, the object of the crush is probably starting from zero and having to learn everything about his or her admirer.

This trope often explores the differences between an imagined lover and the real version of that person or it explores an imagined romantic relationship versus a real one.

It's worth noting that the idealized version of most people rarely lives up to the reality. Often this trope is used as a secondary trope wherein the person with the crush meets the object of their crush, only to be deeply disappointed, but in the meantime meets someone who's genuinely wonderful and who's right under his or her nose until he/she wakes up and realizes a real romantic love is right in front of him or her.

This trope can also explore the insecurities that cause people to be too afraid to tell someone else they're interesting or that they'd like to get to know another person better. If the story is primarily about the person with the secret crush or doing the secret admiring, this story arc explores what it takes to overcome crippling shyness, insecurity, or low self-esteem to take a chance and try to make a romantic connection with someone else.

Because the character with the secret crush has such a major journey of growth and change before he or she can even bring himself/herself to the point of meeting the object of their crush, this is almost always a very slow burn love story. It may be the midpoint of the entire story before the main character and love interest even meet each other.

To remedy the potential boredom of your audience, given how slowly this story has the potential to move, you can start your story well after the main character has developed his or her secret crush and dive into his or her story arc at the point when he or she has lost patience with self and is on the verge of taking the plunge and introducing himself or herself to the love interest.

Alternately, you can combine this trope with an intense, plot-based trope that keeps the action snapping along at a brisk pace while your main character pines for the love interest and they get to know each other in a professional or external setting first.

Another option is to use an active plot to keep the pacing sharp and have your main character and love interest become friends first and only shift into a romantic relationship later in the story when all their common values, interests, trust, and platonic intimacy are well established. In effect, you'll do the emotional relationship work first in this story and let the physical relationship develop last.

. . .

ADJACENT TROPES

- Fear of Intimacy
- Oblivious to Love/Belated Epiphany
- Teen Crush
- Shy Hero/Heroine
- Socially Awkward Hero/Heroine
- Boss-Employee
- In Love With the Wrong Person

WHY READERS/VIEWERS LOVE THIS TROPE

- who *isn't* shy and insecure at the idea of telling someone they've got a crush on that they like them
- the sense of secrecy and anticipation creates a sense of suspense that keeps the audience deeply engaged in will they or won't they get together
- how cool would it be if someone had a secret crush on us? It would mean we're outwardly an attractive and appealing person and that other people see us that way
- many of us have had a secret crush we never acted upon, and this story allows us to live out the fantasy of what might have happened had we said something or acted upon it
- we all relate to having a fear of rejection and can deeply empathize with the main character, hence we vicariously connect deeply with his or her story of overcoming this fear

OBLIGATORY SCENES

. . .

THE BEGINNING:

This story has lots of potential starting points. It may begin:

- When the main character develops his or her secret crush.
- As the main character wallows in the midst of his or her secret crush, paralyzed with fear or insecurity and unable/unwilling to act upon it.
- At the point when the main character is on the verge of jumping off the cliff and approaching the object of his/her affection.
- When the main character decides to confess his/her secret crush to the object of his or her affection.

Of course, these are the main steps in the journey of a person developing, experiencing, and acting upon a secret crush. That is to say, you can start your story anywhere along that journey and make it work.

You may need to include a bit of backstory to catch up your reader on how the main character and love interest met or came into proximity. As always, though, beware of bogging down the forward pacing of your story with too much backstory.

Indeed, you may be able to weave that backstory into your current action by having the love interest express curiosity about how the main character first saw him or her or what drew the main character to him or her.

At any rate, your audience sees the love interest through the rose-colored lens of the main character. And, at the same time, we may get a negatively distorted view of the main character through his or her own lens of self. If nothing else, the beginning usually includes a significant amount of self-flagellation or doubt as the main character agonizes over whether or not to approach the love interest.

Because there are so many possible starting points for this story, the way the beginning climaxes also has a number of variations. The most common ending place, though, is when the main character finally approaches the love interest for the first time. This may an innocuous hello in an elevator, or it may be as bold as an invitation to go out on a date. Either way, the main character has overcome a huge internal obstacle just to speak to the love interest.

You'll probably want to introduce some sort of external plot problem into your story just to keep it moving along while your unhappy main character dithers about whether or not to say anything to his or her secret crush.

Often it is this external problem that finally drives the main character and love interest together and forces the main character to interact with the object of his or her affection.

In the secret admirer story, we typically see the main character and love interest interacting to start dealing with the external plot problem in a purely platonic way while, at the same time, the main character starts corresponding anonymously with the love interest in a romantic fashion.

THE MIDDLE:
This is when your audience will finally get to know the real love interest and not the idealized version from a distance that the main character has been carrying around in his or her head. We see the ways in which the love interest doesn't live up to the imaginary version of himself or herself and the ways in which the real person is much better.

We also get to know the main character through the lens of the love interest and may see a very different person than the main character has portrayed of himself/herself in the beginning.

The hero and heroine spend more time together and as they get to know each other, a romantic spark develops. This may need to happen early in the middle of your story just to keep the story moving along at a pace that doesn't put your audience to sleep.

Meanwhile, the external plot problem is getting steadily worse and more complicated, throwing the main character and love interest together more often and forcing them to work together more closely to deal with it.

The midpoint of this story is especially important. It's when one of three things happens:

- The main character reveals to the love interest that he/she is the author of the anonymous secret admirer correspondence.
- The love interest expresses interest in the main character.

- The main character and love interest have their first romantic spark moment, which can be a look, a touch, or even a kiss. It's probably not much more than that unless you started your story at the point of the main character revealing his/her crush and the real relationship has had half the story to develop already, in which case, this might be a full-blown love scene.

The key to the midpoint in this story is that it's the moment when everything changes and the relationship heads off in a whole new direction. This is when the fantasy relationship finally becomes entirely real.

The last part of the middle of the story is when the real relationship getting to know you, falling in love, passion, conflicts, problems, disagreements, and doubts all have to happen. It's three-quarters of a typical story jammed into one-quarter of it.

It's not uncommon in this trope for the second half of the middle of the story to take up much more than one-quarter of the actual page count of the story because this is where the bulk of the actual relationship has to happen.

At any rate, as the middle draws to a close, the external plot problem explodes into a crisis.

At the same time, the main character's doubts, fears, insecurities, and wounds bubble back up and cause a crisis in the relationship. The love interest's own doubts, fears, insecurities, and wounds may also rise up to cause a crisis in the romantic relationship.

Alternately, the disconnect between the imagined relationship and the reality of the actual one may be the source of a crisis that tears the lovers apart.

BLACK MOMENT:

The hero and heroine fail to successfully resolve the external plot problem. This may be a result of their failure to hold together their romantic relationship. Or the failure to solve the external plot problem may provoke the big break up between the hero and heroine.

The main character may feel guilt and shame and blame himself/herself for everything going wrong. He or she may be deeply disappointed that he/she didn't see the love interest's flaw sooner and hoped for too much from him or her.

Meanwhile, the love interest may feel guilt, shame, or failure for failing to live up to the high opinion the main character once held of him or her. Or the love interest may feel that the expectations the main character placed upon him or her were unrealistic and unattainable.

Meanwhile, both characters realize they had something pretty special between them and they blew it.

THE END:

Both the hero and heroine engage in introspection and experience epiphanies or learn some hard lessons about themselves. They each need to make changes if they're to be a better person, worthy of each other, and able to be together forever in a happy, healthy relationship. They commit to those changes and do the work to start implementing them.

The things they've learned also allow them to have a shot at resolving the previously unresolvable big plot problem. They gather new information, new help, or new perspectives, and then they work together to fix the big plot problem.

As always, the act of getting together to solve the big plot problem may allow the lovers to repair their relationship and reconcile. They may reconcile before attacking the big plot problem or they may wait till afterward to have a serious, adult conversation.

Apologies are exchanged. Grand gestures of love are made. The lessons they've each learned are communicated, and the lovers reconcile. They're now both in a place to move forward into the future, living in a fully real relationship with the fully real—and best—versions of each other.

We get a glimpse of their happily ever after together.

KEY SCENES

- the love interest notices the main character, who freaks out and panics
- the love interest confesses to having noticed the main character before
- the main character confesses how long he or she has had a crush on the love interest
- the main character discovers something wonderful about the love interest that he or she wasn't aware of
- the main character discovers something terrible about the love interest that he or she wasn't aware of
- the love interest tells the main character he or she is more lovable than the main character realizes

- the main character reverts to shy, awkward, insecure behavior...or it may have morphed into jealousy, possessiveness, and suspicion
- the love interest feels the pressure of needing to live up to the main character's inflated expectations of him/her

THINGS TO THINK ABOUT WHEN WRITING THIS TROPE

Who are the main character and love interest and how does the main character know or know of the love interest?

How do their worlds intersect?

Does the love interest know the main character, know who he/she is, or is the love interest oblivious to the main character?

Where in the main character's crush will you begin your story?

Why is the main character afraid to approach or talk to the love interest?

How does the main character's imagined version of the love interest differ from the real person the love interest is? How are these versions of the love interest the same?

How is the love interest better than the person whom the main character imagined?

What are the self-doubts, insecurities, wounds, fears, or misbeliefs the main character holds about himself/herself?

Why is the main character afraid to approach the love interest? Can you make this worse? Much worse?

What causes the main character to decide to and then to act to overcome his/her unwillingness or inability to approach/speak with the love interest?

Is there an external plot problem that's going to push these two characters together? If so, what is it? Why are *they* the two people who have to deal with it?

What does the love interest think of the main character initially? How is he/she right? How is he/she wrong?

What insecurities, wounds, fears, doubts, and misbeliefs does the love interest have about himself/herself?

How does the love interest feel about the imagined version of himself/herself that the main character initially believes of him/her?

Who makes the first move to push the relationship beyond the purely impersonal to a more personal relationship? What's that move? Who asks who out on the first date?

How does the external plot problem get worse? Much worse? How can you make it absolutely terrible?

What will be the consequences if the hero and heroine fail to solve the external plot problem? Can you make these worse? Much worse? Truly terrible?

How do the main character's feelings toward the love interest change as he/she gets to know the real love interest?

What does the main character fall in love with about the love interest? What does he/she fall out of love with?

What does the love interest fall in love with about the main character?

What causes conflict between the hero and heroine?

What threatens to break them up?

Does the plot problem becoming a crisis provoke their breakup or does their breakup provoke the plot crisis? Or are the two unrelated and just happen to occur nearly simultaneously?

Who breaks up with whom? How? Why? Is it mutual or does only one of them dump the other person? If so, who, why, and how?

How do the hero and heroine fail to resolve the big plot problem? What goes wrong? How do they each screw up?

What lessons do the main character and love interest learn about themselves, each other, and love after they've lost each other?

What message are you trying to express to your readers about love, life, insecurity, real love versus imagined love, or something else altogether?

How will you get the hero and heroine back together one more time? To deal with the big plot problem? To talk? Does one of them make a grand gesture that brings them back together?

How will the big plot problem finally be resolved?

What has changed between the end of the middle when the hero and heroine failed to resolve the crisis and now, so they can succeed?

How will you demonstrate to your audience that the hero and heroine have made the changes to themselves so they can be happy together…and that they can stick with these changes for the long term?

What does happily ever after look like for this couple?

TROPE TRAPS

The main character is so painfully shy, introverted, awkward, or wounded that he/she wouldn't plausibly ever come out of his/her shell enough to engage in a relationship.

The main character's shyness/awkwardness looks more like a brain injury or mental health condition that needs professional care and not just a character flaw that he/she can overcome on their own because he/she decides to.

The love interest comes across as arrogant, selfish, or unlikable for not having noticed the main character before now.

The love interest is nothing like the main character imagined and yet the main character is still in love with him or her.

The main character refuses to let go of the idealized version of the love interest and see the real person (for better or worse)

The love interest is too perfect to be plausible to your audience.

The main character and love interest come from such wildly different backgrounds that your audience doesn't believe they'd ever plausibly fall in love or end up together.

The main character becomes so possessive, suspicious, or jealous of the love interest that any sane love interest would break up, walk away, and never look back.

The pace of the development of the love story is so slow it bores your audience into walking away.

There's so much backstory to explain how, why, and when the main character developed a crush on the love interest that your pacing dies a horrible death and your audience walks away from your story.

The romance feels unequal between the hero and heroine. The main character remains an adoring supplicant and the love interest remains the unattainable adored one and they never gain equal footing in the relationship.

The love interest never feels pressure to live up to the lofty image the main character holds of him or her.

The main character never backslides or reverts to insecure, shy, or awkward behavior patterns.

The problems that break up the couple are, in reality, intractable and not likely to be overcome without years of therapy and hard work before they can healthily be together...which is to say the audience doesn't buy the quick lessons learned and easy fixes of the hero and heroine's personal problems.

The big plot problem has nothing to do with the hero and heroine's relationship, has no impact on it, and in no way mirrors or amplifies their problems.

The hero and heroine's personal growth doesn't do anything to help them solve the big plot problem—the two resolutions are completely unrelated.

A simple, honest, adult conversation could have solved al the couple's problems much sooner, but they just never got around to having that talk.

One character forgives the other too easily before the other character makes real amends.

One character is too slow and grudging about forgiving the other character and your audience doesn't want the couple to get back together.

The couple's happily ever after relationship remains unequal and unbalanced and your audience has no faith that it will last for the long term.

SECRET CRUSH/SECRET ADMIRER TROPE IN ACTION
Movies:

- Love, Simon
- You've Got Mail
- Cinderella Story
- Sierra Burgess Is a Loser
- To All the Boys I've Loved Before
- The Truth About Cats & Dogs
- Amelie
- Love Actually

Books:

- Punk 57 by Penelope Douglas
- Spoiler Alert by Olivia Dade
- People We Meet on Vacation by Emily Henry
- The Roommate by Rosie Danan
- Tell Me Three Things by Julie Buxbaum
- The Secret Admirer by Carol Wyer
- The Secret Love Letters of Olivia Moretti by Jennifer Probst
- Dear Ava by Ilsa Madden-Mills
- P.S. I Like You by Kasie West
- The Sweetest Thing by Jill Shalvis
- The Coincidence of Coconut Cake by Amy E. Reichert

29
STOP THE WEDDING

DEFINITION

This story begins with a wedding that's about to happen or may already be in progress.

The main character has a compelling reason for the wedding not to happen or to finish and must take action to stop it. Typically, this is for the good of the future love interest, although the love interest may not see it that way at the time.

NOTE: In the Jilted/Left At the Altar trope, the bride or groom calls off the wedding. In this story, a third party stops it from happening.

A very common version of this trope has the main character and love interest having had a previous relationship. It could have been in the distant or recent past. But either way, it was not fully resolved and fully ended when the pair separated (or at least the main character doesn't think so!).

The love interest has moved on to another relationship and agrees to marry the new partner. When the ex (our main character) hears about these upcoming nuptials, he or she races back to the love interest to find a way to stop the wedding.

Another version of this story is the main character knows something about the person the love interest is about to marry that causes the main character to interfere to stop the wedding. The intended spouse is a criminal, a terrorist, has a terrible secret that makes him or her completely unmarriageable (like another spouse), or something terrible will happen if the love interest and intended marry.

In your story, the main character may work for weeks or months before the wedding to stop it. Or he/she may stop it at the last moment before the I do's are spoken and the couple is declared married. You can time this interference however it works best in your story and creates the most tension or surprise.

The love interest may initially be very angry at the main character for stopping his/her wedding. But, as the story progresses, two things happen to change the love interest's mind. First, he/she learns all the reasons why the main character stopped the wedding and realizes the main character was right to do so. Second, the love interest and main character fall in love, fall back in love, or the love interest realizes they never fell out of love.

The main character may initially conceal his/her feelings for the love interest if they have a romantic past and may only reveal that he/she still has romantic feelings for the love interest after the love interest has forgiven him/her for stopping the wedding.

If they are strangers when the main character stops the wedding, they get to know each other over the course of the story and fall in love the same way most couples do—overcoming external plot problems and internal relationship obstacles until they path is clear for them to be happy ever after.

This trope is, at its core, a love triangle. It's often paired with a strong plot trope that pits the main character against the jilted intended in some way. For example, the intended is a criminal and the main character is a law enforcement official. The intended is an enemy spy and the main character knows it but needs to turn the intended or perhaps kill the intended. The idea is to throw the intended and main character into direct conflict and trap the love interest between them.

ADJACENT TROPES

- Left At the Altar/Jilted
- Love Triangle
- Engaged To/Marrying Someone Else
- In Love With the Wrong Person
- Runaway Bride/Groom

WHY READERS/VIEWERS LOVE THIS TROPE

- weddings are high drama affairs, and we all secretly wonder (and relish) what it would be like to have someone jump up at the last minute, make a shocking revelation, and stop the whole thing
- pursuing someone who's on the verge of being married to someone else is as forbidden a love as you can get, and we love the idea that someone loves us enough to break this taboo
- we all love a story where true love conquers all, and this is a big mountain for true love to have to climb. The love interest is inches away from willingly marrying someone else and that's a long way for his/her true love to have to claw back to win the guy/girl
- it's an interesting exploration of obligation versus love, and some of us may wonder if we married for the right reasons or not. Did we marry from obligation or from a place of real love

OBLIGATORY SCENES

THE BEGINNING:

An engagement happens or has happened, and a wedding is being planned...or is in progress. The main character finds out about it and responds by taking action to stop the wedding. We may or may not see if he/she knows the bride or groom and we may not initially know why he/she takes action to stop the wedding.

Other people may try to stop the main character from stopping the wedding.

The love interest may find out before the wedding that the main character is trying to stop it. The main character may actually approach the love interest before the wedding to ask or tell him/her to call it off. In most cases, the love interest refuses.

The main character may actually kidnap the love interest before the wedding if his/her reason to stop the wedding in compelling enough.

Regardless of when the wedding stoppage occurs, the love interest is usually spitting mad over the interference. He or she doesn't know all that the main character does and only sees the main character interfering with what's supposed to be the happiest day of his or her life. The love interest resists the wedding being stopped but fails to stop the main character from succeeding at halting the wedding.

The main character and love interest are usually thrust together by the big, external plot problem because the love interest typically wants nothing to do with the main character after he/she destroyed the wedding.

Alternately, the main character may insist on forcing the love interest to listen to his/her reasons for stopping the wedding. While the explanation may partially mollify the love interest, it usually doesn't completely. The main character still ruined something he/she was greatly looking forward to.

If the couple has a romantic past, the main character may make a dramatic declaration of love and insist that the love interest give him/her a chance to win the love interest back before the main character will return the love interest to the intended and let the original wedding go through.

If the main character and love interest flee the wedding and/or the intended spouse, this happens in the beginning as well.

The beginning often ends with the first romantic spark or encounter between the main character and love interest. This may be a fiery moment because the love interest isn't won over to the main character's cause yet.

THE MIDDLE:

This is where the main character makes his or her case for why the love interest shouldn't marry the intended. It may involve travel, surveillance, collecting of evidence on the intended or other measures to reveal the truth about the intended—if a flaw in the intended is why the main character broke up the wedding.

This is also where the hero and heroine fall in love if they weren't already at some point in the past.

If they have a past romantic relationship, this is where they fall in love again. Time has passed since they were last together, and they've' both changed since then. They're different people now, and they need to get to know each other again. One or both of them may have matured and grown in positive ways since before. Conversely, one or both of them may have experienced trauma or wounds that have left them scarred and with new issues to work out.

The midpoint of this story is often a love scene that symbolically replaces what would have been the love interest's wedding night... except it's with the main character and not the intended. Sleeping with each other introduces a whole new set of problems, however, that will now dog the couple's steps and cause escalating problems for them.

If they have a past relationship, the middle is where those past problems resurface and the couple remembers why they broke up in the first place. Doubts creep into their romance and the external plot problem strains their relationship even further.

If there's an element of danger, it adds another layer of stress to this new relationship. The love interest may feel guilt at having ditched the bride/groom, and the main character may feel guilt at having made the love interest unhappy. The main character may question whether he/she did the right thing in stopping the wedding before.

To end the middle of the story, the big plot problem and the stresses and conflicts between the hero and heroine explode into crisis.

BLACK MOMENT:

The big plot problem boils over into a crisis that the hero and heroine fail to stop or fix. They may be on the run, in danger or in hiding, outgunned and outmanned. As if that's not enough, their relationship implodes and the couple breaks up.

The big plot crisis may reveal something the main character hasn't been honest with the love interest about, or vice versa. The couple's failure to overcome their old problems or current issues makes them incapable of working together to solve the big plot crisis and they fail to overcome it.

Old, destructive behaviors have ruined their relationship again. Or the love interest's lack of trust in the main character and resentment over the main character destroying the wedding surface and cause the relationship to crumble and mistakes to happen in dealing with the big plot crisis.

All is lost.

The love interest may escape the main character, or the main character may let him/her go. The love interest may angrily return to the intended and declare his or her intent to go through with the wedding now.

Of course, the intended may not want the love interest after he/she took off with the main character, even if the love interest insists he/she didn't go willingly.

THE END:

In the face of losing each other (or possibly losing each other again), the hero and heroine each have to take a long, hard look at themselves and their behavior. They have to acknowledge the mistakes they've made and how they could've handled things differently. They each learn lessons about themselves, about their relationship, and about love and resolve to do things differently going forward. They may also realize they owe the other one an apology.

The main character tacitly or overtly gives the love interest permission to marry whoever he/she wants. Finally free to choose, the love interest chooses (to marry) the main character.

OR

Meanwhile, the intended may force the love interest to go through with the promised wedding from before. Or the love interest may willingly choose to go through with the wedding from before, seeing through an obligation even though the love interest now knows that he/she truly loves the main character.

The main character and love interest may or may not communicate before the second go-round of love interest and intended's wedding. They may communicate obliquely through a third party. Or a third party may approach either the hero or heroine to tell him/her how the other one truly feels without the knowledge of the other lover.

In this case, the main character has yet another wedding between the love interest and intended to stop, and on top of that, now he/she also has the big plot crisis to resolve.

Working together, the hero and heroine resolve the big plot problem and together stop the love interest's wedding to the intended. They run away together and marry each other...or at least there's a suggestion that they'll marry eventually.

Regardless, they're together, they're rid of the intended, and they can now be together forever and finally get their own happily ever after.

KEY SCENES

- the love interest blows his or her stack at the main character for stopping his/her wedding
- a fiery romantic encounter that may be an embrace or kiss while the love interest is still at least somewhat angry with the main character
- the main character reveals the real reason why he/she stopped the wedding
- the love interest saves the main character from doing something stupid that he or she would regret later
- -the intended pleads his or her case to the love interest, trying to convince the love interest to come back and marry him or her
- the love interest responds negatively the morning after the first big love scene (or romantic encounter depending on the heat level of your story)
- if the couple has a past, during a disagreement one or both of them brings back something from the past that drove them crazy about the other one and that's still a big problem
- the main character and the intended have a confrontation

- the past break up repeats itself, or the breaking up of the wedding is mirrored in the breaking up of the main character and love interest

THINGS TO THINK ABOUT WHEN WRITING THIS TROPE

Do the main character and love interest have a romantic past together or not?

Who is the love interest and who is he/she intending to marry? Why is he/she marrying this person? Why is he/she really marrying the intended? Is there an unconscious reason the love interest is marrying this person? If so, what is it?

If the main character and love interest have a romantic past, how does the love interest feel about the main character now?

Is the main character aware of any or all of the reasons the love interest is marrying the intended?

Who's the main character and why is he/she intent on stopping the wedding from happening?

What does the main character know about the intended that the love interest does not?

When does the main character find out a wedding is in the works?

Does the main character work to sabotage the wedding well before it happens, just before it happens, or in the middle of the wedding?

How does the main character stop the wedding?

Does someone try to stop the main character from interfering with or halting the wedding? If so, who, and what do they do?

How does the love interest react to the wedding being stopped?

How does the intended react to the wedding being stopped?

Does the main character kidnap the love interest, flee with the love interest, or help the love interest run away?

How mad is the love interest at the main character when they stop and have time to talk to (or fight with) each other?

What explanation does the main character give the love interest for breaking up the wedding? Is it the truth? Is it the whole truth? If not, what is the main character not telling the love interest?

What big plot problem will drive the main character and love interest together for much of the story? How does it involve the intended?

Is there danger to the love interest and/or main character? If so, from whom? Why?

Will the hero and heroine run away from the site of the wedding and/or from the love interest's family? If so, why and where to?

How does the love interest's family feel about the love interest being around or staying with the main character? What does the family do or do about it?

What attracts the love interest to the main character? What drives the love interest crazy in a bad way about the main character?

What does the main character find irresistible about the love interest?

Should the main character professionally or ethically resist his/her attraction to the love interest? If so, why?

Who makes the first romantic move toward whom—the main character or the love interest? What is it? How does the other character react?

When and how does each character realize they're falling for the other one or falling again?

What does the main character need to convince the love interest is true about the intended for the love interest to be okay with having not married him or her? How will the main character try to do this? Does it work? Why or why not?

Can you put the hero and heroine into close enough physical proximity that their physical relationship can develop or develop more quickly?

What doubts, fears, insecurities, wounds, or misbeliefs do the hero and heroine each bring to this relationship? How do these show up in the story and how do they negatively impact their relationship?

How does the big plot problem get worse? Much worse? Become truly awful?

How does the romantic relationship between the hero and heroine get exponentially more complicated after their first big love scene (or romantic encounter depending on heat level)?

What causes the hero and heroine to have doubts about their relationship lasting?

What does the intended do to try to torpedo the hero and heroine's romance? Does it work?

When does the main character declare his/her love for the love interest and vice versa? (This can happen anywhere from mid-story to the very end.)

How do friends and family react to the hero and heroine getting together?

What do friends and family think of the love interest not following through with marrying the intended? Do they try to talk the love interest into coming back to marry the intended or not? Why or why not?

How do the hero and heroine slide into old, destructive behaviors with each other if they have a shared past?

If they don't have a shared past, how do the current conflicts and disagreements in the relationship blow up into a crisis? Does any outside influence or person help this explosion along?

How does the big plot problem blow up into a crisis?

How do the hero and heroine mess up resolving the big crisis? Who makes mistakes? Why? How did the other partner affect the making of those mistakes?

Does the intended do something to sabotage the effort to fix the big plot problem? If so, what?

What's the event that provokes the hero and heroine into breaking up? Who breaks up with whom?

Do the hero and heroine physically separate when they break up or are they still forced to stay in proximity for safety reasons? How does that work out?

Does the love interest return home?

Does the love interest declare his or her intent to marry the intended? If so, how does the intended react?

Does the intend take back the love interest or is the love interest sullied, untrustworthy, or undesirable now?

What do the hero and heroine learn about themselves after their breakup? How does this dawn on each of them? What provokes the epiphany?

Does the love interest ever decide he or she was settling in marrying the intended or fulfilling an obligation more than marrying for love? If so, when and how does this happen?

What do the hero and heroine do about their epiphanies? How do they decide to change their behaviors? How will they demonstrate to each other and to the audience that they're truly committed to this change and can stick with it for the long term?

Does the main character have another wedding to stop that will bookend the first wedding?

How will the hero and heroine use what they've learned to successfully resolve the big plot problem if they try one more time to fix it?

How will the hero and heroine foil whatever plans the intended has to make the big plot problem go his or her way and not theirs?

How do the hero and heroine work together to solve the big plot problem?

How do the hero and heroine reconcile? Does this happen before, during, or after the climactic struggle to resolve the big plot problem?

What happens to the intended that will keep him or her out of the picture for good?

What does happily ever after look like for the main character and the love interest?

. . .

TROPE TRAPS

The reason the main character stops the wedding is entirely selfish and makes him or her unlikable to your audience.

The love interest is way too willing to let the wedding stop and is unlikable to your audience for not putting up more of a fight for his or her "true love"

The love interest's affections shift way too quickly to the main character and he or she comes across as fickle.

The main character lies so much or for so long to the love interest that he/she comes across as unworthy of the love interest.

The intended is so likable your audience feels bad for him or her and dislikes your love interest and main character for hurting him or her.

The love interest stays in the physical vicinity of the wedding such that friends and family of his/hers and the intended's pester the love interest incessantly about going through with the wedding...and there's no space for the main character to earn the love interest's affections.

The main character and love interest fall in love too fast, making the love interest seem fickle, or too slow, making the pacing lag.

The intended isn't part of the big plot problem.

The intended is just a weird, hanging character at the edge of your story with no real role to play in the story.

The intended and main character never confront each other.

The main character and love interest never have doubts about what they're doing.

The main character and love interest never have any regrets about the other people whom their rash behavior has hurt.

The big plot problem has little or nothing to do with why the main character stopped the wedding.

The intended never does anything active to try to get back the love interest or at least to break up the main character and love interest.

The big plot problem and the new relationship between the main character and love interest don't impact each other enough or at all and feel disconnected.

The reason the main character and love interest break up is lame, immature, or selfish and your audience doesn't think they deserve to be happy together as a result.

The love interest never realizes he/she was making a mistake by marrying the intended.

The hero and heroine don't learn any big lessons.

The hero and heroine don't show your audience or each other their commitment to changing their behaviors.

The hero and heroine don't have to work together to solve the big plot problem. Only one of them does that work, or someone else entirely solves it.

The hero and heroine never apologize to each other. They never forgive each other. Neither makes any big gesture of true love.

The hero and heroine never apologize to the other people they've hurt.

We never see happily ever after for this couple and worry that they won't stay together for the long term. After all, the love interest has ditched one person he/she made a promise to. Why not do the same to someone else?

STOP THE WEDDING TROPE IN ACTION
Movies:

- The Graduate
- The Wedding Singer
- My Best Friend's Wedding
- Sweet Home Alabama
- Made Of Honor
- Runaway Bride

Books:

- It Happened One Wedding by Julie James
- The Runaway Princess by Christina Dodd
- To Have and to Hold by Lauren Layne
- A Kingdom of Dreams by Judith McNaught
- Romancing Mister Bridgerton by Julia Quinn
- The Wedding Crasher by Mia Sosa

30
TERMS OF THE WILL

DEFINITION

In this story, someone is named as the beneficiary of a (substantial) will if and only if they fulfill some specific term. In the romance genre, this requirement typically demands that they do something that's going to lead to romance. They must get married, produce a legitimate heir, or live for a period of time with a specific person, for example.

Wills being executed upon a death are not the only legal documents you could use in this trope. The terms of a trust fund could require the recipient to get married by a certain age to receive it or keep getting funds from it. A contract might have been signed by the main character or in the main character's behalf when he/she was a minor agreeing to marry by a certain age or get cut out of a will that's yet to be executed. Feel free to get creative with these.

You will see stories where a main character has inherited a property and moved into it—a bed and breakfast, a farm, or some business that takes them to a new place. But in this scenario, the terms of the will are a story element as opposed to the driving force of the action in the story. For terms in a will to become a trope, the will must force a main character to *do* something as opposed to merely *being* somewhere.

By far the most common version of this trope is where the main character will not inherit a very large estate unless he or she marries within a certain period of time. This time lock can be generous—several years—or it can be unreasonably short and only last for a few months (or even less if the dead relative is a sadist or was very annoyed with his or her as yet unmarried heir at the time the will was written).

The main character who's now forced to find a mate, and do it fast, may try to break the will. He or she may try to fake a marriage, which adds a whole extra trope to this story. The main character may find a random person and offer him or her a celibate marriage, but a comfortable life in return for a quick marriage to him or her. Or the main character may recruit a friend, acquaintance, or employee to marry him or her, usually in return for a portion of the estate or some sort of financial benefit.

The main character and recruited love interest may strike some other sort of deal—the love interest will get a raise or a career boost or may avoid being fired or having charges pressed against him/her for some transgression he/she has committed. It's purely up to you what the terms of the main character and love interest's deal will be.

Of course, once they're thrown into physical proximity and are technically getting married or already married, the main character and love interest fall in love and ultimately stay married or make their marriage real...just the way the person who wrote the will intended.

This trope is ripe for being combined with other tropes:

- The main character might marry someone in haste to get the estate but only then meet his or her soulmate. Now he or she must choose between a life of wealth or a life of love.
- Fake, pretend, or celibate marriage tropes are obvious candidates to go along with this one.

- The person who wrote the will died and left behind a will with this outrageous condition in it can have faked his or her death and come back after the main character is married.
- The main character may be an extremely grumpy hero/heroine in a Grumpy-Sunshine trope.

At its core, this is a trope of someone being forced into proximity with someone else, and with whom he or she eventually falls in love and lives with happily ever after.

ADJACENT TROPES

- Marriage of Convenience/Fake Marriage
- Arranged Marriage
- Pretend/Celibate Marriage
- Tricked Into Marriage
- Celibate/Unconsummated Marriage

WHY READERS/VIEWERS LOVE THIS TROPE

- we love a story where fate brings together two people who were meant to be together—it gives us hope that there's someone out there who's meant for us
- the shift from a practical bargain to a love match appeals to our romantic natures and gives hope to the pragmatists among us that they, too, can end up in an idyllic relationship that's also logical

- the extreme awkwardness of this situation has lots of opportunities to go hilariously sideways
- the wealthy person in the relationship is not the one with the power in the relationship for a change—he or she comes to the love interest as a supplicant and desperately needs something from the love interest
- this couple's romantic arc will include an overt trust-building element, which we all crave in our own relationships

OBLIGATORY SCENES

THE BEGINNING:

Typically, this story opens with the reading of a will. The grieving (and possibly greedy) family of a wealthy person who has passed away recently gathers to hear who got what. The main character is shocked and appalled to find out he or she inherits only if he or she marries within a certain period of time. Desirous of a life of wealth and ease, the main character goes forth, perhaps angrily and resentfully but he/she goes forth nonetheless, to find a spouse fast.

Alternately, the main character has been aware of the terms of the will or trust and whose proceeds he or she's been using living a wealthy life and becomes aware that his or her fateful birthday is fast approaching or that the date by which the will stipulated he/s he must be married by has snuck up on him or her and is right around the corner. Again, this character has to find a spouse fast.

If this character has a compelling reason to hate the idea of getting married, it's established up front. If this character has some other passion in life that consumes him or her, that's established up front. Whatever the obvious reason why this person hasn't already married is also made clear to your audience right away.

This marriage is always under some sort of deadline that's either very short or that has almost run out, adding a sense of intense urgency to the main character's quest for a spouse.

You may choose to let the entire beginning of your story be the main character's frantic search for someone "okay" to marry—he/she can't afford to be too picky under this time crunch. The perfect person may be right under his or her nose, introducing another trope into the story, of course. But the love interest may lose patience with the main character's fruitless and unproductive search and step in at the end of the beginning to grab the main character by the ear, give him or her a good shake and declare that the two of them are getting married and that's the end of it.

In the absence of a take-charge love interest, the person the main character gets to marry him/her may be someone the main character already knows. Indeed, the love interest may be someone the main character holds power over and can demand that they marry him or her. For example, a secretary, housekeeper, or other employee may get recruited to marry the boss.

You may choose to set up a random meeting between the main character and future love interest. For example, the love interest picks the main character's pocket but gets caught. The main character sees the pickpocket is the right gender for him/her and declares that the pickpocket must marry him/her or get turned in to the police and go to jail. Sky's the limit on how wild you can make this initial meeting.

Regardless of who the main character convinces or coerces into marrying him or her, the pair strike a bargain of some kind. Although the main character almost always brings wealth to the table (hence, the will, trust fund, or contract, and compelling need to meet its terms), the love interest brings himself or herself to the bargain as a spouse.

The beginning usually ends with the bargain being struck, the marriage taking place, and the brand-new spouse triumphantly produced to the executor(s) of the estate.

. . .

THE MIDDLE:

The main character got his/her inheritance, but now he/she is stuck with a spouse he/she doesn't want. However, they have to live together as a married couple now, whether they like it or not. In most cases, the will stipulates something along the lines of the couple having to stay married for a certain number of years or live in the same place, or heaven forbid, produce an heir in a certain amount of time.

The middle of the story then enters into a traditional getting-to-know you, romantic sparks, falling in love arc. Because this couple is already married and consummating the marriage and shifting over from a contractual relationship to a romantic one poses no problems whatsoever, you'll have to manufacture some compelling reason why this couple shouldn't sleep together or why doing so introduces a huge complication to their lives.

For example, the main character has stated his/her intent to divorce the love interest as soon as a child is produced. The love interest, who's fallen in love with the main character, doesn't want to have sex and risk having a baby until *after* the main character has fallen in love with him/her.

At any rate, this complication is typically laid out somewhere in the first half of the middle of the story. Then, after the midpoint—or whenever the hero and heroine actually do consummate the marriage—this complication happens and causes problems for the couple.

If there's a big external plot problem—typically one the main character needs his/her wealth to solve, or one the love interest is hiding from the main character and needs the main character's wealth to solve, or there's some outside force that threatens the continuation of the marriage, this unfolds in the middle of the story. It may be introduced in the beginning, or you may not introduce it until the crisis of racing to get married by the deadline has been solved.

As the hero and heroine get to know each other and fall in love, their own wounds, fear, insecurities, or misbeliefs about themselves, about marriage, about the other person, and about love rear their ugly heads and cause problems for the couple.

If you're running a second trope that provides an obstacle to their love, it also complicates matters. For example, they may be a grumpy-sunshine couple, a May-December couple, come from opposite sides of the track, or clashing cultures.

In most versions of this story, the person who stands to inherit the wealth if the main character doesn't meet the conditions of the will spends the middle of the story trying to prove the marriage isn't real or that the couple hasn't consummated it, or this person tries to break up the marriage in time to cause the will to be invalidated (which also typically has a deadline of some kind, for example, the couple has to stay married for one year for the entire estate to be turned over to the main character).

As the big plot problem blows up into a crisis, all the complications, trust issues, and forces trying to tear apart this couple grow into a crisis that overwhelms the hero and/or heroine's fragile and new romantic relationship.

BLACK MOMENT:

The hero and/or heroine fail to resolve the big plot problem and the thing they were most hoping to avoid happens. The will may be invalidated. Their wealth may be lost or taken away. They fail to help the person(s) they were trying to help.

On top of that devastating failure, the hero and heroine break up. The year the love interest promised to stay married to the hero ends and the love interest leaves as promised. The divorce papers the main character filed the day they got married are delivered on time as originally planned to the love interest. Since this isn't a traditional couple who fell in love, got married, and expected to be happy together forever, you can have fun cooking up a creative reason for the couple to split up or a creative way for it to happen.

Regardless of how it happens, though, the hero and heroine are devastated by the failure of their marriage.

THE END:

The hero may still have his/her wealth and wallow in it, miserable and alone, until he/she realizes that it means nothing without the person he/she loves to share it with. Or the main character may have lost his/her wealth and have to go to work and earn his/her own way in the world for a while. It sucks without the person he/she lives to share it with, but he/she figures it out.

In either case, the main character finally learns the lesson that money isn't everything and that love is what really matters to him/her. The main character also learns whatever other life lessons or personal lessons about himself/herself that need to be learned before he or she can have and sustain a healthy, loving relationship with anyone.

Meanwhile, the love interest has lost everything. Not only has he/she lost the wealth, safety, and affection he/she has grown accustomed to and which were useful in helping others, but more importantly, the love interest has lost the love of his/her life.

Although the love interest may be less interested in the wealth or loss of it, the love interest keenly feels the loss of the main character. The love interest, too, finally learns lessons about himself/herself that finally make him or her capable of having a healthy, loving relationship with someone else going forward.

The hero and heroine must come together to make one last attempt to solve the big plot problem. This may be the thing that forces them back into proximity so they can talk out their problems.

Once they're back together, though, they demonstrate to each other (and to your audience) how they've changed in some obvious and compelling way and are committed to this change. This may involve some sort of grand gesture. In this trope, the grand gesture may not only be one of love but may be one of sacrifice or of eschewing wealth in favor of true love.

The hero and heroine make any apologies owed to each other and forgive each other for their earlier mistakes. They declare their love for each other and decide to resume or restart their marriage, but this time based on a foundation of love and not a contract or bargain.

We get a glimpse of them stepping off into their happily ever after together.

KEY SCENES

- the marriage bargain is negotiated between the main character and love interest
- the wedding night happens and is extremely awkward whether or not they consummate the marriage (and usually they don't, after all they're strangers, or at best acquaintances)
- the couple's first serious argument
- one or both of the partners threatens to renege on the deal
- the moment they each realize they're falling for the other one and why this is a big, big problem
- the couple fakes being happily married in public (and it goes shockingly well or shockingly badly…or maybe one scene of each)
- the couple wants to sleep together and they're each intensely frustrated when it doesn't happen
- there's a mini-crisis they have to work together as a couple to solve that goes well, demonstrating that they can get along with each other and work as a team if they choose to
- the main character reverts to his or her pre-marriage

behaviors that explain why he or she wasn't already married in the first place
- the love interest leaves for some reason (this isn't the final and permanent breakup, but it might look like it) and the main character freaks out

THINGS TO THINK ABOUT WHEN WRITING THIS TROPE

Who's the main character?

Whose will/trust/contract is it and what's this person's relationship to and with the main character?

What are the terms of the will/trust/contract? How much time does the main character have to meets these terms?

What does the main character stand to lose if he/she doesn't meet the terms of the will? Can you make this bigger and more compelling to the main character? A lot bigger and a lot more compelling to the main character?

Who stands to inherit everything if the main character fails to meet the terms of the will? How does this person act as another incentive for the main character to meet the terms of the will? Can you make this person a much bigger incentive, that is, a much bigger jerk or much more charming, and, hence, irritating to the main character?

Who is the love interest? Does the main character know the love interest or not? If not, how do they meet?

How quickly does the main character propose a bargain to the love interest? What's the bargain?

What does the love interest negotiate for himself/herself as part of this bargain?

Does the main character initially tell the love interest about the terms of the will or not? Why or why not? If not, when in the story does the love interest find out about the will and its terms? How angry, hurt, or devastated is the love interest when he/she finds out about it?

What's the wedding like? When, where, and how does it happen? Is it a grand, public affair or a completely unromantic signing of papers in a judge's dreary chambers?

Does the main character and/or love interest (at some point in the story) regret the kind of wedding they had?

Will the marriage be consummated right away or not? If yes, how will you get through the love scenes without squicking out your audience or triggering audience members with barely consensual and very uncomfortable sex?

Does the couple's bargain include some provision about sex or no sex, or compensation if sex happens? If so, what's the provision?

What prevents the main character from leaving immediately after the wedding and abandoning the love interest entirely? Is there some term in the will or some provision in their personal bargain, or some other reason for him or her to stick around, living under the same roof with this near stranger?

What do the hero and heroine each find attractive, appealing, and likable about the other one? How do they feel about noticing these things?

What do the hero and heroine dislike about each other? What are the friction points between them? What are the challenges of living with each other that they encounter?

Who first initiates trying to improve their relationship? What's that person's initial goal? Does he or she want civil conversation, any conversation at all, to seduce the other person, to eventually turn this into a real marriage?

What do the hero and heroine do that puts them into proximity with each other and spending time together?

Do they have to make public appearances together as a married couple? If so, what kinds of appearances and how do those go? How can some go badly and others go better?

What do their family, friends, and coworkers think of this hasty and possibly fake marriage? Do they support the couple or try to sabotage the marriage in some way? If so, how?

How does one partner do little things to ingratiate themselves to the other one?

Does one of the partners want nothing to do with romance and resist the small kindnesses the other one shows to him or her at first? If so, how and why?

What personal wounds, trauma, fears, insecurities, or misbeliefs does each partner bring to this relationship? How will you demonstrate these in actions the characters take (as opposed to relying solely on internal monologue to reveal these)?

Make a list of the steps along the way to this couple falling in love. What qualities do they need to know the other one has before they can fall in love? How does their physical attraction to each other unfold? How do they grow emotionally closer? Now, build events that can happen and scenes that can occur that make possible each of these steps along the way.

What big plot problem(s) do the hero and/or heroine have to deal with over the course of the story?

How does the big plot problem threaten their marriage?

Is the person who stands to inherit if the main character fails to meet the terms of the will involved with or behind the big plot problem? If so, how?

Are other family members meddling in the marriage, trying to destroy it, or trying to keep the terms of the will from being met?

What's the big complication that will happen after the couple consummates their marriage? Can you make it worse? Much worse?

Is there a way you can make it absolutely forbidden for the couple to consummate their marriage? You may not be able to do this in every story, but in the ones where it's possible, by all means, consider doing so.

Does the main character do something before or right after the couple marries (likely in secret or at least secret from the love interest) to destroy the marriage or get out of it at some later date? If so, when does the love interest find out about this? How does he/she feel about it? When does it happen and how much chaos or destruction does it cause?

Does the person who stands to inherit do something to devastate the marriage? If so, what? When? How? How do the hero and heroine each react to it?

How does the big plot problem blow up in the hero and heroine's faces? How do their personal issues and conflicts or lack of trust cause them to fail to halt or resolve the big plot problem and for everything to go horribly wrong with it?

Who breaks up with whom? Who walks out on whom? Has this always been the plan for them to break up after the terms of the will are fulfilled? Or is this a breakup based solely on their internal and external conflicts and on the forces trying to destroy their marriage?

Does breaking up break the will? If so, what happens to all the wealth? What happens to the main character's life and lifestyle in the absence of all the wealth?

What lessons do the hero and heroine each learn about themselves, about each other, about marriage, and about love in the devastating aftermath of their breakup?

How is the devastation bad enough to make the lessons they each learn stick for the long term, meaning how will you convince your audience the lovers are sufficiently traumatized to make real and lasting changes for the better in themselves and in their behaviors?

How will you bring the couple back together physically to work together, talk, and/or start to work out their differences?

How will this wiser couple work together to solve the big plot problem?

Do the hero and heroine work out their differences, make apologies and grand gestures, and reconcile before, during, or after resolving the big plot problem?

What happens to the person who stood to inherit everything? Is he/she taken care of forever, or might he/she come back as a problem at a later date? The answer to this may depend on whether you're writing a series or a stand-alone story.

Does the main character keep the wealth in the end, or does he/she let it go, give it away, or let someone else inherit it?

How do their families, friends, and coworkers react to the couple's reconciliation?

How will you show the will being fully executed, finished, and no longer an issue?

What does happily ever after look like for this couple?

TROPE TRAPS

The main character is such a jerk to begin the story that your audience doesn't want him or her ever to find happiness.

Failing to show at least some small spark of decency or some small, good quality in the main character early enough that your audience sticks around long enough for him or her to change and grow into someone lovable.

The love interest comes across as a gold-digger and is unlikable.

The couple has sex way before they're emotionally ready to and it upsets or triggers your audience.

The bargain the hero and heroine strike is way lopsided in favor of one character over the other and feels exploitative of one character or the other.

The amount of money the main character is entering into a loveless, contract marriage over isn't enough to justify doing this to himself/herself and to someone else.

The terms of the will are so onerous that any reasonable judge would overturn the will and impose less ridiculous conditions upon the main character's inheritance.

The way the main character and love interest meet is so cliché or so outlandish as to be implausible to your audience.

The main character has no good reason to stick around the love interest after the wedding and it doesn't make sense for these two strangers who hate each other's guts to continue living together at all, let alone long enough or closely enough to fall in love.

The love interest has to make all the moves to push the relationship to develop into more than just a business relationship.

The main character does nothing to advance the relationship and comes across as a spoiled, selfish jerk or too lazy to deserve the love interest.

Nobody meddles in the marriage. Families, particularly when there's a lot of money at stake, always meddle.

The big plot problem has nothing to do with the terms of the will.

The person who stands to inherit if the main character doesn't is completely passive and does nothing to try to get the estate...which nobody will believe.

There are no twists or surprises in the storyline. (This is a very straightforward forced proximity story and needs to be spiced up a little not to come across as cliché, dull, or completely predictable.)

The hero and heroine come from such different worlds that they would never plausibly fall in love.

The hero and heroine's core values, morals, ethics, and beliefs are so misaligned that they would never fall in love in the first place, or even like each other, nor would they stay in love for the long term.

Failing to have the main character ever regret making a business deal instead of holding out for true love.

Failing to have the love interest regret getting into this loveless marriage bargain with a person who so clearly didn't want to be married or didn't want to be married to him/her.

Failing to create any complications that result from the couple consummating their marriage.

Failing to create any compelling reason(s) why the couple, once they've fallen in love, shouldn't just stay married and let their marriage transition into being a real one based on love.

The hero and heroine don't have any big epiphanies that make them capable of loving each other and having a healthy relationship in the future.

The main character never learns that love, not money, makes him or her happy and that love is more important by far than money.

Nothing changes from the end of the middle when the hero and/or heroine fail to resolve the big plot problem and the story climax when they successfully solve it. Why couldn't they do that at the end of the middle and void the whole black moment?

The hero and heroine could solve all their relationship problems if they simply sat down sometime in the middle of the story and had an honest, adult conversation with each other. Why didn't they do it then and avoid all the drama and heartache of the black moment?

Neither the hero nor the heroine ultimately makes any sacrifices for the other one.

Being excessively obvious and cliché in the ending, wherein the main character, having finally learned that money isn't everything and love is what really matters is triggers a secret clause in the will and gets back the entire estate, now that he or she is finally married and in love for real. It's okay for the couple to hang on to the inheritance in the end...but try not to be lame about how that happens.

Failing to show the couple happy together in whatever financial circumstances they end up in.

TERMS OF THE WILL TROPE IN ACTION
Movies:

- The Wedding Plan
- This trope is rarely seen in movies, interestingly enough. But there are a lot of variations upon it—marrying to get a green card (The Proposal) or keep custody of a child (Marriage of Convenience) are much more common. My guess is it doesn't play well with the general public simply to marry for money. While marrying for money is often a set-up in film, the main character typically finds love with someone else (Intolerable Cruelty)

Books:

- Marriage of Inconvenience by Penny Reid
- The Marriage Contract by Katee Robert
- Married by Morning by Lisa Kleypas
- The Unwanted Wife by Natasha Anders
- The Marriage Bargain by Jennifer Probst
- The Marriage Merger by Jennifer Probst
- Wayward Wallflower by Mia Marlowe
- The Duke's Shotgun Wedding by Stacy Reid

31

TRICKED INTO MARRIAGE

DEFINITION

As the title of this trope makes clear, the main character is somehow tricked into marrying the love interest. The two may or may not already have a romantic relationship when this trickery happens. Classically, the female love interest claims to be pregnant and the main character feels obliged or is obliged by a shotgun to marry her.

But there are a whole lot more ways than that for one person to trick or coerce another person into marrying him or her, and I encourage you to be creative in coming up with this reason.

It's also possible for a third party to trick or coerce both the main character and love interest into marrying each other. For example, a beloved person to both the hero and heroine might claim to be dying and his or her last wish is to see them marry...after which, the beloved person stages a miraculous recovery, of course.

At any rate, the main movement and conflict in this trope are provided by the trick itself. What is it, how reprehensible is it, when is it revealed, how does everyone react, and is it forgivable or not?

And of course, once tricked into marriage, the hero and heroine begin to fall in love. The trick and/or trickster may keep up the trick long enough for the couple not only to fall in love but to consummate the marriage. But regardless of when the trick is revealed, it causes a crisis in the relationship, which is revealed to have been based on a lie.

In the end, of course, the couple realizes their love is true and real regardless of how they were brought together, they resolve their differences, and they live happily ever after.

The one huge monkey wrench to this is if one of the partners tricked the other one into marrying him or her. Now that journey of forgiveness is a much harder one to make. Not only must the other partner forgive the trick, but they both must reckon with the fact that the foundation of their marriage is, in fact, a lie. Is their love true and real at all, or is the other partner still lying when he or she swears to love him or her?

This version of the trope often requires some sort of major sacrifice or grand gesture on the part of the partner who tricked the other one into the marriage in the first place before the tricked partner is willing to believe and forgive the trickster partner.

ADJACENT TROPES

- Accidental Pregnancy
- Drunk/Vegas Wedding
- Fling/One Night Stand
- Enemies to Lovers
- Estranged Spouses/On the Rocks
- Forgiveness

WHY READERS/VIEWERS LOVE THIS TROPE

- this forced marriage creates immediate and intense sparks of conflict that are exciting and fascinating

- the fantasy of finding love without having to all the hard work of finding the perfect partner
- the notion that two people who have good reason to despise each other can still find things in common and even true love
- we love seeing and knowing these two people are really meant to be together long before they do and building anticipation of when they'll finally realize it
- we've all lied about something in our life and would like to think, even if it was a whopper, that if it was revealed the people who love us would forgive us and still love us

OBLIGATORY SCENES

THE BEGINNING:

We may see both the hero and heroine living their ordinary lives before the trick happens. They may or may not know each other, and they may or may not already be involved in a romantic relationship. Whatever this status quo is, though, you may choose to show your audience a snippet of it before all hell breaks loose.

In a way, this story has two inciting incidents. The first one is whatever event happens that makes the trickster decides to trick the hero and/or heroine into getting married to each other. This could be a one-night stand, a financial crisis, physical danger or a threat where one of the partners feels a need for the protection of marriage, or simple impatience that these two stubborn people who are clearly in love aren't getting around to saying I do.

The second inciting incident is the trick itself. It's the scene where the person tricking the other one into marriage launches the ruse and the hero and heroine agree to get married.

Typically this wedding happens very quickly. The trickster wants it to happen fast before anyone backs out of the agreement to get married and before anyone finds out about the lie behind the trick. Part of the trick is often some sort of implied or overt deadline for it to happen. The couple needs to be married before the pregnancy shows. The couple needs to be married before their feuding families find out they slept together and kill them both. The couple needs to be married before a loved one dies.

The beginning of this story usually ends with the wedding itself happening.

Alternately, it might end with someone who would have otherwise harmed or killed the hero or heroine finding out about the wedding and being enraged. Or the wedding may simply go public. A wealthy, powerful or famous person who's been tricked into marriage might simply be seen in public and introduce his or her new spouse to the world, causing an uproar.

THE MIDDLE:

Trick complete, the couple suddenly find themselves thrust into a marriage neither or them expected and that one or both of them didn't want. The person(s) tricked into marriage may be deeply resentful of being married and there may be a lot of friction, disagreements, or open conflict between the lovers.

If the love interest tricked the main character into marriage, he or she may do their best to be conciliatory and to make the marriage as pleasant as possible for the main character...not that it does any good. The main character is mad and may very well try to make the marriage as miserable as possible for the love interest who forced him/her into this against their will.

If a third party tricked both the hero and heroine into marrying, they may both be angry and resent being force to marry, but at least they have that in common and aren't likely to take out their anger on each other. They may find their first companionship, commiseration, and commonality in their shared resentment, in fact.

It may take a big, external plot problem to force the hero and heroine into any kind of truce or cooperation early on in their relationship. This problem unfolds and gets worse through the middle of the story, forcing the hero and heroine to work more and more closely together to try to contain or fix it.

Even though the hero and heroine may be reluctant to admit it, they start to find things about each other that they like, admire, and are attracted to. Into their fragile truce a spark of attraction ignites. In spite of their resentments, reluctance, and anger, their attraction grows.

How long it takes the couple to actually fall in love and to consummate their marriage is up to you and will vary from story to story. Some may have done the deed by the midpoint. Others may hold off until right before the black moment.

If the couple was already romantically involved before they got married, they may get back together romantically as soon as their resentment and anger begin to cool and their previous attraction and chemistry reassert themselves. They are married now, after all.

However, the lie that the marriage is based on looms larger and larger the more in love they fall and the closer they become.

If someone else knows about the lie, he or she may threaten to reveal it.

If one of the partners lied to trick the other into this marriage, his or her guilt may overwhelm him or her into finally admitting what he or she did.

The middle almost always ends with the revelation of the lie, which leads to a huge blow-up and immediately breaks up the couple.

The big external plot problem may reach a crisis that forces or causes the revelation of the lie, or vice versa, the revelation of the lie and subsequent huge fight between the hero and heroine may provoke the big external plot problem to explode into a crisis.

Either way, everything goes as badly as it's possible for it to go.

. . .

BLACK MOMENT:

The character who has been lied to feels completely betrayed. The person he or she loves—loved—tricked or coerced them into doing something life changing. Marriage isn't a little trick. It's one of the biggest tricks someone can pull on another human being. The love interest respected him or her so little that the love interest was willing to do this utterly reprehensible and unforgivable thing to him or her. What does that say about their entire relationship?

For his or her part, the trickster love interest is utterly devastated. He or she took a chance at revealing the truth, trusting that the main character loved him or her enough to forgive the trick. But he or she miscalculated. The love interest is kicked out of the main character's life and actively punished for the trick.

Friends, family, and coworkers may also shun the love interest after his/her terrible trick is revealed. The guilt and shame may be very public and the consequences may also be very public. The love interest may lose their job, their income, their standing in society, their friends and family—indeed, the love interest may lose absolutely everything of importance to him or her.

It may be this utter destruction of the love interest that finally breaks through the main character's rage and desire for revenge. However, this utter destruction may also cause the love interest to have serious second thoughts about his/her relationship with the main character whether or not he/she wants it back.

Not only has the trick and its revelation caused the big plot problem not to be successfully resolved, but things may be even worse now with regard to the plot problem than they were even when the plot crisis first happened.

THE END:

Into this righteous fury and hurt, the tricked main character registers missing the trickster love interest. And, if the love interest had a compelling and logical reason for lying and tricking him/her into the marriage, the main character may begin to see why the love interest felt compelled to trick him or her. The main character may not forgive it yet, but at least understanding dawns.

Into this emotional stew, the main character takes a hard look at himself/herself and finally sees where he/she made mistakes in the relationship. It's possible the main character's actions or behaviors pushed the love interest into their desperate gambit in some way, and the main character finally sees and acknowledges his or her role in the trick.

If a third party tricked the hero and heroine into marriage, their mutual anger may initially cause them to break up, if for no other reason than to show the third party that they won't be manipulated in that way and that it was a rotten thing to do to anyone.

However, once they're apart, the hero and heroine miss each other and realize that they really did love each other. Maybe their relationship and their love was more real than they realized. In this scenario, the hero and heroine are likely to arrive at a place of forgiveness much faster than in the scenario where one of the partners tricked the other one into the marriage.

The big plot problem may bring them back together to finally talk out why the love interested tricked the main character and how they feel about it, now. Using the lessons they've learned about themselves as a result of this whole mess, they now have what it takes to resolve the big plot problem. The hero and/or heroine successfully resolve the big plot problem.

OR

The third party who tricked them both may bring them back together to apologize to them in person. In this case, reconciliation may happen fairly quickly. The hero and heroine confess to each other how much they missed each other and hated being apart. And, as angry as they both are at the person who tricked them, they have to admit they're grateful to that person for bringing them together.

OR

If the love interest tricked the main character into marriage, he or she is likely to initiate their first contact with each other after the dramatic break up. The love interest may reach out directly to the main character who may or may not initially accept the invitation to talk. Indeed, the main character may want the love interest to suffer a while longer before agreeing to speak with him or her.

The love interest may enlist the aid of an outside person to help him or her get the main character into the same room as the love interest to hear out the love interest's explanation and apology for what he/she did.

Or the love interest may make some grand and risky gesture, often in a very public way, to get the main character's attention and force him or her to at least listen to what the love interest has to say. Be careful about having the love interest manipulate or coerce the main character into anything at this point in the story, however.

Regardless of how they physically get back together, the love interest profusely and sincerely apologizes to the main character, or the third party who tricked them both sincerely apologizes.

The hero and heroine express their feelings about the trick. They express what they've learned while being apart, and any remaining apologies get made. Last but not least, the hero and heroine express still loving each other and wanting to give their marriage another try... but this time completely honestly.

We see them finally get their happily ever after together.

KEY SCENES

- the hero and/or heroine react with fury to being tricked like this
- the tricked character(s) nearly walks out on the wedding or nearly refuses to go through with it

- the very angry, unromantic wedding night
- the hero and/or heroine wonders if they've lost their mind for developing romantic feelings toward the other one
- the tricked character walks out on the trickster character in a foreshadowing of the black moment later
- the love interest does something very kind or makes a sacrifice mid-marriage that demonstrates feelings of real affection, love, or respect toward the main character
- the trickster's guilt almost but not quite pushes him or her into confessing the trick
- a friend or family member who knows about the trick almost but not quite reveals the trick to the tricked party but stops at the last second
- the tricked character's basic decency and goodness are on display when he or she does something altruistic or kind in the story
- the main character makes a mistake, does or says something rotten in the marriage that he or she feels bad about after they've broken up

THINGS TO THINK ABOUT WHEN WRITING THIS TROPE

Who are the hero and heroine? Do they know each other when the story begins? If so, how?

Are the hero and heroine already dating when the story begins? If so, why haven't they gotten married before now?

Who's tricking whom into marriage?

If the love interest is tricking the main character into marriage, is his or her reason for doing it so compelling that your audience can understand and forgive why he or she is taking this drastic action?

If a third party tricks both the hero and heroine into getting married, why does he or she feel compelled to take this drastic action? What does this person know about the hero and heroine that they don't each know about themselves?

If the hero and heroine are not dating when the story begins, why does the trickster choose this particular person to trick into marrying them or choose this particular pair of people to trick into marriage?

What's the trick? How is it delivered?

How does the tricked party push back against the trick initially? What evidence does the trickster offer to prove that the trick is real and true?

Why does the tricked party believe the trick? Does any part of him or her doubt the veracity of the trick? If so, why does he she go through with the wedding anyway?

What kind of wedding is it? Who attends? When and where is it?

Where will the couple live after they get married? What other details of their hasty marriage have yet to be worked out that must be worked out after they marry?

Where do they spend their wedding night? How bad is it? Just how angry is the tricked party(ies)?

How uncomfortable or unpleasant are the first few days of this unplanned, unexpected, unwanted marriage? Who's making it unpleasant for whom?

Who tries to ease the tension and make the best of the situation? How does the other partner react?

What's the big plot problem that's going to force the couple together to work as a team?

What about each other do the hero and heroine like? What do they have in common? How will they discover these things about each other in ways that don't seem contrived or fake?

What core values, moral, ethics, and beliefs do the hero and heroine have in common?

How will you set up a spark of attraction and romance between the hero and heroine that feels natural and unforced when it happens, particularly in light of how mad at least one of them is to be trapped in this marriage in the first place?

What's the big complication that happens in the wake of the hero and heroine consummating their marriage? Can you make it bigger? Worse? More dangerous? More devastating?

How does the trick and the lie behind it eat away at the trickster? How does this guilt eat at him or her and how does it manifest itself in how he or she acts?

How do friends and family react to this hasty marriage? Do they know the details of why the marriage happened and that someone tricked one or both of them into it?

Do family and friends know the identity of the trickster? If so, how do they act around and toward the trickster?

When in the story is the trick or lie revealed?

Does the big plot crisis cause the lie to be revealed, or does the revelation of the lie behind the trick cause the big plot crisis?

How does the implosion of the marriage cause the hero and heroine to fail to resolve the big plot crisis successfully?

Who walks out on whom? Where does he or she go?

Who feels what in the aftermath of the couple's big breakup?

What lessons do the hero and heroine each learn in the wake of their big breakup?

Does the trickster have something he or she needs to tell the tricked character that he or she desperately needs that character to believe...but which the main character refuses to believe, even though it is true this time?

What finally brings the hero and heroine back together in the same place? Is it the big plot problem? Does someone trick them into the same room? Does someone they can't refuse summon them both? Does the love interest arrange it? Does the love interest get help from a third party to arrange the meeting? Does the third party who tricked them both arrange the meeting?

Who apologizes to whom and for what?

What feelings, epiphanies, and lessons learned do they confess to each other?

How will the hero and heroine each prove their honesty and trustworthiness going forward to each other?

At what point does the tricked party forgive the trickster and vice versa, since by now, the tricked person has hurt the trickster plenty, too?

Why do the hero and heroine agree to give their relationship another chance...more to the point, why do they each believe the other one is being honest now and will be honest with him or her going forward?

What does a glimpse of this couple's happily ever after look like?

TROPE TRAPS

The love interest is so self-serving and selfish the audience hates him or her.

The main character is so gullible, naïve, and trusting that, in the eyes of the audience, he or she deserves to get tricked.

No matter how great the love interest treats the main character, he or she will never make up to the main character how thoroughly he/she wrecked the main character's life with the trick.

If the love interest tricked the main character into marriage, his or her reason for doing so isn't sympathetic enough for your audience to understand why he or she did it, and the audience hates him or her and roots for the marriage to end.

The tricked party(ies) get over being angry at being tricked into marriage way too quickly or easily. This is a huge betrayal and not one that many people could forgive at all, let alone quickly or easily.

If a third party tricks the couple into getting married, he/she isn't believable in delivering the ruse, doesn't stick with the ruse for long enough, or isn't close enough and influential enough in the lives of the hero and heroine to plausibly manipulate these two adults in *marrying* each other.

Once married, the couple bickers too little or too much, depending on how angry they each should logically be, in the eyes of your audience.

Relying too much on sex to stop the arguments in this couple's rocky marriage.

Portraying angry sex that upsets or triggers your audience. While the hero or heroine may have good reason to be angry...don't take that into the bedroom if there's any chance your audience might be triggered by how that anger gets expressed sexually.

The character tricked into marriage has no plausible reason to stick around day in and day out, living in close quarters, and going through the motions of being married.

The reason the love interest tricked the main character into marriage isn't understandable or compelling enough to the main character to justify him or her forgiving the love interest for it, and the main character seems weak or stupid for forgiving the love interest.

The trickster doesn't pay a heavy enough price for his or her trick to satisfy your audience.

The trickster is punished too much or too harshly for what he/she did in the eyes of your audience, particularly if the reason he/she did it is sympathetic to most audience members.

The tricked party(ies) trust the trickster again way too easily or quickly, particularly if the trickster does nothing grand or special to earn back the tricked party's trust.

Relying solely on a grand gesture by the love interest to win back the wronged main character.

Failing to have the love interest make a sincere and heartfelt apology worthy of the main character and commensurate with the scale of the lie and trick.

Failing to have the main character apologize for the mistakes he/she made in the marriage. No marriage is perfect, and no person is always perfect.

The hero and heroine forgive each other too quickly or too slowly.

The couple dives back whole hog into their marriage with no period of first earning each other's trust back, and your audience thinks that's a dumb decision by both of them.

Failing to give the audience a peek at the couple's happily ever after once they have resumed their now happy and healthy marriage based on honesty and mutual trust.

TRICKED INTO MARRIAGE TROPE IN ACTION
Movies:

- What Happens in Vegas
- Laws of Attraction
- Overboard
- The Decoy Bride
- Fools Rush In
- Knocked Up
- Nine Months

Books:

- The Unwanted Wife by Natasha Anders
- The Wedding Night by Kati Wilde
- The Tycoon's Pregnant Mistress by Maya Banks
- The Marriage Trap by Sandra Marton
- Devil in Spring by Lisa Kleypas
- The Greek's Christmas Baby by Lucy Monroe
- A Reason To Believe by Maureen McKade

32
UNREQUITED LOVE

DEFINITION

In this story, two people already know each other, usually for a long time, and usually intimately. They're good friends, roommates, or coworkers and have spent a great deal of time together before your story begins. In what started out as a platonic friendship or working relationship, though, the main character has developed romantic feelings for the love interest. However, the love interest doesn't return those romantic feelings and may not be aware that the main character harbors romantic feelings for him or her.

Over the course of the story, the main character may patiently wait for the love interest to grow to love him or her. Or the main character may launch some sort of campaign to get the love interest to fall in love with him/her. Or the main character may set out to get the love interest to figure out that he or she also already loves the main character and that they'd be perfect together romantically.

This is a trope of timing more than anything else. In a traditional friends to lovers story, the friends fall in love together as their friendship blossoms into something more. In this story, one of the friends falls in love well before the other one.

SIDE NOTE: In an oblivious to love story, the main character is oblivious to all love. In this story, the main character is merely oblivious to the fact that his or her best friend or close coworker is in love with him or her and to the fact that he or she is also in love with the best friend/coworker.

This story explores the main character's complex feelings and frustrations as they cope with their unreturned love and try not to ruin the friendship. The main character may experience frustration and pain as well, but it unable to express these feelings to the love interest for much of the story for fear of driving away the person he/she loves entirely.

As for the love interest, his or her story is typically a slow burn realization that his or her friendship with the main character is more than simple friendship, and a slow journey to falling in love. Oddly, in this trope, only the love interest falls in love over the course of the story.

However, as the love interest finally gets a clue and falls in love, the couple's romantic relationship can then develop following usual patterns of attraction and growing romantic involvement.

By the end of the story, best friends have turned into lovers who are also best friends, which is a recipe for a wonderful happily ever after if there ever was one.

ADJACENT TROPES

- Oblivious to Love/Belated Epiphany
- Friends to Lovers
- Everyone Else Can See It
- In Love With the Wrong Person
- Right Under Your Nose
- Secret Crush/Secret Admirer

WHY READERS/VIEWERS LOVE THIS TROPE

- Many of us have had feelings for someone who doesn't return them, so this is a highly relatable story
- For those of us who've experienced this, we want the fantasy of this lopsided relationship working out and turning into true love
- We all desperately want to be seen, appreciated, and loved and this trope speaks directly to that
- Your audience is aware of the unrequited love well before the main character, which creates strong anticipation and engagement in the, "will they, won't they?" question
- The ah ha moment when the oblivious person in the relationship finally gets it is one of the most satisfying in all of romance stories for audience members

OBLIGATORY SCENES

THE BEGINNING:

This story almost always begins by establishing the friendship or close proximity of the future lovers. We see them as best friends or close coworkers and establish what the status quo has been for a long time.

The audience then is shown the main character's secret feelings for the love interest. This may be done in some sort of internal monologue, or the main character may pain for the love interest in some visual way that's obvious to the audience...but to which the love interest reacts with blissful ignorance. The main character may even go so far as to try to tell the love interest that he/she is in love with the love interest. But the love interest either misses the message, mishears, or thinks it's a joke.

We see the main character back off and not press the point. As soon as this happens, your audience knows exactly the story it's getting, and the anticipation begins to build of when will the love interest catch a clue, and will the relationship survive when he or she finally does catch on.

Typically, some external plot problem is introduced in the beginning of the story that will force the hero and heroine to interact even more frequently and closely than usual, a development that's sure to strain the main character's ability to stay silent about his or her true feelings, and which provides the love interest with ample opportunities to remain clueless and miss the abundant hints the main character commences dropping about his or her true feelings.

The beginning often ends with the first big crisis or development in the external plot story, in which the audience clearly sees that the main character is in love with the love interest, who does not return those feelings.

Although the ah ha moment for the love interest traditionally happens at the midpoint of the story, you may choose to end the beginning with the love interest finally catching on and realizing the main character loves him or her.

THE MIDDLE:

Shenanigans ensue. The external plot problem provides lots of opportunities for humor or suspense. Action relating to the external plot problem becomes important to keeping the middle of the story moving along at a decent pace while the love interest drags his or her emotional feet and continues to be clueless.

The main character may refrain from dropping any more hints about his or her romantic love for the love interest and may sit back and wait for the love interest to fall in love with him or her. Or the main character may commence a subtle (or not so subtle) campaign to help the love interest fall in love with him or her.

Somewhere in the middle of the story, the love interest finally starts to notice that he or she is having feelings he or she hasn't felt before toward the main character. It may take a while for the love interest to identify them as romantic, however.

It's not uncommon for there to be a scene where the hero and heroine end up in an embrace or may even kiss—all in good fun, of course—except the love interest feels something more than awkwardness or humor. Even then, he or she may not fully catch on, depending on how dense and stubborn you choose to make him or her...and how much you plan to torture both your main character and your audience before you finally give them both the love interest's big ah ha moment.

Traditionally, the ah ha moment of it finally dawning on the love interest that the main character is in love with him or her happens at the midpoint of the story. As soon as this revelation hits the love interest, often like a sledgehammer between the eyes, everything about the hero and heroine's relationship changes.

NOTE: If you've chosen to have the ah ha moment happen at the end of the beginning, the middle of the story will be taken up by the evolution of the friendship into a romance and the complications that ensue. Which means your middle would start with the following events...

The love interest sees the main character in an entirely new light. The love interest sees his or her own feelings in an entirely new light. And the love interest may look back on past interactions with the main character and belatedly realize that the main character has been trying to tell or show him/her for a very long time that the main character loves him or her.

And of course, the fact that the main character loves the love interest and the love interest may return those feelings launches a whole new set of complications to their lives and friendship. Their work together to resolve the big plot problem may become tense, uncomfortable, or fraught with sexual tension. The love interest may not know how to behave around the main character anymore. Whatever fears, doubts, insecurities, or misbeliefs the love interest have about himself/herself, about his/her lovability, and about love itself may rise up and cause problems.

The introduction of love into the equation makes what was an easy, relaxed, comfortable relationship abruptly risky. If the pair doesn't get this romance thing right, not only do they each lose a potential romance, but they also stand to lose their long-time best friend. Everything is on the line, now. This will either go very well or very, very badly.

Situations that used to be casual and comfortable are suddenly charged with romantic tension and unfamiliar to the hero and heroine. They have to build a whole new relationship and learn a whole set of new things about each other now that they're seeing each other through the lens of romance and deciding if this is a relationship that could last forever as a romantic one.

The hero and heroine may act differently around each other. Old patterns of friendship are disrupted as they start to treat each other as romantic interests and not just friends. The friendship itself grows wobbly, and they may start to keep secrets from each other, stop confiding their feelings, and make other changes to how they act around each other.

Into this heightened anxiety and fragile new romance, the big external plot problem rears its ugly head and builds toward a crisis that puts even more strain on the relationship.

It all becomes too much, and the friendship implodes along with the romantic relationship. The big crisis in the external plot problem may provoke this implosion, or vice versa. Regardless, the external plot problem goes as badly as it's possible to go in the midst of or because of the complete disaster in the couple's romantic relationship and friendship.

BLACK MOMENT:

The couple breaks up and the friends fall apart. As they've both feared, they've lost not only a lover but also their best friend, which makes the loss all the more keen, painful, and devastating emotionally.

The main character kicks himself/herself for rocking the boat. He or she should have left well enough alone and just stayed friends with the love interest. This is all his or her fault for pushing the relationship to be more. He/She knew better and got greedy.

The love interest kicks himself/herself for not realizing sooner, much sooner, that the main character was in love with him or her and for not realizing much sooner that he or she returned those feelings. If only he or she had acted earlier, maybe this whole mess and disastrous ending wouldn't have happened.

On top of all that guilt and self-recrimination, they both must grapple with the fact that their failings have also caused the external plot problem to go horribly, terribly wrong. Worse, without their best friend, they can't individually fix the problem on their own.

THE END:

As they each wallow in their misery, the hero and heroine take a hard look at themselves and sees the mistakes they made and their flaws, fears, doubts, insecurities, or misbeliefs that led to the breakup.

New information, new help, a new perspective, or one last opportunity to fix the external plot problem presents itself, and the hero and heroine get back together one last time to take one last shot at resolving the external plot problem. Indeed, this may be what brings them back together to work out their relationship.

Or the act or getting back together to work out their relationship may give them a chance to work together to fix the external plot problem.

The ex-lovers and ex-friends express missing each other. They confess to the mistakes they each made, and they may apologize to each other. One or both of them may make a grand gesture in a last-ditch attempt to repair their broken relationship.

In particular, the love interest tends to make a dramatic demonstration of how much he or she loves the main character romantically. The main character may make a grand gesture to the love interest to demonstrate how much he/she values their friendship.

Although their grand gestures may get their wires crossed yet again, at the same time, these are exactly the gestures they both need to feel comfortable being both best friends and lovers. They can now go forward into the future as both and have the best of both worlds of friendship and romantic love.

KEY SCENES

- the main character tells the clueless love interest "I love you" and the love interest blows it off
- the love interest tells the main character "I love you" but clearly means it as a joke or a casual remark and the main character reacts intensely…but can't show the reaction to the love interest
- the first inkling the love interest has of missing something in his/her interactions with the main character
- it dawns on the love interest that the main character might be in love with him/her but the love interest blows off the idea as ridiculous
- a romantic encounter or love scene where the pair's friendship comes through and makes the encounter endearing, sweet, or funny
- they argue as lovers, not as friends
- the first time they go out in public as a romantic couple
- they mourn the loss of their friendship individually or together but before they break up romantically
- they're warned by a third party that they'll lose even their friendship if they let the relationship become romantic
- a warning shot across the bow that one or both of them is not good at doing romance with the other person

- they see a side of their best friend as a lover that they've never seen before, which may not be good or healthy, and they now understand why the other person's relationships always go badly

THINGS TO THINK ABOUT WHEN WRITING THIS TROPE

Who are your main character and love interest and how do they know each other?

What's their long-time relationship like?

How did they meet? How long have they been best friends/close coworkers?

What are some inside jokes between them? What are some shorthand comments or observations they make to each other that they understand but outsiders might not?

What events, actions, or things become recurring themes, symbols, or actions in your story and which demonstrate how close they are to each other as friends, how well they know each other, or how much they have in common?

Who loves whom?

Will you tell this story primarily from one of the character's point of view or will you tell it from both of their points of view?

Where's your best starting point for this story?

Will you show your audience a montage of their friendship? Is there one event or scene that best demonstrates the kind of friends they are?

How will you show your audience that the main character is in love with the love interest but that the love interest is clueless?

What's the inciting incident that launches the big external plot problem? Will you put this before, simultaneously, or after showing the audience the main character's unrequited love?

How does the love interest react to the first demonstration or declaration that the main character loves him or her?

What's the main character's state of mind just before and just after his or her first demonstration or declaration of love for the love interest?

What does the main character decide to do or not do as a result of how the love interest reacts cluelessly to his or her attempt to reveal his/her true feelings of love? NOTE: This is a big question and will shape a lot of the middle of your story, so maybe make a list of ways the main character will try to lead the love interest to realizing that the main character loves him or her. A few examples:

- overt actions that demonstrate love
- subtle hints
- conversations about love and romance
- dates that get progressively more romantic
- using what the main character knows about the love interest's love languages to say or do things the love interest perceives as loving
- progressively more physically intimate interactions

How does the external plot problem force the hero and heroine into even closer and more frequent proximity with each other?

How physically intimate, albeit casually, are the couple before the love interest figures out the main character loves him or her? How does this change after the love interest realizes the main character loves him/her?

When does the love interest get a first inkling that maybe the main character has romantic feelings for him or her? What's the situation? Why does it dawn on him or her now? How does the love interest react to this inkling?

When is the full-blown ah ha moment for the love interest? What's the scene and situation, and are these big enough, symbolic enough, and appropriate to the importance of this moment, realizing it's one of the key moments in your whole story?

How does the main character feel and react (which may be very different) to the love interest finally catching on?

How does the love interest feel react to the ah ha moment?

What complications does the shift from friendship to romance introduce into the story? Into dealing with the external plot problem? Into the hero and heroine's internal thoughts and feelings?

How does the relationship change as it shifts from friendship to romance? Again, this will define a big chunk of your story's movement, so you might make a list of steps of the evolution of the relationship. This shift may happen very quickly or it may happen very slowly depending on where in your story you choose to place the ah ha moment.

How do the hero and heroine each act differently toward each other when they start to treat each other as lovers instead of friends?

What do the hero and heroine learn about each other when they see each other in this new light? NOTE: The main character has already spent a while thinking of the love interest as a potential lover and may have a head start on this...but he or she has not seen the love interest act like a girlfriend or boyfriend before now, so the main character is still going to have a significant learning arc.

What do they dislike about each other as friends? How about as romantic interests? Are these the same or different lists? Do the friendship dislikes get better or worse as romantic dislikes?

What core values, morals, ethics, and beliefs are most pronounced and important to their friendship? How do these carry over into their romantic relationship?

What do they like best about each other as friends? As romantic partners? Are these the same or different? Why?

What do their friends, family, and coworkers think of the shift in their relationship from friends to lovers? Do they support the shift? Sabotage the shift? How and why?

What conflicts threaten to break up their romantic relationship?

What conflicts threaten to break up their entire relationship—both as friends and as romantic partners?

How does the external plot problem threaten to break them up?

What are the consequences of failing to resolve the external plot problem? Can you make these worse? Much worse?

Does the big crisis in the external plot problem provoke the couple's breakup or the other way around?

How does the breakup itself happen? Is there a big fight? No fight at all? Despair? Fury? Jealousy? Accusations?

If they fight, do the hero and heroine take the worst possible shots at each other, given that they know each other well enough to know exactly how to hurt each other the worst, or do they exercise some restraint in their climactic breakup fight? Why?

Who walks out on whom or is it mutual?

How does their breakup help or cause the couple to fail to resolve the big plot crisis?

What epiphanies do they each have or lessons do they each learn about themselves, their friendship, and the romantic relationship after they break up? What provokes or enables these realizations?

What do they each do about their lessons learned? How do they change? What would they do differently if they had it to do over?

What new information, help, or perspectives come to light that make it possible for them to resolve the big plot problem now when they couldn't do so before?

Will the hero and heroine come together to solve the big plot problem and then solve their personal issues, or will they resolve their relationship issues and then deal with the big plot problem?

What needs to be said to repair their friendship?

What needs to be said to repair their romantic relationship?

Do they make grand gestures to each other? If so, what are they? How, when, and where do they happen?

How do they each react to the grand gestures?

How will they rebuild their relationship? Will they start with just friendship? Will they resume their romantic relationship? Both?

How will you demonstrate that they've both repaired their friendship and their romantic relationship by the end of the story?

How will you give your audience, who's suffered a lot along the way, a glimpse of happily ever after for this couple?

TROPE TRAPS

The love interest is so dense that he/she is never plausibly going to catch on to the main character's real feelings.

The main character hints so loudly that he/she loves the love interest that a telephone pole could catch the clue…and your audience doesn't buy that the love interest is actually missing these hints.

The main character is so insecure, so anxious, so self-effacing, and so long-suffering that your audience finds them weak and unlikable.

No sane person would wait around as long as this main character for anyone to figure out how they feel and your audience doesn't buy how long the main character has stuck around.

The main characters don't have enough in common to be believable best friends, let alone believable true loves.

Nothing changes in the couple's relationship when they initially transition from being best friends to lovers.

The ah ha moment happens too soon or too late to make sense in your story.

The external plot problem has no bearing on the couple's relationship and feels disjointed or disconnected from the love story.

The external plot problem puts no pressures or strains on the couple's relationship.

There are nor or not enough consequences to failing to resolve the big plot problem and your audience and your hero and heroine don't care if it gets fixed or not.

The couple goes from platonic friends to hot and heavy lovers too fast.

The couple spends no time learning about each other as romantic partners—they go from friends to deep into a romantic relationship way too fast to feel believable, even if they do know each other very well.

They never date or do the sorts of things new couples do. They go straight to "old married couple" behaviors.

The friends never fight, and the romantic couple never makes up.

The couple knows everything about each other before they get romantically involved and there's no sense of discovery at all to the relationship.

The couple's fights are very ugly because they know each other so well, and they say the sorts of hurtful things to each other that shouldn't be forgiven and forgotten.

The consequences for failing to resolve the big plot problem never happen or aren't bad enough for the hero and heroine to care that they've happened.

The hero and heroine don't learn anything from their breakup and don't make any changes in behavior or attitude that would give them a better shot at staying together after they reconcile.

The hero and heroine never apologize to each other or they apologize for the wrong things.

Failing to show the hero and heroine as both friends and lovers by the end of the story.

Failing to give your audience of this couple's hard-earned happily ever after.

UNREQUITED LOVE TROPE IN ACTION
Movies:

- Love, Rosie
- 10 Things I Hate About You
- The Notebook
- When Harry Met Sally
- Bridget Jones's Diary
- 13 Going On 30

- Clueless
- Some Kind of Wonderful
- She's All That

Books:

- Persuasion by Jane Austen
- Jane Eyre by Charlotte Bronte
- The Convenient Marriage" by Georgette Heyer
- Attachments" by Rainbow Rowell
- Bet Me" by Jennifer Crusie
- The Friend Zone" by Abby Jimenez
- From Lukov with Love" by Mariana Zapata
- Act Like It" by Lucy Parker

APPENDIX A – UNIVERSAL ROMANCE TROPES LISTED BY VOLUME

Volume 1, THE TROPOHOLIC'S GUIDE TO INTERNAL ROMANCE TROPES

Accidental Pregnancy
    Amnesia
    Anti-Hero
    Bad Boy/Girl Reformed
    Beauty-and-the-Beast
    Burdened by Beauty/Talent
    Celibate Hero
    Clumsy/Thoughtless/Bumbling Hero/Heroine
    Cold/Serious/Uptight Hero/Heroine
    Commitment Phobia
    Damaged Hero/Heroine
    Dangerous Secret
    Disabled Hero/Heroine
    Fear of Intimacy
    Fresh Start/Do-Over
    Goody Two Shoes

Hero/Heroine in Disguise
Makeover
Nerdy/Geek/Genius
Newcomer/Outsider/Stranger
Oblivious to Love/Last to Know
Only One Not Married
Plain Jane/John
Plus Size Love
Rebellious Hero/Heroine
Reclusive Hero/Heroine
Shy Hero/Heroine
Single Parent
Socially Awkward Hero/Heroine
Transformation/Fixer Upper
Ugly Duckling
Virgin Hero/Heroine
Widowed Hero/Heroine

Volume 2, THE TROPOHOLIC'S GUIDE TO EXTERNAL ROMANCE TROPES

Across the Tracks/Wrong Side of the Tracks
    Best Friend's Sibling/Sibling's Best Friend
    Best Friend's/Sibling's Ex
    Best Friend's Widow/Widower
    Childhood Sweethearts/Friends
    Couples Therapy
    Cross-Cultural/Interethnic/Interracial
    Divided Loyalties
    Everyone Else Can See It
    Evil/Dysfunctional Family
    Feuding Families

Fish Out of Water/Cowboy in the City
Following Your Heart
Forbidden Love
Friends to Lovers
Girl/Boy Next Door
Hero/Heroine in Hiding
Hidden/Secret Wealth
Home for the Holiday/Vacation Fling
Long Distance Romance
Love Triangle
Marriage Pact/Bargain Comes Due
Marriage of Convenience/Fake Marriage
No One Thinks It Will Work
Nursing Back to Health
On the Run/Chase
Quest/ Search for MacGuffin
Rags to Riches/Cinderella
Rescue Romance/Damsel or Dude in distress
Riches to Rags
Rivals/Work Enemies
Secret Baby
Secret Identity
Secret Organization/Secret World

Twins Switch Places/Lookalikes

Volume 3, THE TROPHOLIC'S GUIDE TO BACKSTORY ROMANCE TROPES

Back From the Dead
    Billionaire

Bully Turned Nice
Burned By Love
Dangerous Past
Enemies to Lovers
Engaged to/Marrying Someone Else
Estranged Spouses/On the Rocks
Ex-Convict Hero/Heroine
Finding a Home
First Love
Forgiveness
Guardian/Caretaker
Instant Family
In Love With the Wrong Person
Is the Baby Mine
Left At the Altar/Jilted
Lone Wolf Tamed
Mafia Romance
Not Good Enough for Him/Her
Rebound Romance
Reconciliation/Second Chance
Recovery/Rehabilitation
Redemption
Reunion
Revenge
Ruined/Scandalous Reputation
Runaway Bride/Groom
Spinster/Bluestocking/On the Shelf
Stepsiblings/Stepparent Romance
Survivor's Guilt/PTSD
Teenage Crush

Volume 4, THE TROPOHOLIC'S GUIDE TO HOOK ROMANCE TROPES

THE TROPOHOLIC'S GUIDE TO HOOK ROMANCE TROPES

. . .

Arranged Marriage
- Baby On the Doorstep
- Boss-Employee
- Celibate/Unconsummated Marriage
- Coming Home
- Deathbed Confession
- Disguised as a Male
- Drunk/Vegas Wedding
- Fake Fiancé(e)/Boyfriend/Girlfriend
- False Identity
- Fated Mates/Soul Mates
- Fling/One Night Stand
- Grumpy/Sunshine
- Hate/Snark to Love
- Innocent Cohabitation
- Love At First Sight
- Love-Hate Relationship
- Matchmaker/Matchmaker Gone Wrong
- May-December Romance
- Mistaken Identity
- Nanny/Teacher & Single Parent
- Online Love/Pen Pals
- Opposites Attract
- Raising a Child Together
- Right Under Your Nose
- Road Trip/Adventure
- Running Away From Home
- Secret Crush/Secret Admirer
- Stop the Wedding
- Terms of the Will
- Tricked into Marriage
- Unrequited Love

ALSO BY CINDY DEES

THE TROPOHOLIC'S GUIDES:

UNIVERSAL ROMANCE TROPES

Volume 1, The Tropoholic's Guide to Internal Romance Tropes

Volume 2, The Tropoholic's Guide to External Romance Tropes

Volume 3, The Tropoholic's Guide to Backstory Romance Tropes

Volume 4, The Tropoholic's Guide to Hook Romance Tropes

The Tropoholic's Guide to Universal Thriller Tropes

NOTE: I've chosen not to make future Tropoholic's Guides available as pre-orders because I'm committed to getting each book right instead of hurrying to meet deadlines.

If you'd like to be notified when the next volume goes on sale, please visit www.cindydees.com/tropes and sign up for my (rather infrequent) tropes newsletter.

FICTION

Second Shot, A Helen Warwick Thriller

Double Tap, A Helen Warwick Thriller

The Medusa Project

The Medusa Game

The Medusa Prophecy

The Medusa Affair

The Medusa Seduction

Medusa's Master

The Medusa Proposition

I've received and heard your requests (with great delight, I might add) for more books covering the tropes of specific genres of fiction.

I'm currently developing lists of tropes for what I expect will amount to something like a dozen more genre fiction books covering genres including but not limited to:

- The Tropes of Spicy Romance
- Historical and Paranormal Romance Tropes
- Sweet, Clean & Wholesome, and Inspirational Romance Tropes
- Cozy Mystery Tropes
- Noir Mystery Tropes
- Crime Fiction Tropes
- Thriller Tropes
- Horror Tropes
- Science Fiction Tropes
- Fantasy Tropes
- Paranormal Tropes
- Action/Adventure Tropes
- Melodrama Tropes
- Western Tropes

If I've missed any genres you'd like to see books on, please feel free to contact me at www.cindydees.com and let me know!

ABOUT THE AUTHOR

New York Times and USA Today bestselling author of over a hundred books, Cindy Dees has sold over two million books worldwide. She writes in a variety of genres, including thrillers, military adventure, romantic suspense, fantasy, and alternate history.

Cindy is the creator and executive producer of an upcoming Netflix television series based on her Helen Warwick thriller novel series about a woman assassin, and Cindy has multiple additional television and film projects in development.

A two-time RITA winner and five-time RITA finalist, she is also a two-time Holt Medallion winner, two-time winner of Romantic Times' Romantic Suspense of the Year Award and a Career Lifetime Achievement Award nominee from Romantic Times.

Copyright © 2024 by Cynthia Dees Publishing, Inc.

All rights reserved. No part of this book may be reproduced in any form or by any electronic or mechanical means, including information storage and retrieval systems, AI, or AI training, without written permission from the author, except for the use of brief quotations in a book review.

www.ingramcontent.com/pod-product-compliance
Lightning Source LLC
Chambersburg PA
CBHW070124080526
44586CB00015B/1542